THE WRITING
EXPERIENCE

THE WRITING EXPERIENCE

THE WRITING EXPERIENCE

THIRD EDITION

Carol Schoen

Nila Gandhi-Schwalto

James Vaughn

Herbert H. Lehman College of the
City University of New York

Scott, Foresman and Company

Glenview, Illinois   Boston   London

LIBRARY OF CONGRESS
Library of Congress Cataloging-in-Publication Data

Schoen, Carol.
The writing experience / Carol Schoen, Nila Gandhi-Schwalto, James
Vaughn.—3rd ed.
p.   cm.
Previous eds. cataloged under title.
Includes index.
ISBN 0-673-39910-9
1. English language—Rhetoric.   2. College readers.   I. Gandhi-
Schwalto, Nila.   II. Vaughn, James.   III. Title.
PE1417.S3617 1989
808'.042—dc19   88-17783
                                                                             CIP

Copyright © 1989 by Carol Schoen, Nila Gandhi-Schwalto, and
James Vaughn

1 2 3 4 5 6 7 8 9 10–MVN–94 93 92 91 90 89 88

Printed in the United States of America

CREDITS
Pages 6–8. Excerpts from "Natural Boundaries" reprinted from *Crossing the
Border* by Joyce Carol Oates by permission of the publisher, Vanguard Press, Inc.
Copyright © 1976, 1975, 1974 by Joyce Carol Oates.
Pages 8–15. "A Tree, A Rock, A Cloud" from *The Ballad of the Sad Cafe and
Collected Short Stories* by Carson McCullers. Copyright 1936, 1941, 1942, 1950, ©
1955 by Carson McCullers, Copyright renewed © 1979 by Floria V. Lasky. Re-
printed by permission of Houghton Mifflin Company.
Page 16. "First Love" from Henry Miller, *Stand Still Like the Hummingbird.*
Copyright © 1962 by Henry Miller. Reprinted by permission of New Directions
Publishing Corporation.
Page 16. Excerpt from *Children of Violence: Vol. 1, Martha Quest* by Doris Less-
ing. Copyright 1952, 1954, © 1964 by Doris Lessing. Reprinted by permission of
Simon & Schuster, Inc. and Grafton Books Ltd.
Page 17. "Sinew" from *Ultramarine* by Raymond Carver. Copyright © 1986
by Raymond Carver. Reprinted by permission of Random House, Inc.
Pages 18–22. Ernest Hemingway, "Hills Like White Elephants" from *Men
Without Women.* Copyright 1927 Charles Scribner's Sons; copyright renewed 1955
Ernest Hemingway. Reprinted with the permission of Charles Scribner's Sons.
Pages 24–25. Excerpt from *Music for Chameleons* by Truman Capote. Copy-
right © 1980 by Truman Capote. Reprinted by permission of Random House,
Inc.
(continued on p. 258)

Preface

Our experiences in the classroom have been the motivating guide for this third edition of *The Writing Experience*, as they have since we first considered writing a developmental composition text. The approach reflects the continuing changes we have noted as we experiment with new ideas, rejecting some and modifying others. Although the growing body of compositional theory has provided indispensable counsel, we have continued to rely primarily on what our interactions with our students have taught us. We have added new material, removed some that now seems outmoded, and revived other pieces that we had temporarily rejected.

A major change has been the elimination of separate units for description and narration within the text. We had always been aware that these forms rarely appeared in isolation and that our students seldom understood the necessity for treating them as distinct entities. Nor did the division reflect our primary concern of viewing student papers from a holistic perspective. Under the new arrangement, each assignment assumes a total approach to a given situation rather than the fragmented one that our previous classification may have suggested.

This change also permits us to emphasize those aspects of teaching writing that we have always considered basic. The new organization of the book contains separate sections on writing about one's past, present, and future, thus making our experiental focus immediately apparent. By asking students to write out of their own experiences, we believe we can tap material that is most deeply felt and will produce the most interesting compositions.

An additional change brought about by the new classification is the creation of a fourth section devoted to those writing strategies most frequently called upon in writing for college courses. Both comparison/contrast and process papers are common forms for examinations and reports, and the in-class writing test has become a standard measure of student achievement throughout the country. By devoting a full chapter to each of these concerns, we are able to provide a necessary and useful guide to students and teachers.

A change of a different sort has been our decision to restore readings as a major portion of the text. Although in the second edition we had eliminated many of the writings of professionals as being probable interferences with student creativity, we have found that our students missed the sense of possibility that those readings had inspired. Some of the readings we have added appeared originally in the first edition; others are excerpted from recent publications. These readings are not included as models, but instead as ways of showing students what others have felt about the subjects on which they have been asked to write. The renewed awareness of the close connection between reading and writing that the current research has exposed has strengthened our resolve in this area.

Along with the addition of writings by professional authors, we have, for the first time, included work by student writers. Seeing the example of their peers has, we feel, helped many of our students come to a better understanding of what they themselves may achieve. At the same time these student writings are reassuring in that they are proof that freshmen are not expected to be able to produce masterpieces.

Teaching our students to revise has always been a problem and, as a partial solution, we have made provision for student reading and feedback sessions. Using techniques developed by the New York City Writing Project, we have adopted only those strategies that offer positive reinforcement and constructive guidance. These sessions are in no sense a substitute for teacher input, but they do allow for a middle step between first draft and final copy.

Since the encouragement of writing per se is a basic need in all composition courses, we have added assignments for a Writer's Log to our text. Unlike a journal, which we have found frequently misused by students, the entries for the Writer's Log are specifically prescribed and deal with subjects directly related to the topic of the chapter in which they appear.

Despite these many changes, the basic format of our text remains the same. Each chapter begins with a group activity related to the subject matter of the chapter and designed to break down the barriers that usually make students feel isolated in academic situations. The writing assignments grow out of students' own experiences, encouraging them in the belief that they, as unique individuals, have contributions to make. Each assignment, regardless of "subject matter," reinforces the students' awareness of how the writing process, once begun with questions meaningful to the writer, results in a written product that can and does become meaningful to the world outside. Students are given a chance to think through an issue, as well as to explore ways of presenting their ideas in words before the final assignment.

Even though we have broken down the writing skills into small, easily learned segments that build on one another, we have also attempted to integrate the material with the awareness of the process of writing as a whole. In most cases, the initial activity is the basis for the in-class writing assignment; it provides a rough draft for the formal paper at the end of the chapter. The activity provides the preliminary thought; the in-class writing provides a working, prewriting, or first draft experience; the language learning and rhetoric learning segments are a natural outgrowth of the material being treated. The desire for uniformity has not, however, assumed greater importance than the integrity of the chapter itself, so that the construction of each chapter has been true to the needs of that chapter rather than to any demand that it be arranged like every other chapter in the book.

Despite our concern for integration, we have maintained flexibility. There is ample room for instructors to rearrange the material to suit their own teaching needs. There is, in fact, far more material than can be covered in any one semester. In our own use of the book not one of the three of us has ever been able to use more than four or five chapters, basing our selection on the differing needs of courses and classes.

We have used certain terms that may need clarification:

Activity—The activities are essentially group experiences that stimulate student participation and focus on a particular topic that will be the subject of the final formal writing assignment. The time spent on any one activity can vary from a few minutes to a whole class period, to suit the individual instructor's preference.

In-Class Writing—These are usually focused, freewriting situations and should be handled as such. In most cases they treat subjects that will be written about in the formal papers, so that in effect, students are given the opportunity to explore ideas on paper as they prepare a preliminary draft. Students should be encouraged to share and discuss their ideas to stimulate each other, and to share and discuss their drafts to stimulate further thought on the subject.

Revision—This refers to the process of rethinking the entire approach of a particular paper. It can involve changing the ideas and examples that are used to support an idea, changing the order in which the ideas are presented, or even changing the main idea of a composition completely.

Editing—This refers to the process of correcting a paper. It involves checking to see that proper spelling, grammar, and punctuation have been used.

In creating this text, we have been fortunate to have had the help of a great many people. Although we regret Elaine Avidon's decision to withdraw from this enterprise, we have retained much of the material she originated from the previous two editions, and the intelligence and sensitivity that she brought to that work continues to inform our thinking.

We particularly thank our students who suffered through our efforts to redefine our techniques, and we express our appreciation to our colleagues in the Academic Skills Department at Lehman College, who generously offered their suggestions and ideas. We thank our editors at Scott, Foresman and Company, Joe Opiela and Brad Gray, for their efforts on our behalf. Finally, we could not end without special thanks to our friends and families whose encouragement helped us through some difficult times.

We are grateful to those who critiqued the manuscript for this edition: Helen C. Covington, North Harris Community College; Sallyanne H. Fitzgerald, University of Missouri at St. Louis; C. Jeriel Howard, Northeastern Illinois University; Carol Simonson, Tacoma Community College; and Marti Singer, Georgia State University. We continue to acknowledge also those who read the manuscript for the previous editions and offered their suggestions: Peter Lindblom, Miami-Dade Community College; Roberta S. Matthews, LaGuardia Community College; Joseph E. Trimmer, Ball State University; Betsy Brown, Pennsylvania State University; Mary Cignarelli, Illinois Central College; Linda Feldmeier, Northeastern University; Ellen Friedman, Trenton State College; Phyllis Levy, California State University at Northridge; Joanne McCarthy, Tacoma Community College; Joyce Melville, University of Illinois at Chicago Circle; Charlotte Miller, California State University at Northridge; also Richard S. Beal and most especially Karl K. Taylor, who in a "fatherly, precise" way guided our initial ideas into a workable, finished form.

Contents

Part Four
USEFUL STRATEGIES 187

Part One

DESCRIPTION AND NARRATION— BEING IN COLLEGE

The writing you will do in Part One concentrates almost exclusively on narratives and descriptions. Together they form the two most basic reasons a writer has to write — to tell what happened and to describe the way in which it happened, to whom it happened, and where. Whether your purpose is to entertain or to inform, what you write usually ends up somehow telling a story, because stories are often the most accessible form in which to render information, be it the evening news or the substance of an official document. Since the narrative — whether entertaining or informative, whether oral or written, or whether factual or fictional — is such an early form, it seems to fill a basic human instinct as a way of communicating and thus offers an appropriate starting point for instruction. Yet a story barren of description is like a painting without color, like a beautiful dress on a hanger rather than on the body of the girl for whom it was sewn. Narration and description share a similar intimacy.

As you move through Part One, you will most likely notice the many references to the word *now.* Notice how at one point it means a fraction of a second; at another, two days or so; and at still another, an entire semester. In fact, *now* defines not just time but place as well, for now you are "here," in a college classroom. Part One, then, is intended to help you see just how involving being in college can be.

Chapter 1 goes directly to the physical experience of sitting in a classroom and meeting new people.

Where Chapter 1 concentrates on people, especially those in new or strange situations, Chapter 2 focuses specifically on place — how it either impacts on us radically or only subtly influences our behaviors, even the way we speak. The activities in Chapter 2 get you outside and keep you moving, jotting down information as you go along observing people and places on your campus and in your neighborhood. The writing assignments encourage you to use the detail you gather as a way of creating a dominant impression. Because mood and atmosphere tend to dominate here, narrative is not so important. Reporting your impressions accurately and choosing the right words highlight everything you do in these assignments.

The writing assignments in Chapter 3 lessen the need for descriptive writing but emphasize narration as a way of keeping you aware of the changes you are beginning to recognize in yourself because of your new life focus. Recording all the changes you are presently experiencing adds up to a story — a narrative others can read.

Writing About People in New Situations

Why You Must Write in the First Place

The reason you write is to record a communication that may have occurred only in a world of your own private thoughts — just between you and you. You may never seek to share it with another living being. Nevertheless, you have a record of that transaction, that thought, and because you wrote it down, it is always available to you. For this reason, many writers keep diaries and journals — written communications that they can share with no one at all, with just one or a few others, or with five thousand others.

Most of what you write — indeed, *must* write on or about — involves far more external and socially demanding reasons. For example, you must leave a note on the kitchen table explaining your absence and the approximate time of your return. You had to write a letter to request admission into the college you're now attending. Soon you will write essay exams and term papers describing, defining, and evaluating what you saw, what you read, and what you understood. No, writing isn't easy to do — to do well, that is.

Chapter 1 helps you to get started so that whatever your doubts and inhibitions about writing, you can at least feel comfortable in the presence of others who most likely feel much the same as you. Look at the faces around you. Don't they show some of the discomfort you feel now?

ACTIVITY   **Introducing a Stranger.** One way to get to know everyone in the class is to begin by meeting one other person in the class. Pick out a stranger in the room and talk with him or her for about ten minutes. First, let's think about the kinds of questions you might want to ask. Some questions will occur to almost everyone — "What school did you come from?" "How many brothers and sisters do you have?" But are these really helpful or interesting? Do they really aid you in getting to know the person you are talking to?

Below are some questions that may serve your purpose better:

1. What kinds of jobs have you held? Which job did you like most? Why? What was unpleasant about the one you disliked?
2. What would you do if you had a million dollars?
3. What kind of people do you like to be with?
4. What makes you angry, sad, happy, bored?
5. What was the greatest experience you ever had? the worst?
6. What do you like to do in your free time?
7. What kind of music do you prefer? Who are your favorite performers?
8. What do you expect your life to be like ten years from now?

See if you can think of more unusual questions that might give you an insight into the other person's character. As the members of the group suggest new questions, your instructor or a classmate can write the most interesting ones on the board.

Once the questions have been selected, find a person you don't know and start an interview. You may ask all your questions first and then answer all the other person's, or the two of you may alternate; use any order that makes sense to both of you. If one of the questions leads you into an interesting discussion, don't hesitate to follow it up with related questions. You might find it helpful to take notes during the conversation. After the interview, spend five minutes writing up your thoughts.

At the end of the time period, reassemble as a group. You may use your notes to help you introduce your partner to the class, but tell about the interview rather than read from your notes. Introduce your partner to the class by telling your classmates some of the things you have discussed. If you think of any questions as other members of the group are being introduced, feel free to ask them.

Discussion

Now that you know a little more about one another than you did at the beginning of the session, let's talk about this activity.

1. During this activity, did you hesitate to ask certain questions that came to mind? What does this tell you about yourself? about the other person?
2. How did it feel to introduce a person who until a few minutes ago had been a stranger to you?
3. Did this experience tell you anything about how people behave in a classroom?
4. Did this activity break down some of the barriers to communication? If so, how and why? If not, what ways might have worked better?
5. How differently do you feel now about this class from the way you did when you first walked into the room?

IN-CLASS WRITING

Catching First Impressions by Freewriting. You're at the point now that you are asked to shift from the act of talking — generally with its easy flow of give and take — to the act of writing, specifically to write about the person you have just talked with. The transition from one to the other is rarely easy. In talking, someone is there to complete the give-and-take situation; you act and react immediately in each other's presence. Not so in writing; you create your audience; and then wait — sometimes quite a while — for a response. That's why writers need more time to think, to gather together what they think so as to help them know what they are going to write.

It is during this period of getting to know what you're thinking when freewriting can be of most help. Rather than thinking before you write, freewriting lets you write before you think. Perhaps it warms up the fingers, hand, and arm, introducing them to the pen and paper and explaining their function. In that instant, you begin writing words, even your name, as a way of getting the hand to move the pen across the paper. Then you keep writing and you keep writing, thinking of nothing at all as you do. Just don't stop writing. Fill a page or so before you stop. And that's just about all there is to freewriting. When you read back over to see what's there, most likely you'll discover that sense overtook nonsense much earlier than you might expect. What helps to make freewriting free is that it's exempt from evaluation — the scrutiny and judgment of others.

What Did You Get? Once you've finished freewriting, you will want to look over what you got down on paper. If your teacher asks, you might agree to read to the class some of what you wrote. You'll want to share some of the impressions you wrote. Were you able to catch all the strangeness, all the newness? What is worth holding on to, to come back to at a later date for revising, reworking?

READINGS In the two readings that follow, an excerpt from "Natural Boundaries," by Joyce Carol Oates, and "A Tree • A Rock • A Cloud," by Carson McCullers, a meeting of two strangers is portrayed, an event not very different from the kind you just wrote about in your In-Class Writing exercise. In all three instances, it is not only the fact that two people are strangers but also the situation of their meeting that accentuates the event.

NATURAL BOUNDARIES   Joyce Carol Oates

Renée, twenty-six years old, with dark-red hair sometimes worn loose on her shoulders and sometimes drawn back into a knot, had the look, she supposed, of a university student: one of those tall, startled-looking, quite often very attractive girls whose bearing—both submissive and striking—make them popular with men of a certain type. Never extravagantly dressed, never ostentatiously "pretty," their appeal is almost intellectual: even their beauty, if they are beautiful, is an arrangement of facial bones, strong elegant cheekbones, strong graceful body. Renée's complexion was milky pale and freckled. Her forehead was rather wide, so she wore bangs to disguise it; her red-blond eyebrows were scant and light, making her eyes appear larger than they were. Her nose was small and ordinary. Her mouth was ordinary. She was convinced that her appearance was an ordinary one, and most of the time she didn't bother to exaggerate her good features—to outline her eyes in black or to paint her eyelids green or blue, as many of the girls here tonight had—so it always surprised her, it truly flattered her, when men approached her; *it must be for herself, herself alone.* Tonight Renée did feel pretty; she was flushed, excited. Karl spoke enthusiastically to her about a recent provincial grant that had come their way—"their" referring to his circle of poet-friends, she assumed—that would subsidize readings in local high schools and in several institutions, a home for the blind, a home for elderly people, a half-

way house for young people near the university, and as he spoke he
leaned toward her, urgent, yet still casual, with his mannered infor-
mality, so that she lost the thread of his conversation and began to
feel, uneasily, that this man had somehow recognized her . . . there
was a kind of agreement between them . . . But she must have been
imagining it. Only near the end of their conversation did he say
something odd, meant to be amusing: *I can tell you're married, you
couldn't not be married . . . right? . . . How do you like my son Ja-
mie, the brat crawling under the table there, see him, about to surface by that lady's legs? . . . that's how I looked at his age.*

Later, Renée wished she had drawn closer to Mrs. Davies, after
Karl excused himself and returned to her and his friends . . . she
wished she had made an effort to see what the woman looked like,
up close. *Evie,* her name was; Renée had overheard it. *Evie.* She
was a pretty woman in her mid-thirties, though rather flush-faced—
her cheeks reddened with the pleasure of conversation, of laughter—blond, the hair too severe, too short, for her plump face. She
wore scarlet slacks and a silkish scarlet and green blouse . . . The
kind of woman everyone liked, and Renée herself would probably
have liked her; she knew suddenly that she would never meet her.
Renée watched the group, watched Karl with them, sliding his arm
around his wife's shoulders . . . and, without glancing back at Renée, he drifted with the group across the room, to meet someone
else. Renée stared after them, her cup still in her hand, the coffee
cold, thinking that it did not matter; it really did not matter . . . *You
couldn't not be married.*

He had nothing to do with her loneliness, or with the river out
there, nothing to do with the infinitely changing sky and the waves
that were now fierce and white-capped, now flattened, shallow,
washing up on the beach. Yet when he telephoned her the first
time, a few days after the reading, she stumbled with the telephone
across the kitchen, as far as the cord would let her, to stare wildly
out the window. She hardly heard what he was saying; she hardly
heard her own hesitant, confused replies, *No I don't think so. No,
really.* . . . It was a shock, though she had been thinking of him. She
had even endured a puzzling and possibly humiliating dream about
him, which she could not quite remember. *No, Karl, really . . . I . . .
I don't think so.* . . . She laughed at her own timidity. He laughed
also, nervously. She had the idea he was extremely nervous. . . . He
forced himself to speak more casually, asking her fairly routine
questions about how she and her husband liked living where they
did: any discrimination against them, as Americans? . . . he hoped
not, he liked Americans, he identified with them, for some reason
. . . not with the government, of course, but with Americans . . . that
is, the Americans he ran into, here and in Toronto. They were
rather like himself, he thought. Did she agree? . . . Renée didn't
know; she told him *Yes.* He was overbearing even when seemingly

deferential. It must always be easier to agree with him, she thought. Always easier to agree. . . . Then he asked her what she did all day long: she hadn't a baby, eh? Somehow he knew she hadn't. Her body, her stance, the way she'd been standing there . . . something about the tilt of the pelvis, he knew, he could tell . . . she was certainly someone's wife, but not a young mother, was that right? . . . Renée was too confused to be offended; she stared out at the river, not seeing it, aware of one of the barges edging into the corner of her vision, aware of something happening, something mysterious and alarm-

ing . . . she stared out there, as if Karl were there.

Finally she told him, embarrassed, that she had to hang up.

Discussion

1. A casual meeting at a party — have you ever experienced one? Have friends told you about ones they've had? Have you read about or seen in films or on television memorable first meetings?
2. Renée seems to feel a sense of déjà vu. Do you think she uses it to justify her attraction to Karl?
3. What other strategies do people use to explain to themselves why they are attracted to or offended by a person they are meeting for the first time?
4. In writing about a casual encounter, how would you direct the course of events (if any) that follow?

A TREE • A ROCK • A CLOUD   Carson McCullers

It was raining that morning, and still very dark. When the boy reached the streetcar café he had almost finished his route and he went in for a cup of coffee. The place was an all-night café owned by a bitter and stingy man called Leo. After the raw, empty street, the café seemed friendly and bright: along the counter there were a couple of soldiers, three spinners from the cotton mill, and in a corner a man who sat hunched over with his nose and half his face down in a beer mug. The boy wore a helmet such as aviators wear. When he went into the café he unbuckled the chin strap and raised the right flap up over his pink little ear; often as he drank his coffee someone would speak to him in a friendly way. But this morning Leo did not look into his face and none of the men were talking. He paid and was leaving the café when a voice called out to him:

"Son! Hey Son!"

He turned back and the man in the corner was crooking his finger and nodding to him. He had brought his face out of the beer mug and he seemed suddenly very happy. The man was long and pale, with a big nose and faded orange hair.

"Hey Son!"

The boy went toward him. He was an undersized boy of about twelve, with one shoulder drawn higher than the other because of the weight of the paper sack. His face was shallow, freckled, and his eyes were round child eyes.

"Yeah Mister?"

The man laid one hand on the paper boy's shoulders, then grasped the boy's chin and turned his face slowly from one side to the other. The boy shrank back uneasily.

"Say! What's the big idea?"

The boy's voice was shrill; inside the café it was suddenly very quiet.

The man said slowly: "I love you."

All along the counter the men laughed. The boy, who had scowled and sidled away, did not know what to do. He looked over the counter at Leo, and Leo watched him with a weary, brittle jeer. The boy tried to laugh also. But the man was serious and sad.

"I did not mean to tease you, Son," he said. "Sit down and have a beer with me. There is something I have to explain."

Cautiously, out of the corner of his eye, the paper boy questioned the men along the counter to see what he should do. But they had gone back to their beer or their breakfast and did not notice him. Leo put a cup of coffee on the counter and a little jug of cream.

"He is a minor," Leo said.

The paper boy slid himself up onto the stool. His ear beneath the upturned flap of the helmet was very small and red. The man was nodding at him soberly. "It is important," he said. Then he reached in his hip pocket and brought out something which he held up in the palm of his hand for the boy to see.

"Look very carefully," he said.

The boy stared, but there was nothing to look at very carefully. The man held in his big, grimy palm a photograph. It was the face of a woman, but blurred, so that only the hat and the dress she was wearing stood out clearly.

"See?" the man asked.

The boy nodded and the man placed another picture in his palm. The woman was standing on a beach in a bathing suit. The suit made her stomach very big, and that was the main thing you noticed.

"Got a good look?" He leaned over closer and finally asked: "You ever seen her before?"

The boy sat motionless, staring slantwise at the man. "Not so I know of."

"Very well." The man blew on the photographs and put them back into his pocket. "That was my wife."

"Dead?" the boy asked.

Slowly the man shook his head. He pursed his lips as though

about to whistle and answered in a long-drawn way; "Nuuu — " he said. "I will explain."

The beer on the counter before the man was in a large brown mug. He did not pick it up to drink. Instead he bent down and, putting his face over the rim, he rested there for a moment. then with both hands he tilted the mug and sipped.

"Some night you'll go to sleep with your nose in a mug and drown," said Leo. "Prominent transient drowns in beer. That would be a cute death."

The paper boy tried to signal to Leo. While the man was not looking he screwed up his face and worked his mouth to question soundlessly: "Drunk?" But Leo only raised his eyebrows and turned away to put some pink strips of bacon on the grill. The man pushed the mug away from him, straightened himself, and folded his loose crooked hands on the counter. His face was sad as he looked at the paper boy. He did not blink, but from time to time the lids closed down with delicate gravity over his pale green eyes. It was nearing dawn and the boy shifted the weight of the paper sack.

"I am talking about love," the man said. "With me it is a science."

The boy half slid down from the stool. But the man raised his forefinger, and there was something about him that held the boy and would not let him go away.

"Twelve years ago I married the woman in the photograph. She was my wife for one year, nine months, three days, and two nights. I loved her. Yes . . . " He tightened his blurred, rambling voice and said again: "I loved her. I thought also that she loved me. I was a railroad engineer. She had all home comforts and luxuries. It never crept into my brain that she was not satisfied. But do you know what happened?"

"Mgneeow!" said Leo.

The man did not take his eyes from the boy's face. "She left me. I came in one night and the house was empty and she was gone. She left me."

"With a fellow?" the boy asked.

Gently the man placed his palm down on the counter. "Why naturally, Son. A woman does not run off like that alone."

The café was quiet, the soft rain black and endless in the street outside. Leo pressed down the frying bacon with the prongs of his long fork. "So you have been chasing the floozie for eleven years. You frazzled old rascal!"

For the first time the man glanced at Leo. "Please don't be vulgar. Besides, I was not speaking to you." He turned back to the boy and said in a trusting and secretive undertone: "Let's not pay any attention to him. O.K.?"

The paper boy nodded doubtfully.

"It was like this," the man continued. "I am a person who feels many things. All my life one thing after another has impressed me. Moonlight. The leg of a pretty girl. One thing after another. But the point is that when I had enjoyed anything there was a peculiar sensation as though it was laying around loose in me. Nothing seemed to finish itself up or fit in with the other things. Women? I had my portion of them. The same. Afterwards laying around loose in me. I was a man who had never loved."

Very slowly he closed his eyelids, and the gesture was like a curtain drawn at the end of a scene in a play. When he spoke again his voice was excited and the words came fast—the lobes of his large, loose ears seemed to tremble.

"Then I met this woman. I was fifty-one years old and she always said she was thirty. I met her at a filling station and we were married within three days. And do you know what it was like? I just can't tell you. All I had ever felt was gathered together around this woman. Nothing lay around loose in me any more but was finished up by her."

The man stopped suddenly and stroked his long nose. His voice sank down to a steady and reproachful undertone: "I'm not explaining this right. What happened was this. There were these beautiful feelings and loose little pleasures inside me. And this woman was something like an assembly line for my soul. I run these little pieces of myself through her and I come out complete. Now do you follow me?"

"What was her name?" the boy asked.

"Oh," he said, "I called her Dodo. But that is immaterial."

"Did you try to make her come back?"

The man did not seem to hear. "Under the circumstances you can imagine how I felt when she left me."

Leo took the bacon from the grill and folded two strips of it between a bun. He had a gray face, with slitted eyes, and a pinched nose saddled by faint blue shadows. One of the mill workers signaled for more coffee and Leo poured it. He did not give refills on coffee free. The spinner ate breakfast there every morning, but the better Leo knew his customers the stingier he treated them. He nibbled his own bun as though he grudged it to himself.

"And you never got hold of her again?"

The boy did not know what to think of the man, and his child's face was uncertain with mingled curiosity and doubt. He was new on the paper route; it was still strange to him to be out in the town in the black, queer early morning.

"Yes," the man said. "I took a number of steps to get her back. I went around trying to locate her. I went to Tulsa where she had folks. And to Mobile. I went to every town she had ever mentioned to me, and I hunted down every man she had formerly been connected with. Tulsa, Atlanta, Chicago, Cheehaw, Memphis. . . . For the better part of two years I chased around the country trying to lay hold of her."

"But the pair of them had vanished from the face of the earth!" said Leo.

"Don't listen to him," the man said confidentially. "And also just forget those two years. They are not important. What matters is that around the third year a curious thing begun to happen to me."

"What?" the boy asked.

The man leaned down and tilted his mug to take a sip of beer. But as he hovered over the mug his nostrils fluttered slightly; he sniffed the staleness of the beer and did not drink. "Love is a curious thing to begin with. At first I thought only of getting her back. It was a kind of mania. But then as time went on I tried to remember her. But do you know what happened?"

"No," the boy said.

"When I laid myself down on a bed and tried to think about her my mind became a blank. I couldn't see her. I would take out her pictures and look. No good. Nothing doing. A blank. Can you imagine it?"

"Say Mac!" Leo called down the counter. "Can you imagine this bozo's mind a blank!"

Slowly, as though fanning away flies, the man waved his hand. His green eyes were concentrated and fixed on the shallow little face of the paper boy.

"But a sudden piece of glass on a sidewalk. Or a nickel tune in a music box. A shadow on a wall at night. And I would remember. It might happen in a street and I would cry or bang my head against a lamppost. You follow me?"

"A piece of glass . . . " the boy said.

"Anything. I would walk around and I had no power of how and when to remember her. You think you can put up a kind of shield. But remembering don't come to a man face forward—it corners around sideways. I was at the mercy of everything I saw and heard. Suddenly instead of me combing the countryside to find her she begun to chase me around in my very soul. *She* chasing *me*, mind you! And in my soul."

The boy asked finally: "What part of the country were you in then?"

"Ooh," the man groaned. "I was a sick mortal. It was like smallpox. I confess, Son, that I boozed. I fornicated. I committed any sin that suddenly appealed to me. I am loath to confess it but I will do so. When I recall that period it is all curdled in my mind, it was so terrible."

The man leaned his head down and tapped his forehead on the counter. For a few seconds he stayed bowed over in this position, the back of his stringy neck covered with orange furze, his hands with their long warped fingers held palm to palm in an attitude of prayer. Then the man straightened himself; he was smiling and suddenly his face was bright and tremulous and old.

"It was in the fifth year that it happened," he said. "And with it I started my science."

Leo's mouth jerked with a pale, quick grin. "Well none of we boys are getting any younger," he said. Then with sudden anger he balled up a dishcloth he was holding and threw it down hard on the floor. "You draggle-tailed old Romeo!"

"What happened?" the boy asked.

The old man's voice was high and clear: "Peace," he answered.

"Huh?"

It is hard to explain scientifically, Son," he said. "I guess the logical explanation is that she and I had fleed around from each other for so long that finally we just got tangled up together and lay down and quit. Peace. A queer and beautiful blankness. It was spring in Portland and the rain came every afternoon. All evening I just stayed there on my bed in the dark. And that is how the science come to me."

The windows in the streetcar were pale blue with light. The two soldiers paid for their beers and opened the door—one of the soldiers combed his hair and wiped off his muddy puttees before they went outside. The three mill workers bent silently over their breakfasts. Leo's clock was ticking on the wall.

"It is this. And listen carefully. I meditated on love and reasoned it out. I realized what is wrong with us. Men fall in love for the first time. And what do they fall in love with?"

The boy's soft mouth was partly open and he did not answer.

"A woman," the old man said. "Without science, with nothing to go by, they undertake the most dangerous and sacred experience in God's earth. They fall in love with a woman. Is that correct, Son?"

"Yeah," the boy said faintly.

"They start at the wrong end of love. They begin at the climax. Can you wonder it is so miserable? Do you know how men should love?"

The old man reached over and grasped the boy by the collar of his leather jacket. He gave him a gentle little shake and his green eyes gazed down unblinking and grave.

"Son, do you know how love should be begun?"

The boy sat small and listening and still. Slowly he shook his head. The old man leaned closer and whispered:

"A tree. A rock. A cloud."

It was still raining outside in the street: a mild, gray, endless rain. The mill whistle blew for the six o'clock shift and the three spinners paid and went away. There was no one in the café but Leo, the old man, and the little paper boy.

"The weather was like this in Portland," he said. "At the time my science was begun. I meditated and I started very cautious. I would pick up something from the street and take it home with me. I bought a goldfish and I concentrated on the goldfish and I loved it. I graduated from one thing to another. Day by day I was getting this technique. On the road from Portland to San Diego—"

"Aw shut up!" screamed Leo suddenly. "Shut up! Shut up!"

The old man still held the collar of the boy's jacket; he was trembling and his face was earnest and bright and wild. "For six years now I have gone around by myself and built up my science. And now I am a master. Son. I can love anything. No longer do I have to think about it even. I see a street full of people and a beautiful light comes in me. I watch a bird in the sky. Or I meet a traveler on the road. Everything, Son. And anybody. All stranger and all loved! Do you realize what a science like mine can mean?"

The boy held himself stiffly, his hands curled tight around the counter edge. Finally he asked: "Did you ever really find that lady?"

"What? What say, Son?"

"I mean," the boy asked timidly. "Have you fallen in love with a woman again?"

The old man loosened his grasp on the boy's collar. He turned away and for the first time his green eyes had a vague and scattered look. He lifted the mug from the counter, drank down the yellow beer. His head was shaking slowly from side to side. Then finally he answered: "No, Son. You see that is the last step in my science. I go cautious. And I am not quite ready yet."

"Well!" said Leo. "Well well well!"

The old man stood in the open doorway. "Remember," he said. Framed there in the gray damp light of the early morning he looked shrunken and seedy and frail. But his smile was bright. "Remember I love you," he said with a last nod. And the door closed quietly behind him.

The boy did not speak for a long time. He pulled down the bangs on his forehead and slid his grimy little forefinger around the rim of his empty cup. Then without looking at Leo he finally asked:

"Was he drunk?"

"No," said Leo shortly.

The boy raised his clear voice higher. "Then was he a dope fiend?"

"No."

The boy looked up at Leo, and his flat little face was desperate, his voice urgent and shrill. "Was he crazy? Do you think he was a lunatic?" The paper boy's voice dropped suddenly with doubt. "Leo? Or not?"

But Leo would not answer him. Leo had run a night café for fourteen years, and he held himself to be a critic of craziness. There were the town characters and also the transients who roamed in from the night. He knew the manias of all of them. But he did not want to satisfy the questions of the waiting child. He tightened his pale face and was silent.

So the boy pulled down the right flap of his helmet and as he turned to leave he made the only comment that seemed safe to him, the only remark that could not be laughed down and despised:

"He sure has done a lot of traveling."

Discussion

1. The least prominent character in the story, Leo, is given a name, and we are told the kind of person he is but not what he looks like. Neither of the two main characters is given a name, but we are told what they look like as clearly as in a photograph. Why do you think McCuller did this?
2. What might be the author's reason for describing a person only a little at a time as the story progresses, rather than describing him or her all at once? How did you go about describing the person you interviewed for the In-Class Writing assignment? How will you approach your description for your Formal Writing?

LANGUAGE LEARNING

Choosing the Right Words (1). In the two stories you've just read, the authors bring you directly into the scenes; they create the illusion that you're there. The right choice of words is largely responsible for this cutting through of reality to draw the reader into the story. And it is the force of the storytelling that also pulls the reader along. The language in these readings, though, consists of just everyday vocabulary — you don't need a dictionary to understand what is going on.

READINGS

The four readings that follow — two very brief excerpts, a poem, and a Hemingway story — reveal a more vivid use of language. Like painters, these authors use broad strokes of color and brilliance to make their descriptions sharp and vivid. Bright images, similes, and metaphors draw attention to themselves. All the senses are registered, communicating how keenly our senses respond not only to direct stimuli and contact but also to precise and economical description.

Notice how all the senses — touch, sight, sound, taste, and smell — are described here.

FIRST LOVE   Henry Miller

In my mind's eye I can see her today just as vividly as when I first
met her, which was in one of the corridors of Eastern District High
School (Brooklyn) as she was going from one classroom to another.
She was just a little shorter than I, well built, that is to say rather
buxom, radiant, bursting with health, head high, glance at once im-
perious and saucy, concealing a shyness which was disconcerting.
She had a warm, generous mouth filled with rather large, dazzling
white teeth. But it was her hair and eyes which drew one first.
Light golden hair it was, combed up stiff in the form of a conch. A
natural blonde such as one seldom sees except in an opera. Her
eyes, which were extremely limpid, were full and round. They
were a China blue, and they matched her golden hair and her ap-
ple-blossom complexion. She was only sixteen, of course, and not
very sure of herself, though she seemed to give the impression that
she was. She stood out from all the other girls in the school, like
someone with blue blood in her veins. Blue blood and icy, I am
tempted to say.

MARTHA QUEST   Doris Lessing

Mr. Jasper Cohen already owned her heart because of a quality one
might imagine would make it impossible: he was hideously ugly.
No, not hideously: he was fantastically ugly, so ugly the word
hardly applied. He was short, he was squat, he was pale: but these
were words one might as justly use for Joss, his nephew, or for his
brother, Max. His body was broad beyond squareness: it had a
swelling, humped look. His head was enormous: a vast, pale,
domed forehead reached to a peak where the hair began, covering a
white, damp scalp in faint oily streaks, and breaking above the ears
into a black fuzz that seemed to Martha pathetic, like the tender,
defenceless fuzz of a baby's head. His face was inordinately broad,
a pale, lumpy expanse, with a flat, lumpy nose, wide, mauvish lips,
and ears rioting out on either side like scrolls. His hands were
equally extraordinary: broad, deep palms puffed themselves into
rolls of thick white flesh, ending in short, spatulate fingers almost
as broad as long. They were the hands of a grotesque; and as they
moved clumsily in a drawer, looking for something, Martha
watched them in suspense, wishing she might offer to help him.
She longed to do something for him; for this ugly man had something so tender and sweet in his face, together with the stubborn
dignity of an afflicted person who intends to make no apologies or
claims for something he cannot help, that she was asking herself,
What is ugliness? She was asking it indignantly, the protest di-
rected against nature itself; and, perhaps for the first time in her life
she wondered with secret gratitude what it would be like to be born

plain, born ugly, instead of into, if not the aristocracy, at least the middle classes of good looks.

The poem that follows is steeped in sensory data — well, all but one. It describes an encounter that might also be seen as two strangers meeting.

SINEW   Raymond Carver

The girl minding the store.
She stands at the window
picking a piece of pork
from her teeth. Idly
watching the men in serge suits,
waistcoats, and ties,
dapping for trout in Lough Gill,
near the Isle of Innisfree.
The remains of her midday meal
congealing on the sill.
The air is still warm.
A cuckoo bird calls.

Close in, a man in a boat,
wearing a hat, looks
toward shore, the little store,
and the girl. He looks, whips
his line, and looks some more.
She leans closer to the glass.
Goes out then to the lakeside.
But it's the cuckoo in the bush
that has her attention.

The man strikes a fish,
is all business now.
The girl goes on working
at the sinew in her teeth.
But she watches this well-dressed
man reaching out
to slip a net under his fish.

In a minute, shyly, he floats near,
holds up his catch for the girl's pleasure
Doffs his hat. She stirs and smiles,
a little. Raises her hand.
A gesture which starts the bird
in flight, toward Innisfree.

The man casts and casts again.
His line cuts the air. His fly
touches the water, and waits.
But what does this man
really care for trout?
What he'll take
from this day is the memory of
a girl working her finger
inside her mouth as their glances
meet, and a bird flies up.

They look at each other and smile.
In the still afternoon.
With not a word lost between them.

Discussion

1. The poem is a catalogue of concrete nouns and active verbs that together depict a scene of ceaseless activity. What is it that really happens?
2. From which of the five senses do data seem absent? Are they really absent?
3. How would you describe the encounter between the man and the girl?

HILLS LIKE WHITE ELEPHANTS   Ernest Hemingway

The hills across the valley of the Ebro were long and white. On this side there was no shade and no trees and the station was between two lines of rails in the sun. Close against the side of the station there was the warm shadow of the building and a curtain, made of strings of bamboo beads, hung across the open door into the bar, to keep out flies. The American and the girl with him sat at a table in the shade, outside the building. It was very hot and the express from Barcelona would come in forty minutes. It stopped at this junction for two minutes and went on to Madrid.

"What should we drink?" the girl asked. She had taken off her hat and put it on the table.

"It's pretty hot," the man said.

"Let's drink beer."

"Dos cervezas," the man said into the curtain.

"Big ones?" a woman asked from the doorway.

"Yes. Two big ones."

The woman brought two glasses of beer and two felt pads. She put the felt pads and the beer glasses on the table and looked at the man and the girl. The girl was looking off at the line of hills. They were white in the sun and the country was brown and dry.

"They look like white elephants," she said.

"I've never seen one," the man drank his beer.

"No, you wouldn't have."

"I might have," the man said. "Just because you say I wouldn't have doesn't prove anything."

The girl looked at the bead curtain. "They've painted something on it," she said. "What does it say?"

"Anis del Toro. It's a drink."

"Could we try it?"

The man called "Listen" through the curtain. The woman came out from the bar.

"Four reales."

"We want two Anis del Toro."

"With water?"

"Do you want it with water?"

"I don't know," the girl said. "Is it good with water?"

"It's all right."

"You want them with water?" asked the woman.

"Yes, with water."

"It tastes like licorice," the girl said and put the glass down.

"That's the way with everything."

"Yes," said the girl. "Everything tastes of licorice. Especially all the things you've waited so long for, like absinthe."

"Oh, cut it out."

"You started it," the girl said. "I was being amused. I was having a fine time."

"Well, let's try to have a fine time."

"All right. I was trying. I said the mountains looked like white elephants. Wasn't that bright?"

"That was bright."

"I wanted to try this new drink. That's all we do, isn't it—look at things and try new drinks?"

"I guess so."

The girl looked across at the hills.

"They're lovely hills," she said. "They don't really look like white elephants. I just meant the coloring of their skin through the trees."

"Should we have another drink?"

"All right."

The warm wind blew the bead curtain against the table.

"The beer's nice and cool," the man said.

"It's lovely," the girl said.

"It's really an awfully simple operation, Jig," the man said. "It's not really an operation at all."

The girl looked at the ground the table legs rested on.

"I know you wouldn't mind it, Jig. It's really not anything. It's just to let the air in."

The girl did not say anything.

"I'll go with you and I'll stay with you all the time. They just let the air in and then it's all perfectly natural."

"Then what will we do afterward?"

"We'll be fine afterward. Just like we were before."

"What makes you think so?"

"That's the only thing that bothers us. It's the only thing that's made us unhappy.'

The girl looked at the bead curtain, put her hand out and took hold of two of the strings of beads.

"And you think then we'll be all right and be happy."

"I know we will. You don't have to be afraid. I've known lots of people that have done it."

"So have I," said the girl. "And afterward they were all so happy."

"Well," the man said, "if you don't want to you don't have to. I wouldn't have you do it if you didn't want to. But I know it's perfectly simple."

"And you really want to?"

"I think it's the best thing to do. But I don't want you to do it if you don't really want to."

"And if I do it you'll be happy and things will be like they were and you'll love me?"

"I love you now. You know I love you."

"I know. But if I do it, then it will be nice again if I say things are like white elephants, and you'll like it?"

"I'll love it. I love it now but I just can't think about it. You know how I get when I worry."

"If I do it you won't ever worry?"

"I won't worry about that because it's perfectly simple."

"Then I'll do it. Because I don't care about me."

"What do you mean?"

"I don't care about me."

"Well, I care about you."

"Oh, yes. But I don't care about me. And I'll do it and then everything will be fine."

"I don't want you to do it if you feel that way."

The girl stood up and walked to the end of the station. Across, on the other side, were fields of grain and trees along the banks of the Ebro. Far away, beyond the river, were mountains. The shadow of a cloud moved across the field of grain and she saw the river through the trees.

"And we could have all this," she said. "And we could have everything and every day we make it more impossible."

"What did you say?"

"I said we could have everything."

"We can have everything."

"No, we can't."

"We can have the whole world."

"No, we can't."

"We can go everywhere."

"No, we can't. It isn't ours any more."

"It's ours."

"No, it isn't. And once they take it away, you never get it back."

"But they haven't taken it away."

"We'll wait and see."

"Come on back in the shade," he said. "You musn't feel that way."

"I don't feel any way," the girl said. "I just know things."

"I don't want you to do anything that you don't want to do —"

"Nor that isn't good for me," she said. "I know. Could we have another beer?"

"All right. But you've got to realize —"

"I realize," the girl said. "Can't we maybe stop talking?"

They sat down at the table and the girl looked across at the hills on the dry side of the valley and the man looked at her and at the table.

"You've got to realize," he said, "that I don't want you to do it if you don't want to. I'm perfectly willing to go through with it if it means anything to you."

"Doesn't it mean anything to you? We could get along."

"Of course it does. But I don't want anybody but you. I don't want any one else. And I know it's perfectly simple."

"Yes, you know it's perfectly simple."

"It's all right for you to say that, but I do know it."

"Would you do something for me now?"

"I'd do anything for you."

"Would you please please please please please please please stop talking?"

He did not say anything but looked at the bags against the wall of the station. There were labels on them from all the hotels where they had spent nights.

"But I don't want you to," he said. "I don't care anything about it."

"I'll scream," said the girl.

The woman came out through the curtains with two glasses of beer and put them down on the damp felt pads. "The train comes in five minutes," she said.

"What did she say?" asked the girl.

"That the train is coming in five minutes."

The girl smiled brightly at the woman, to thank her.

"I'd better take the bags over to the other side of the station," the man said. She smiled at him.

"All right. Then come back and we'll finish the beer."

He picked up the two heavy bags and carried them around the station to the other tracks. He looked up the tracks but could not see the train. Coming back, he walked through the barroom, where people waiting for the train were drinking. He drank an Anis at the bar and looked at the people. They were all waiting reasonably for the train. He went out through the bead curtain. She was sitting at the table and smiled at him.

"Do you feel better?" he asked.

"I feel fine," she said. "There's nothing wrong with me. I feel fine."

Discussion

1. The simile that forms the story's title, "Hills Like White Elephants," also plays a key role in the dialogue between the man and the girl. How does the girl explain how she came to choose the simile she used?
2. What effect does her explanation seem to have on the course of their conversation?
3. What similes might you use to describe distant hills?

LANGUAGE LEARNING

Choosing the Right Words (2). If you saw them on the street, you would have no trouble recognizing the schoolboy's "first love" or Mr. Cohen, because the writers, Henry Miller and Doris Lessing, use vivid words to describe the striking characteristics in the appearance of both characters. For instance, when Miller describes the girl's body, he uses the word *buxom*, and when Lessing depicts Mr. Cohen's fingers, she calls them *lumpy*. The dictionary defines *buxom* as plump and *lumpy* as fat. However, the phrases *a plump body* and *fat fingers* do not arouse sensory and emotional responses. They provide the literal scene but not the emotional flavor.

The literal meaning of words is called *denotation*. A denotative word names or identifies an object, but it does not elicit a sensory image or an emotional response. In vivid writing, the good writer tries to evoke strong feelings in the reader. To achieve this purpose, the writer looks for words that excite, shock, or in some way stir up the audience. The ability of words to arouse this kind of response is called *connotative*.

Below are several denotative words frequently used to describe people. Next to each is a series of more vivid, connotative words. As you read through them, you will notice that some of them arouse pleasant images, while others are distinctly unpleasant. Try to decide which ones you would use for someone you like and which you would use for someone you dislike.

fat	chubby, buxom, overweight, robust, heavy, stout, corpulent, obese, thick, plump, pudgy
thin	slim, slender, willowy, spindly, scrawny, wizened, lean, emaciated, wispy
smooth	silky, glassy, velvety, sleek, glazed, satiny
short	stumpy, tiny, squat, dwarfish, puny, petite, little, stunted, runty, diminutive
tall	lanky, rangy, towering, gangling, stringy, statuesque
colorless	pallid, ashen, pasty, white, anemic, pale

When you are writing a description, it is useful to know that your choice of using either denotative or connotative words depends largely on your attitude toward or distance from the person or object being described. A preference for denotative words suggests a neutral or objective approach to your subject, while a leaning toward connotative words creates a description in which the observer's feelings and attitudes are absorbed into the object being described. This is to say that the former leans toward the factual account, whereas the latter presents a personal interpretation of what is being described.

Exercise

"He was overbearing even when seeming deferential." These are the words Joyce Carol Oates uses about Karl in the story on p. 6. But why does she not give us a physical description of him, since she took such care to make us see Renée? She doesn't hesitate to tell us what he is like as a person. Still, we'd like to know what he looks like. Perhaps Oates would prefer that we describe Karl for ourselves, attempting to see him as Renée and the author do.

On the lines below, describe Karl as you see him. To help you do this, we have provided the same structure and word order that Oates uses to describe Renée. Simply fill in the blank spaces with your own choices of words that describe Karl as he looks to you.

Karl, _____ _____ _____ _____, with _____
_____ hair sometimes worn _____ to his shoulders and sometimes _____ _____ _____ _____ _____ _____,
had the look, he supposed of, of a university student; one of

those _____ _____ _____ quite often _____ guys whose
bearing — both _____ and _____ — make them popular
with women of a certain type. Never extravagantly dressed,
never ostentatiously _____, their appeal is almost _____:
even their _____, if they are _____, is an arrangement of
facial bones, _____ _____ cheekbones, _____ _____
body. His forehead was _____ _____. His eyebrows were
_____ and _____, making his eyes appear _____ than
they were.

FORMAL WRITING

Describing Someone You Recently Met. Through the interview with your classmate, the two of you have become acquainted in such a way that the word *friend* might aptly describe the regard that now exists — no longer strangers. Though you still have the notes for that interview, you may want to choose someone else to write about for this assignment, someone who is also accessible to you, at least occasionally, so that you can spend an hour, perhaps more, in that person's company. Think about the person's most distinctive quality, what gesture seems to be his or her trademark, and which attributes he or she shares with your other friends. Make the portrait you draw vivid. To give your description a narrative bent, you might want to begin by describing the situation that drew the two of you together as strangers.

Although your meeting occurred in the past, your story will bring us up to the present time: now. In a sense, then, you are in the process of learning who your new friend is. You are discovering a person.

READING

The following excerpt from "Music for Chameleons," by Truman Capote, offers a clear model for you to see and hear how stories written in the present tense strike the eye as well as the ear. It may also offer a hint as to how your own narrative develops.

MUSIC FOR CHAMELEONS   Truman Capote

She is tall and slender, perhaps seventy, silver-haired, soigné, neither black nor white, a pale golden rum color. She is a Martinique aristocrat who lives in Fort de France but also has an apartment in Paris. We are sitting on the terrace of her house, an airy, elegant house that looks as if it was made of wooden lace; it reminds me of certain old New Orleans houses. We are drinking iced mint tea slightly flavored with absinthe.

Three green chameleons race one another across the terrace; one pauses at Madame's feet, flicking its forked tongue, and she comments: "Chameleons. Such exceptional creatures. The way they change color. Red. Yellow. Lime. Pink. Lavender. And did you know they are very fond of music?" She regards me with her fine black eyes. "You don't believe me?"

During the course of the afternoon she had told me many curious things. How at night her garden was filled with mammoth night-flying moths. That her chauffeur, a dignified figure who had driven me to her house in a dark green Mercedes, was a wife-poisoner who had escaped from Devil's Island. And she had described a village high in the northern mountains that is entirely inhabited by albinos. "Little, pink-eyed people white as chalk. Occasionally one sees a few on the streets of Fort de France."

"Yes, of course I believe you."

She tilts her silver head. "No, you don't. But I shall prove it."

So saying, she drifts into her cool Caribbean salon, a shadowy room with gradually turning ceiling fans, and poses herself at a well-tuned piano. I am still sitting on the terrace but I can observe her, this chic, elderly woman, the product of varied bloods. She begins to perform a Mozart sonata.

Eventually, the chameleons accumulated; a dozen, a dozen more, most of them green, some scarlet, lavender. They skittered across the terrace and scampered into the salon, a sensitive, absorbed audience for the music played. And then not played, for suddenly my hostess stood and stamped her foot, and the chameleons scattered like sparks from an exploding star.

Now she regards me. "*Et maintenant? C'est vrai?*"

"Indeed. But it seems so strange."

Raising my eyes from the mirror's demonic shine, I notice my hostess has momentarily retreated from the terrace into her shadowy salon. A piano chord echoes, and another. Madame is toying with the same tune. Soon the music lovers assemble, chameleons, scarlet, green, lavender, an audience that, lined out on the floor of the terra-cotta terrace, resembles a written arrangement of musical notes. A Mozartean mosaic.

CHAPTER 2

Describing a Place
Familiar and Unfamiliar

Each day, each minute, we are assaulted by sense impressions. Whether we are in a rural setting with the sight of its vast expanse of land, the smells of new-mown hay, and the sounds of birds, animals, and farm machinery, or in a crowded city with the wail of police car sirens, the vivid colors of neon signs, and the pressure of people crowded against each other on a rush-hour bus — we are constantly receiving messages from the environment. Even when we sit alone in our own homes, the messages from the outer world are always invading our consciousness.

Most of the time we are not aware of these signals. We must, in fact, ignore them in order to function. When we drive down a busy highway, we do not notice the myriad sights, sounds, and smells; if we did, we might end up in an accident.

But though it may be vital to concentrate on the traffic when we are driving, there are many other occasions when we might enjoy responding to our environment if only we would give ourselves a chance. As we pass by a clump of trees in summer, we might be fascinated by the different shades of green. Or on a walk down Main Street, we could be intrigued by the pattern of cracks in the sidewalk. The smell of freshly baked bread, the sound of friends chatting, the glow of an airplane's jet stream in the late afternoon sky — such small details can add a moment's brightness to an otherwise boring day. Even unpleasant sense impressions — the jarring rattle of a jackhammer, the rusting frame of an abandoned pickup truck, the puckering sourness of an unripe apple — can remind us of the vitality of the world.

In the Readings in Chapter 1, you read how writers create —
out of ordinary words, out of vivid ones — scenes so real that they
give you the illusion of being there. Impressions received from all
their five senses they recorded with accuracy and sureness.

Here in Chapter 2, it is you who must do what the writers did
for you in Chapter 1, for the writing assignments in this chapter
keep you busy looking at familiar and unfamiliar things, naming
them as briefly and precisely as you can. Your objective here is to
create for *your* readers, from the impressions you gather, the illusion that they, too, are there. So, as you walk around your campus,
keep all five senses alert, recording and reporting. Your first task
is to describe your college.

READING   Before you make your tour of your campus, this excerpt from
Ralph Ellison's novel *The Invisible Man* might inspire you to look
more intently at what you see, for at some point in your life you
might find the images drifting back to you. This is what happens
to the "invisible man"; though his stay at the college had been
brief, we read his remembrance of it.

From THE INVISIBLE MAN   Ralph Ellison

It was a beautiful college. The buildings were old and covered with
vines and the roads gracefully winding, lined with hedges and wild
roses that dazzled the eyes in the summer sun. Honeysuckle and
purple wisteria hung heavy from the trees and white magnolias
mixed with their scents in the bee-humming air. I've recalled it
often, here in my hole: How the grass turned green in the springtime and how the mocking birds fluttered their tails and sang, how
the moon shone down on the buildings, how the bell in the chapel
tower rang out the precious short-lived hours; how the girls in
bright summer dresses promenaded the grassy lawn. Many times,
here at night, I've closed my eyes and walked along the forbidden
road that winds past the girls' dormitories, past the hall with the
clock in the tower, its windows warmly aglow, on down past the
small white Home Economics practice cottage, whiter still in the
moonlight, and on down the road with its sloping and turning, par-
alleling the black powerhouse with its engines droning earth-shak-
ing rhythms in the dark, its windows red from the glow of the furnace, on to where the road became a bridge over a dry riverbed,
tangled with brush and clinging vines; the bridge of rustic logs,
made for trysting, but virginal and untested by lovers; on up the
road, past the buildings, with the southern verandas half-a-city-
block long, to the sudden forking, barren of buildings, birds, or
grass, where the road turned off to the insane asylum.

It's so long ago and far away that here in my invisibility I wonder if it happened at all. Then in my mind's eye I see the bronze
statue of the college Founder, the cold Father symbol, his hands
outstretched in the breathtaking gesture of lifting a veil that flutters
in hard, metallic folds above the face of a kneeling slave; and I am
standing puzzled unable to decide whether the veil is really being
lifted, or lowered more firmly in place; whether I am witnessing a
revelation or a more efficient blinding. And as I gaze there is a rus-
tle of wings and I see a flock of starlings fighting before me and,
when I look again, the bronze face, whose empty eyes look upon a
world I have never seen, runs with liquid chalk — creating another
ambiguity to puzzle my groping mind: Why is a bird-soiled statue
more commanding than one that is clean?

Oh, long green stretch of campus, Oh, quiet songs at dusk, Oh, moon that kissed the steeple and flooded the perfumed nights, Oh, bugle that called in the morning, Oh, drum that marched us militarily at noon — what was real, what solid, what more than a pleasant, time-killing dream? For how could it have been real if now I am invisible? If real, why is it that I can recall in all that island of greenness no fountain but one that was broken, corroded and dry? And why does no rain fall through my recollections, sound through my memories, soak through the hard dry crust of the still so recent past? Why do I recall, instead of the odor of seed bursting in springtime, only the yellow contents of the cistern spread over the lawn's dead grass? Why? And how? How and why?

ACTIVITY   **Getting Acquainted with Your College.** The In-Class Writing that follows this Activity will test your skills for noticing details — significant details — and finding a way to organize them into increasingly larger units of description.

You and your classmates will work in teams of about four persons each. Each team will describe an important part of your college — a building, a monument, a plaza. From the notes you gather, your team will produce a paragraph, and the combined paragraphs of all the teams will then result in a well-organized descriptive essay. With this in mind, strive to make your pictorial composition accurate enough so that it could serve as a guide to a visitor in search of your school's points of interest.

What follows is the work of a basic writing class during its first semester at Lehman College in New York. On two mornings for two class periods, five groups of four students apiece each headed for different destinations — the college library, the fine arts building, the student cafeteria, the faculty cafeteria, and the campus plaza. Their instructions were the same as those above. What follows are the notes of three groups who visited the fine arts building and the faculty cafeteria.

The team visiting the fine arts building gathered the following notes:

Building with tinted windows. White walls with sloping roof. Chairs. Kids engaging in artwork. Glass doors throughout building. Abstract art, wooden art, stone and clay art. Nobody in gallery. Vertical blinds. Air conditioning. African & Indian Art. Clothes, shoes, necklace jewelry. Photos of people. Exit signs, doors, track lighting, electric outlets, statues, beads, feathers, white statues with no form, white statues in form of chicken with egg, also of a dog. There was cardboard dog, old sneakers, paintings mostly of fruit, vase and flower (painted by students). Bewt Hammon picture of women naked, checker board paintings. Classrooms in art gallery, security guard in building. The alarm system. The walls had yellow tiles and blue tiles on different sides. There was a wooden floor, carpeting, tile floor. Staircase. Typewriter noise. Voices of people. Light switches on wall.

The two teams who gathered notes on the faculty cafeteria described the scenery and the occupants, respectively:

Scenery
wood tables and chairs
(orange and brown) walls painted
carpet on the floor
very clean
atmosphere (comfortable, quiet, very relaxing)
notice most teachers sit alone, when empty, except when with
    a friend
not crowded
chandeliers from the ceiling
very classy looking
looks like an elegant restaurant
table secluded from the rest
only one with a tablecloth
looks like it is used for banquets
tables seat two and four in dining area
every table was clean except for a few tables

Occupants
A woman just entered the cafeteria.
She opens her sandwich, puts butter on her sandwich.
Recloses her sandwich inside the plastic.
She places everything inside a brown paper bag (soup, sand-
    wich, coffee).
Placed the tray on the rack and left.
Opposite the table, the two women are sitting.
There is an older lady drinking tea, sitting down.
Eating a piece of bread gazing out the window all by herself.
She has finished her food and is getting ready to eat dessert.
Got lime jello with whipped cream on top.
She's having a difficult time opening the top of the cover. She's
struggling.
She finally got it open
She is wiping the spoon and is now eating the jello.

Two women are sitting down talking to each other.
One has coffee, soup, and a sandwich.
One took a bite into her sandwich while the other is talking.
One is beginning to sip her soup and now she has sipped her
    soup and bit her sandwich.
The conversation is very low.
It's very quiet in the faculty cafeteria.

**RHETORIC
LEARNING**

Writing as a Decision-Making Process. Now that you have returned from your exploration, you will find that each team has
collected a mass of detail — information your senses have fed you,
mainly as impressions but also as more specific and direct contacts
with objects (statues, benches) and people on the move. Your task
now, as individuals working in a team, is to decide how you will
convert a mass of notes into a unified and coherent piece of writing.

It is here that the real process of writing begins. Now you must
make all those decisions which ultimately dictate the quality of
your final product. It is fair to warn you that the decisions you
make for this assignment are more diverse and complex than the
ones you confronted in the Formal Writing at the end of Chapter
1. There you were telling a story that was self-generated; you were
its creator, basing it for the most part on what you alone experienced. In this assignment, your experiences may be challenged by
how others have experienced objects and chosen words to describe
them. Having to make decisions of this kind will test almost every
skill you currently possess. It will, however, also point to all those
aspects of writing which later chapters, in Part Two and Part Three,
will expand on and clarify for you — especially expository writing,
where you make objective use of information, excluding what you
might think or feel about it. This is the kind of writing that will
most often be demanded of you throughout college and beyond.

**RHETORIC
LEARNING**

Making a Paragraph. Comparing the completed paragraph with
the quite voluminous team notes gathered by the students at Lehman College, you can see how many decisions had to be made.
Below is the paragraph the two groups who visited the faculty cafeteria came up with.

As we first enter the Faculty Cafeteria, we see a blackboard
which lists the day's specials. People standing by the blackboard are discussing the choices of food listed on the black-

board. As we enter the dining area, the atmosphere seems passive, comfortable, and relaxing. We seat ourselves near the entrance to the dining area. While we sit we notice the floor is carpeted, air-conditioning cooled the room; then we look at the golden yellow chandeliers. These accessories make the dining area look like an elegant restaurant. One table stands out among the others. It was covered with a tablecloth as if it were used for special occasions like banquets. While we're sitting, an elderly woman catches all of our attention. She is sitting alone gazing out of a window, drinking tea and nibbling on a piece of bread. She finishes her main course and then turns to her dessert, which is lime jello with whipped cream on top. She has a look of frustration on her face. She is having a hard time getting the container opened. After a while of struggling with the container the woman gets it opened. A look of relief covers her face immediately. She then wipes her spoon with a napkin and starts to eat.

IN-CLASS WRITING

Writing a Group Description. You have now made all the decisions necessary to reach the point where actual writing can begin. Keep in mind that you and your teammates are together writing just one paragraph, and that your paragraph, along with those of the other teams, will help create a composite portrait of your campus in the form of a descriptive essay that is both unified and coherent, with all the pieces fitting snugly into place.

Once your team completes the actual writing of its paragraph, each team member should read it over individually to make certain all the decisions made are the best ones. Word choice, phrasing, and sentence structure are among the most important aspects to consider. You will want agreement that all the elements move toward producing a dominant impression. If you don't have total agreement on what is written, then rewriting your paragraph may be your only recourse. Here is where you discover that rarely will you get a piece of writing correct or to your satisfaction the first time. Whether done individually or as a group, writing is, for the most part, re-writing.

LANGUAGE LEARNING

Improving Verbs. One way to sharpen the image you wish to convey is by using lively, precise verbs as modifiers when you are writing descriptive sentences. For instance, in the description of a person, you might have sentences like the following:

Maria has full, pale lips. Her small teeth are white.

Look what happens, though, when these two features are seen in relation to each other and a more concrete verb is used:

Maria's full, pink lips *frame* her small, white teeth.

Exercise

Look at the picture of the old house at the bottom of this page. Write sentences of description combining the listed features by using the verb in parentheses.

1. the small triangle on the right side
   the large triangle of the main part of the house
   (echo)
2. the worn shabby columns on either side of the door
   the fresh painted door
   (frame)

3. the downstairs windowpanes
   the bare branches of trees
   (reflect)
4. off-white shades in the upper windows
   the contents of the house
   (conceal)

Present Tense

In addition to stating the action, verbs also give an indication of when an action takes place; that is, they tell whether it is taking place now (present tense), took place at some earlier time (past tense), or will take place in the future (future tense). Within these broad categories are a number of variations, and a full discussion of all verb forms appears in the Appendix.

Causing trouble for some people is the fact that there are two present tenses — the simple present and present continuous that is formed by combining the correct form of the verb *to be* with the verb + *ing* as in

The wife enters the room as the husband *sleeps* soundly.
The husband *is sleeping* soundly as the wife enters the room.

The present continuous form is used primarily when there are two actions occurring in a sentence but one is an ongoing action interrupted by the other.

Others have difficulty if their native language is one in which the ending of the verb changes with almost every change in subject (the doer of the action) or noun. In Spanish, for instance, the changes in the verb *to speak* — *hablar* — are:

I speak	yo hablo	we speak	nosotros hablamos
you speak	tu hablas	you (plural) speak	ustedes hablan
you (formal) speak	usted habla	they speak	ellos, ellas hablan
he, she, it speaks	el, ella habla		

Similar changes existed hundreds of years ago in English, but gradually most of them have dropped out. Today English retains only one such change in the present tense — the one used when the subject is *he, she, it,* or words that substitute for them, such as *John, the lady, the radio, this, that.*

The present tense form in English of *speak* is:

I speak		we speak
you speak		you speak
he, she, it }	speak<u>s</u>	they speak

The change we make, as you can see, is adding *-s*. If you have difficulty with this form, you will have to learn to check your writing carefully whenever you are using the present tense.

Some verbs do not follow the regular rules completely. One of the most common is the verb *to be.* The present tense is given below:

I am		we are
you are		you are
he, she, it }	is	they are

You can see, however, that *to be* does retain the *-s* ending for *he, she,* and *it.*

Because English makes only this one change in the present tense, it is easy to forget it; nevertheless, you need to make an extra effort to remember it.

Exercise

The following passage is from *Zen and the Art of Motorcycle Maintenance,* by Robert M. Pirsig. Although it was written in the past tense, you should now rewrite it, substituting the proper present tense form for the verbs in parentheses.

He (had) _____ been having trouble with students who (had) _____ nothing to say. At first he (thought) _____ it (was) _____ just laziness but later it (became) _____ apparent that it (wasn't) _____. They just (couldn't) _____ think of anything to say.

One of them, a girl with strong-lensed glasses, (wanted) _____ to write a five-hundred-word essay about the United States. He (was) _____ used to the sinking feeling that comes from statements like this, and (suggested) _____ without disparagement that she narrow it down to just Bozeman.

When the paper (came) _____ due she (didn't) _____ have it and (was) _____ quite upset. She (had) _____ tried and tried but she just (couldn't) _____ think of anything to say. . . .

It just (stumped) _____ him. Now he (couldn't) _____ think of anything to say. A silence (occurred) _____, and then a peculiar answer: "Narrow it down to the *main street* of Bozeman." It (was) _____ a stroke of insight.

She (nodded) _____ dutifully and (went) _____ out. But just before her next class she (came) _____ back in real distress, tears this time, distress that (had) _____ obviously been there for a long time. She still (couldn't) _____ think of anything to say, and (couldn't) _____ understand why, if she (couldn't) _____ think of anything about all of Bozeman, she should be able to think of something about just one street.

He (was) _____ furious. "You're not *looking!*" he (said) _____. She really (wasn't) _____ looking and yet somehow (didn't) _____ understand this. He (told) _____ her angrily, "Narrow it down to the *front* of one building on the main street of Bozeman. The Opera House. Start with the upper left-hand brick."

Her eyes, behind the thick-lensed glasses, (opened) _____ wide.

She (came) _____ in the next class with a puzzled look and (handed) _____ him a five-thousand word essay on the front of the Opera House on the main street of Bozeman, Montana. "I sat in the hamburger stand across the street," she (said) _____, "and started writing about the first brick and the second brick, and then by the third brick it all started to come and I couldn't stop. They thought I was crazy, and they kept kidding me, but here it all is. I don't understand it."

Neither (did) _____ he, but on long walks through the streets of town he (thought) _____ about it and (concluded) _____ she (was) _____ evidently stopped with the same kind of blockage that had paralyzed him on his first day of teaching. She (was) _____ blocked because she (was) _____ trying to repeat, in her writing, things she (had) _____ already heard, just as on the first day he had tried to repeat things he had already decided to say. She (couldn't) _____ think of anything to write about Bozeman because she (couldn't) _____ recall anything she had heard worth repeating. She (was) _____ strangely unaware, that she (could) _____ look and see freshly for herself, as she (wrote) _____ without primary regard for what (had) _____ been said before. The narrowing down to one brick (destroyed) _____ the blockage because it (was) _____ so obvious that she (*had*) _____ to do some original and direct seeing.

Discussion

1. What was the student's problem?
2. Why was the girl's discovery a useful one?
3. What have you learned from her experience?
4. What problems might she now have as she writes her paper on the bricks of the building?

ACTIVITY   **Exploring Your Neighborhood.** This second activity sets up a task quite similar to the one you did in Chapter 1. In this instance, however, the purpose is not to explore a new place as a way of learning your way around, but instead to help you reexamine a place you believe you already know quite well — your neighborhood. "Neighborhood is a word that has come to sound like a Valentine," says Jane Jacobs, author of *The Life and Death of Great American Cities.* Whether you view your own neighborhood as a Valentine or a prison, it does form a focal point in your life. Writing largely about city neighborhoods, Jacobs continues:

> Even the most urbane citizen does care about the atmosphere of the street where he lives, no matter how much choice he has of pursuits outside it; and the common run of city people do depend greatly on their neighborhoods for the kind of everyday lives they lead.
>
> Let us assume (as is often the case) that city neighbors have nothing more fundamental in common with each other than that they share a fragment of geography.
>
> A city's very wholeness in bringing together people with communities of interest is one of its greatest assets, possibly the greatest.

As you walk your "fragment of geography," try to experience it as if for the first time. Focus more sharply on everything you see, hear, feel, smell, and taste, enjoying the full force of the inrush of stimuli. We suggest that you take two walks over the weekend, spacing them about twelve hours apart — one in the morning, one in the evening.

First Walk. To go walking in your neighborhood, you should start out as relaxed as possible. Wear comfortable shoes, and be unburdened of schedules, deadlines, and pressing engagements. Simply be relaxed. Take a long, leisurely walk down your block and around a corner or two. Consider the number of times you've walked the length and breadth of the block you live on and the streets that run perpendicular to it, just above and just below the house or apartment building you live in. How many times have you walked or run up and down these streets? Yet has it ever occurred to you just how much you've actually seen, heard, felt, smelled? Have you ever noticed anything special about your block? In how many ways could you distinguish it from any other town or city block? Are you uniquely different from any other person you've ever met or seen? If you are, is that uniqueness related to where you live? These are the kinds of questions you might mull over when, bright and early on Saturday morning, you take your first walk around your neighborhood. On this walk you are going to open up your five senses and let the stimuli waft into your consciousness. Don't force anything to happen; just walk and be relaxed in the activity itself. For this first experimental and experiential walk of, say, about twenty minutes, let the enjoyment of the stimuli as they press into your consciousness take over.

Second Walk. Either later in the same day or early Sunday morning, take a second walk. This time you will be deliberately focusing. Here, be more aware of what your senses tell you. You can call it a sensory trip, because you will consciously exercise your senses, which, in turn, will automatically heighten your awareness of what you are seeing, hearing, feeling, smelling. (If you want to exercise your taste, buy a pizza or a hot dog, or drink a soda or a cup of coffee, and devour it with zest!) When you get home, rummage through the imagery you collected. What things stand out most sharply?

Next, get out your paper and pencil and write a list of twenty objects you recall. Remember, however, that this is a list of *things*. Use a minimum of descriptive words; they will come later. You are being a materialist; you are concerned only with objects. Now you are ready to bring your list to class and read it to the group.

READINGS   In "Theme for English B," Langston Hughes invokes Harlem to hear him and talk to him as he sits down to write his theme. Hughes remained a Harlem resident until his death in 1967. The intimacy that exists between writers and their place is also evident in the subsequent story by Eudora Welty.

THEME FOR ENGLISH B   Langston Hughes

The instructor said,

> Go home and write
> a page tonight.
> And let that page come out of you —
> Then, it will be true.

I wonder if it's that simple?
I am twenty-two, colored, born in Winston-Salem.
I went to school there, then Durham, then here
to this college on the hill above Harlem.
I am the only colored student in my class.
The steps from the hill lead down into Harlem,
through a park, then I cross St. Nicholas,
Eighth Avenue, Seventh, and I come to the Y,
the Harlem Branch Y, where I take the elevator
up to my room, sit down, and write this page:

It's not easy to know what is true for you or me
at twenty-two, my age. But I guess I'm what
I feel and see and hear, Harlem, I hear you:
hear you, hear me — we two — you, me, talk on this page.
(I hear New York, too.) Me—who?

Well, I like to eat, sleep, drink, and be in love.
I like to work, read, learn, and understand life.

I like a pipe for a Christmas present,
or records — Bessie, bop, or Bach.
I guess being colored doesn't make me *not* like
the same things other folks like who are other races.
So will my page be colored that I write?
Being me, it will not be white.
But it will be
a part of you, instructor.
You are white —
yet a part of me, as I am a part of you.
That's American.
Sometimes perhaps you don't want to be a part of me.
Nor do I often want to be a part of you.
But we are, that's true!
As I learn from you,
I guess you learn from me —
although you're older — and white —
and somewhat more free.

This is my page for English B.

As you read "A Worn Path," by Eudora Welty, keep in mind the following quotation from the preface of *The Collected Stories of Eudora Welty:* "In general, my stories as they've come along have reflected their own present time . . . they came out of my response to it. . . . If they have any special virtue in this respect, it would lie in the fact that they, like the others, are stories written from within. They come from living here — they were part of living here, of my long familiarity with the thoughts and feelings of those around me, in their many shadings and variations and contradictions." (p. x)

A WORN PATH   Eudora Welty

It was December — a bright frozen day in the early morning. Far out in the country there was an old Negro woman with her head tied in a red rag, coming along a path through the pinewoods. Her name was Phoenix Jackson. She was very old and small and she walked slowly in the dark pine shadows, moving a little from side to side in her steps, with the balanced heaviness and lightness of a pendulum in a grandfather clock. She carried a thin, small cane made from an umbrella, and with this she kept tapping the frozen earth in front of her. This made a grave and persistent noise in the still air, that seemed meditative, like the chirping of a solitary little bird.

She wore a dark striped dress reaching down to her shoetops, and an equally long apron of bleached sugar sacks, with a full pocket; all neat and tidy, but every time she took a step she might have fallen over her shoelaces, which dragged from her unlaced shoes. She looked straight ahead. Her eyes were blue with age. Her skin had a pattern all its own of numberless branching wrinkles and as though a whole little tree stood in the middle of her forehead, but a golden color ran underneath, and the two knobs of her cheeks were illuminated by a yellow burning under the dark. Under the red rag her hair came down on her neck in the frailest of ringlets, still black, and with an odor like copper.

Now and then there was a quivering in the thicket. Old Phoenix said, "Out of my way, all you foxes, owls, beetles, jack rabbits, coons, and wild animals! . . . Keep out from under these feet, little bobwhites. . . . Keep the big wild hogs out of my path. Don't let none of those come running my direction. I got a long way." Under her small black-freckled hand her cane, limber as a buggy whip, would switch at the brush as if to rouse up any hiding things.

On she went. The woods were deep and still. The sun made the pine needles almost too bright to look at, up where the wind rocked. The cones dropped as light as feathers. Down in the hollow was the mourning dove — it was not too late for him.

The path ran up a hill. "Seem like there is chains about my feet, time I get this far," she said, in the voice of argument old people keep to use with themselves. "Something always take a hold on this hill — pleads I should stay."

After she got to the top she turned and gave a full, severe look behind her where she had come. "Up through pines," she said at length. "Now down through oaks."

Her eyes opened their widest and she started down gently. But before she got to the bottom of the hill a bush caught her dress.

Her fingers were busy and intent, but her skirts were full and long, so that before she could pull them free in one place they were caught in another. It was not possible to allow the dress to tear. "I in the thorny bush," she said. "Thorns, you doing your appointed work. Never want to let folks past — no sir. Old eyes thought you was a pretty little green bush."

Finally, trembling all over, she stood free, and after a moment dared to stoop for her cane.

"Sun so high!" she cried, leaning back and looking, while the thick tears went over her eyes. "The time getting all gone here."

At the foot of this hill was a place where a log was laid across the creek.

"Now comes the trial," said Phoenix.

Putting her right foot out, she mounted the log and shut her eyes. Lifting her skirt, leveling her cane fiercely before her, like a festival figure in some parade, she began to march across. Then she opened her eyes and she was safe on the other side.

"I wasn't as old as I thought," she said.

But she sat down to rest. She spread her skirts on the bank around her and folded her hands over her knees. Up above her was a tree in a pearly cloud of mistletoe. She did not dare to close her eyes, and when a little boy brought her a little plate with a slice of marble-cake on it she spoke to him. "That would be acceptable," she said. But when she went to take it there was just her own hand in the air.

So she left that tree, and had to go through a barbed-wire fence. There she had to creep and crawl, spreading her knees and stretching her fingers like a baby trying to climb the steps. But she talked loudly to herself; she could not let her dress be torn now, so late in the day, and she could not pay for having her arm or her leg sawed off if she got caught fast where she was.

At last she was safe through the fence and risen up out in the clearing. Big dead trees, like black men with one arm, were standing in the purple stalks of the withered cotton field. There sat a buzzard.

"Who you watching?"

In the furrow she made her way along.

"Glad this not the season for bulls," she said, looking sideways, "and the good Lord made his snakes to curl up and sleep in the winter. A pleasure I don't see no two-headed snake coming around that tree, where it come once. It took a while to get by him, back in the summer."

She passed through the old cotton and went into a field of dead corn. It whispered and shook, and was taller than her head. "Through the maze now," she said, for there was no path.

Then there was something tall, black, and skinny there, moving before her.

At first she took it for a man. It could have been a man dancing in the field. But she stood still and listened, and it did not make a sound. It was as silent as a ghost.

"Ghost," she said sharply, "who be you the ghost of? For I have heard of nary death close by."

But there was no answer, only the ragged dancing in the wind.

She shut her eyes, reached out her hand, and touched a sleeve. She found a coat and inside that an emptiness, cold as ice.

"You scarecrow," she said. Her face lighted. "I ought to be shut up for good," she said with laughter. "My senses is gone. I too old. I the oldest people I ever know. Dance, old scarecrow," she said, "while I dancing with you."

She kicked her foot over the furrow, and with mouth drawn down shook her head once or twice in a little strutting way. Some husks blew down and whirled in streamers about her skirts.

Then she went on, parting her way from side to side with the cane, through the whispering field. At last she came to the end, to a wagon track, where the silver grass blew between the red ruts. The quail were walking around like pullets, seeming all dainty and unseen.

"Walk pretty," she said. "This the easy place. This the easy going."

She followed the track, swaying through the quite bare fields, through the little strings of trees silver in their dead leaves, past cabins silver from weather, with the doors and windows boarded shut, all like old women under a spell sitting there. "I walking in their sleep," she said, nodding her head vigorously.

In a ravine she went where a spring was silently flowing through a hollow log. Old Phoenix bent and drank. "Sweetgum makes the water sweet," she said, and drank more. "Nobody knows who made this well, for it was here when I was born."

The track crossed a swampy part where the moss hung as white as lace from every limb. "Sleep on, alligators, and blow your bubbles." Then the track went into the road.

Deep, deep the road went down between the high green-colored banks. Overhead the live-oaks met, and it was as dark as a cave.

A black dog with a lolling tongue came up out of the weeds by the ditch. She was meditating, and not ready, and when he came at her she only hit him a little with her cane. Over she went in the ditch, like a little puff of milk-weed.

Down there, her senses drifted away. A dream visited her, and she reached her hand up, but nothing reached down and gave her a pull. So she lay there and presently went to talking. "Old woman," she said to herself, "that black dog come up out of the weeds to stall you off, and now there he sitting on his fine tail, smiling at you."

A white man finally came along and found her — a hunter, a young man, with his dog on a chain.

"Well, Granny!" he laughed. "What are you doing there?"

"Lying on my back like a June-bug waiting to be turned over, mister," she said, reaching up her hand.

He lifted her up, gave her a swing in the air, and set her down, "Anything broken, Granny?"

"No sir, them old dead weeds is springy enough," said Phoenix, when she had got her breath. "I thank you for your trouble."

"Where do you live, Granny?" he asked, while the two dogs were growling at each other.

"Away back yonder, sir, behind the ridge. You can't even see it from here."

"On your way home?"

"No, sir, I going to town."

"Why, that's too far! That's as far as I walk when I come out myself, and I get something for my trouble." He patted the stuffed bag he carried, and there hung down a little closed claw. It was one of the bobwhites, with its beak hooked bitterly to show it was dead. "Now you go on home, Granny!"

"I bound to go to town, mister," said Phoenix. "The time come around."

He gave another laugh, filling the whole landscape. "I know you colored people! Wouldn't miss going to town to see Santa Claus!"

But something held Old Phoenix very still. The deep lines in her face went into a fierce and different radiation. Without warning she had seen with her own eyes a flashing nickel fall out of the man's pocket on to the ground.

"How old are you, Granny?" he was saying.

"There is no telling, mister," she said, "no telling."

Then she gave a little cry and clapped her hands, and said, "Git on away from here, dog! Look! Look at that dog!" She laughed as if in admiration. "He ain't scared of nobody. He a big black dog." She whispered, "Sick him!"

"Watch me get rid of that cur," said the man. "Sick him. Pete! Sick him!"

Phoenix heard the dogs fighting and heard the man running and throwing sticks. She even heard a gunshot. But she was slowly bending forward by that time, further and further forward, the lids stretched down over her eyes, as if she were doing this in her sleep. Her chin was lowered almost to her knees. The yellow palm of her hand came out from the fold of her apron. Her fingers slid down and along the ground under the piece of money with the grace and care they would have in lifting an egg from under a sitting hen. Then she slowly straightened up, she stood erect, and the nickel was in her apron pocket. A bird flew by. Her lips moved. "God watching me the whole time. I come to stealing."

The man came back, and his own dog panted about them. "Well, I scared him off that time," he said, and then he laughed and lifted his gun and pointed it at Phoenix.

She stood straight and faced him.

"Doesn't the gun scare you?" he said, still pointing it.

"No, sir, I seen plenty go off closer by, in my day, and for less than what I done," she said, holding utterly still.

He smiled, and shouldered the gun. "Well, Granny," he said, "you must be a hundred years old, and scared of nothing. I'd give you a dime if I had any money with me. But you take my advice and stay home, and nothing will happen to you."

"I bound to go on my way, mister," said Phoenix. She inclined her head in the red rag. Then they went in different directions, but she could hear the gun shooting again and again over the hill.

She walked on. The shadows hung from the oak trees to the road like curtains. Then she smelled wood-smoke, and smelled the river, and she saw a steeple and the cabins on their steep steps. Dozens of little black children whirled around her. There ahead was Natchez shining. Bells were ringing. She walked on.

In the paved city it was Christmas time. There were red and green electric lights strung and crisscrossed everywhere, and all turned on in the daytime. Old Phoenix would have been lost if she had not distrusted her eyesight and depended on her feet to know where to take her.

She paused quietly on the sidewalk, where people were passing by. A lady came along in the crowd, carrying an armful of red-, green-, and silver-wrapped presents; she gave off perfume like the red roses in hot summer, and Phoenix stopped her.

"Please, missy, will you lace up my shoe?" She held up her foot.

"What do you want, Grandma?"

"See my shoe," said Phoenix. "Do all right for out in the country, but wouldn't look right to go in a big building."

"Stand still then, Grandma," said the lady. She put her packages down carefully on the sidewalk beside her and laced and tied both shoes tightly.

"Can't lace 'em with a cane," said Phoenix. "Thank you, missy. I doesn't mind asking a nice lady to tie up my shoe when I gets out on the street."

Moving slowly and from side to side, she went into the stone building and into a tower of steps, where she walked up and around and around until her feet knew to stop.

She entered a door, and there she saw nailed up on the wall the document that had been stamped with the gold seal and framed in the gold frame which matched the dream that was hung up in her head.

"Here I be," she said. There was a fixed and ceremonial stiffness over her body.

"A charity case, I suppose," said an attendant who sat at the desk before her.

But Phoenix only looked above her head. There was sweat on her face; the wrinkles shone like a bright net.

"Speak up, Grandma," the woman said. "What's your name? We must have your history, you know. Have you been here before? What seems to be the trouble with you?"

Old Phoenix only gave a twitch to her face as if a fly were bothering her.

"Are you deaf?" cried the attendant.

But then the nurse came in.

"Oh, that's just old Aunt Phoenix," she said. "She doesn't come for herself — she has a little grandson. She makes these trips just as regular as clockwork. She lives away back off the Old Natchez Trace." She bent down. "Well, Aunt Phoenix, why don't you just take a seat? We won't keep you standing after your long trip." She pointed.

The old woman sat down, bolt upright in the chair.

"Now, how is the boy?" asked the nurse.

Old Phoenix did not speak.

"I said, how is the boy?"

But Phoenix only waited and stared straight ahead, her face very solemn and withdrawn into rigidity.

"Is his throat any better?" asked the nurse. "Aunt Phoenix, don't you hear me? Is your grandson's throat any better since the last time you came for the medicine?"

With her hand on her knees, the old woman waited, silent, erect and motionless, just as if she were in armor.

"You mustn't take up our time this way, Aunt Phoenix," the nurse said. "Tell us quickly about your grandson, and get it over. He isn't dead, is he?"

At last there came a flicker and then a flame of comprehension across her face, and she spoke.

"My grandson. It was my memory had left me. There I sat and forgot why I made my long trip."

"Forgot?" The nurse frowned. "After you came so far?"

Then Phoenix was like an old woman begging a dignified forgiveness for waking up frightened in the night. "I never did go to school — I was too old at the Surrender," she said in a soft voice. "I'm an old woman without an education. It was my memory fail me. My little grandson, he is just the same, and I forgot it in the coming."

"Throat never heals, does it?" said the nurse, speaking in a loud, sure voice to Old Phoenix. By now she had a card with something written on it, a little list. "Yes. Swallowed lye. When was it — January — two — three years ago —"

Phoenix spoke unasked now. "No, missy, he not dead, he just the same. Every little while his throat begin to close up again, and he not able to swallow. He not get his breath. He not able to help himself. So the time come around, and I go on another trip for the soothing medicine."

"All right. The doctor said as long as you came to get it you could have it," said the nurse. "But it's an obstinate case."

"My little grandson, he sit up there in the house all wrapped up, waiting by himself," Phoenix went on. "We is the only two left in the world. He suffer and it don't seem to put him back at all. He got a sweet look. He going to last. He wear a little patch quilt and peep out, holding his mouth open like a little bird. I remembers so plain now. I not going to forget him again, no, the whole enduring time. I could tell him from all the others in creation."

"All right." The nurse was trying to hush her now. She brought her a bottle of medicine. "Charity," she said, making a check mark in a book.

Old Phoenix held the bottle close to her eyes and then carefully put it into her pocket.

"I thank you," she said.

"It's Christmas time, Grandma," said the attendant. "Could I give you a few pennies out of my purse?"

"Five pennies is a nickel," said Phoenix stiffly.

"Here's a nickel," said the attendant.

Phoenix rose carefully and held out her hand. She received the nickel and then fished the other nickel out of her pocket and laid it beside the new one. She stared at her palm closely, with her head on one side.

Then she gave a tap with her cane on the floor.

"This is what come to me to do," she said. "I going to the store and buy my child a little windmill they sells, made out of paper. He going to find it hard to believe there such a thing in the world. I'll march myself back where he waiting, holding it straight up in this hand."

She lifted her free hand, gave a little nod, turned round, and walked out of the doctor's office. Then her slow step began on the stairs, going down.

Discussion

1. Discuss the ways in which the student in "Theme for English B" and Aunt Phoenix reveal an intimacy with and knowledge of the neighborhoods they inhabit.
2. Welty has said, "My imagination takes its strength and guides its direction from what I see and hear and learn and feel and remember of my living world." How is this statement borne out in "A Worn Path"?
3. In "Theme for English B" the student invokes Harlem: ". . . hear me — we two — you, me, talk, on this page." How might you write such a dialogue?
4. Make lists of the visual (sight), auditory (sound), and tactile (touch) descriptions in "A Worn Path." How might you use this imagery to describe Aunt Phoenix's return?

IN-CLASS WRITING   **Writing About My Neighborhood: Getting Started.** Rely largely on freewriting to accomplish this exercise. Let it be a kind of spontaneous draft, a way of getting started on your Formal Writing.

Language may be your most important consideration. On your list of twenty objects noted during your walk, you'll find that the words you chose have either a denotative value (are objective) or reflect a sentiment of your own (are subjective). In thinking about your approach to describing your neighborhood, you might want to give attention to achieving a balance between these two ways of looking at your neighborhood.

FORMAL WRITING   **Describing a Walk Through Your Neighborhood.** Your major writing assignment for this chapter will enable you to make use of what you've done up to now — your walk and your list of twenty objects.

1. Now, you will want to expand that paragraph into a three-paragraph essay, focusing on as much detail as possible. Not only will you be describing what you saw, but you will be quite literally telling a story of your walk. Since nearly all stories have a beginning, a middle, and an end, your three paragraphs will be divided in just that way and in just that order — your first paragraph describing what you saw in the initial phase of your walk, your second paragraph describing

you in middle passage, and your third paragraph describing your final phase and concluding your essay.

2. Before you begin writing, get out your list and your paragraph and reread both. Remember, in this essay you are striving for specificity; you want to make each image so clear and sharp that your reader feels able to reach out and touch everything you describe.

3. Once you have completed the essay to your satisfaction, read it through (or have a friend or a family member read it to you), keeping in mind all you've learned about precision and specificity in descriptive writing.

4. To help you get started on your own, read the following account of a neighborhood walk. It, too, began with a list of twenty things observed, which in turn were absorbed into ten sentences. Now you see those sentences — revised, expanded, and more richly detailed — organized into an essay.

Pay particular attention to Jim Vaughn's organization: He begins by leaving his gate and tripping on a beer can and ends by returning a friendly growl to a neighbor's dog.

A SATURDAY'S WALK AROUND MY NEIGHBORHOOD
Jim Vaughn

Although I have always lived in a big city, I am generally not aware of it as a fact or what that fact means. But Saturday morning when I left my house for my walk through my neighborhood, even with the first step I took outside my gate, my foot clomped down on a half-flattened Schlitz beer can, but then when I counted four more before reaching the corner, I began to consider who I was and where I lived. But then I crossed the street, and there leaning against a No Parking sign was an old porcelain kitchen sink, browned by two generations of stains. Next to it was the weathered torso of an ancient Singer sewing machine. I thought that if a person is what he or she eats, then a neighborhood is what throws away.

I continued up the block, noticing or at least being aware of for the first time how much of my neighborhood consists of row houses, some built straight up, some protruding with bellylike bay windows. My mother tells my father that this is not architectural but is from too much beer. Reaching the corner of this short block, I looked up at the tall, dark, and brooding St. John's Hospital, which impresses me more as Count Dracula's Home for Aged Vampires. Opposite it and diagonally across from where I stood was a tiny, tree-studded park enclosing a statue of John Hancock. Remembering what he was famous for, I looked to see if he had his quill in his hand. But no, his arms were folded in a posture that suggested "I dare you." He seemed to be gazing off into the distance, probably into Pauline's Beauty Parlor.

Turning to my right, I advanced slowly up the next block that runs parallel to mine. It, too, consists of brownstone row houses. The attention-getter here was the hulk of a blue 1957 Pontiac that strippers had reduced to a gaping skeleton. But why a copy of *Prevention* on the back seat? I pondered this rounding the corner, again to my right, when oh! sweet distraction, the heavy wafting smell of oil and flour informed me that Alvarez's Pizza Hut was not far off. Imagining was enough: I bit into one of his crisp, saucy pizza slices, with the melted cheese gripping my upper palate, the hot tomato sauce swooshing against the sides of my mouth like a thick, spicy shower. I let imagination suffice. The noise of the early baseball players caught my attention over in the school ground. Just across from it, facing Alvarez's, is the entrance to the park. Elderly residents were out walking their dogs, while alongside the park front favorite benches were already in occupancy by morning sitters.

On my side of the street, in front of the vacant lot next to Alvarez's, I stopped to admire those beautiful blue flowers (or were they weeds?) growing randomly and profusely. Next to this lot, or rather a part of it, is an old frame house, the only one for blocks around: dark, secluded and shuttered, it sits far back off the street, almost concealed by two gigantic oak trees. I think I've heard it's become a museum or some other kind of city monument. Adjacent to it is one of those big-city apartment buildings. If buildings dream of their past, this one ought never to be reminded of its present.

At this point, I've reentered the block I live in. The pastor of Zion A.M.E. greeted me with a hello as he locked the side door. But already my eye was on Peter, the mangy, toothless mutt that belongs to a family living two doors from me. Peter growled, bared his purple gums, and arched his back as if he thought he were a cat. I said, "Hi, Peter." He sniffed and wagged his tail. It was a greeting of return from my trip around my neighborhood.

CHAPTER 3

Stopping to Look Ahead

You have now reached the third and final chapter of Part One. You are still a freshman, though maybe a little less fresh. This first of many endings provides for one "pause that refreshes" so that you can stop and look, yes, ahead, not back. What you have learned already is itself a part of your future. Now you can look ahead and learn still more.

No better opportunity exists than now to take stock of and reflect on whether or not things are going as you hoped. Writing offers you the most convenient entrance into your deeper thoughts, into what you really think. Some say that you write to find out just what you do know, while others say that if you can't write it, you probably don't know it. Proven or not, these observations ought to encourage you to write as a way of keeping open the lines of communication that are now in the process of opening up for you.

What better way to express your view at a major turning point in your life than to tell it in narrative form, using a narrator who can represent mostly what you think but what someone else may be thinking as well. The letter to a friend that you write at the end of this chapter will give you just such an opportunity to discover what you are learning. In addition are ample readings that represent opposing viewpoints on the present state of American colleges and universities and the students who attend them.

ACTIVITY   Attempt to answer some or most of the questions asked on the opposite page. Whether in small groups or as a class, you may find it useful to give your responses a visual or schematic representa-

Before you grit your teeth and plunge ahead, stop. Vague notions of buckling down, getting through college, and launching a career don't quite add up to direction. Before you go much further, you ought to determine where, approximately, you are going.

Do you know when, where, and how to study? the time? the place? and the techniques that produce the best results?

That means getting organized. It means setting your sights on the future and planning your college career accordingly, down to your semesters, weeks, and days.

Are You Getting Organized?

Are you handling the big assignments? Do you understand term papers and other major projects—the point of it all and some some pointers on mastering the process?

Are you making the grade on tests? Do you know what they're for? how to ease the anxiety over them? prepare for them? take them? and get the most out of them?

Are you making college "it"? Are you coping with the competition for your college time and energy—like jobs and family—and how to deal with the freedom of it all?

Do you know why (and how) to plan your future? your college career? your schedules? your weeks and days?

Are you solving the big problems? overcoming personal pressures? course difficulties? overloads—how to avoid giving up?

tion. For example, use a flow chart as a way of giving the correct sequence and a direction to the questions you answer. The answer to your first question should flow directly into your response to the second question and so on. If there are questions you would like answers to but they are not on the page, add them to your chart. Note at what point your chart ends — at the end of the current academic year? four years later? after college?

READINGS The following readings ought to help you further crystallize your thinking about why you have come to college, what to expect now that you're here, and how to go about doing what has to be done to make your years here rewarding.

The first reading is an essay that describes some of the pressures you are likely to confront. The three that follow, each in distinctive ways, present sobering views of what it takes today to adjust to the world of higher learning.

COLLEGE PRESSURES   William Zinsser

I see four kinds of pressure working on college students today; economic pressure, parental pressure, peer pressure, and self-induced pressure. It is easy to look around for villains — to blame the colleges for charging too much money, the professors for assigning too much work, the parents for pushing their children too far, the students for driving themselves too hard. But there are no villains; only victims.

"In the late 1960s," one dean told me, "the typical question that I got from students was 'Why is there so much suffering in the world?' or 'How can I make a contribution?' Today it's 'Do you think it would look better for getting into law school if I did a double major in history and political science, or just majored in one of them?' " Many other deans confirmed this pattern. One said: "They're trying to find an edge — the intangible something that will look better on paper if two students are about equal."

Note the emphasis on looking better. The transcript has become a sacred document, the passport to security. How one appears on paper is more important than how one appears in person. *A* is for Admirable and *B* is for Borderline, even though, in Yale's official system of grading, *A* means "excellent" and *B* means "very good." Today, looking very good is no longer good enough, especially for students who hope to go on to law school or medical school. They know that entrance into the better schools will be an entrance into the better law firms and better medical practices where they will make a lot of money. They also know that the odds are harsh.

The pressure is almost as heavy on students who just want to graduate and get a job. Long gone are the days of the "gentleman's C," when students journeyed through college with a certain relaxation, sampling a wide variety of courses — music, art, philosophy, classics, anthropology, poetry, religion — that would send them out as liberally educated men and women. If I were an employer I would rather employ graduates who have this range and curiosity than those who narrowly pursued safe subjects and high grades. I know countless students whose inquiring minds exhilarate me. I like to hear the play of their ideas. I don't know if they are getting As or Cs, and I don't care. I also like them as people. The country needs them, and they will find satisfying jobs. I tell them to relax. They can't.

Nor can I blame them. They live in a brutal economy. Tuition, room, and board at most private colleges now comes to at least $7,000, not counting books and fees. This might seem to suggest that the colleges are getting rich. But they are equally battered by inflation. Tuition covers only 60 percent of what it costs to educate a student, and ordinarily the remainder comes from what colleges receive in endowments, grants, and gifts. Now the remainder keeps being swallowed by the cruel costs — higher every year — of just opening the doors. Heating oil is up. Insurance is up. Postage is up. Health-premium costs are up. Everything is up. Deficits are up. We are witnessing in America the creation of a brotherhood of paupers — colleges, parents, and students, joined by the common bond of debt.

Along with economic pressure goes parental pressure. Inevitably, the two are deeply intertwined.

I see many students taking pre-medical courses with joyless tenacity. They go off to their labs as if they were going to the dentist. It saddens me because I know them in other corners of their life as cheerful people.

"Do you want to go to medical school?" I ask them.

"I guess so," they say, without conviction, or "Not really."

"Then why are you going?"

"Well, my parents want me to be a doctor. They're paying all this money and . . ."

Poor students, poor parents. They are caught in one of the oldest webs of love and duty and guilt. The parents mean well; they are trying to steer their sons and daughters toward a secure future. But the sons and daughters want to major in history or classics or philosophy — subjects with no "practical" value. Where's the payoff on the humanities? It's not easy to persuade such loving parents that the humanities do indeed pay off. The intellectual faculties developed by studying subjects like history and classics — an ability to synthesize and relate, to weigh cause and effect, to see events in perspective — are just the faculties that make creative leaders in business or almost any general field. Still, many fathers would rather put their money on courses that point toward a specific profession — courses that are pre-law, pre-medical, pre-business, or, as I sometimes heard it put, "pre-rich."

But the pressure on students is severe. They are truly torn. One part of them feels obligated to fulfill their parent's expectations; after all, their parents are older and presumably wiser. Another part tells them that the expectations that are right for their parents are not right for them.

Peer pressure and self-induced pressure are also intertwined, and they begin almost at the beginning of freshman year.

"I had a freshman student I'll call Linda," one dean told me, "who came in and said she was under terrible pressure because her roommate, Barbara, was much brighter and studied all the time. I couldn't tell her that Barbara had come in two hours earlier to say the same thing about Linda."

The story is almost funny — except that it's not. It's symptomatic of all the pressures put together. When every student thinks every other student is working harder and doing better, the only solution is to study harder still. I see students going off to the library every night after dinner and coming back when it closes at midnight. I wish they could sometimes forget about their peers and go to a movie. I hear the clacking of typewriters in the hours before dawn. I see the tension in their eyes when exams are approaching and papers are due: *Will I get everything done?*

Probably they won't. They will get sick. They will get "blocked." They will sleep. They will oversleep. They will bug out. *Hey Carlos, help!*

Part of the problem is that they do more than they are expected to do. A professor will assign five-page papers. Several students will start writing ten-page papers to impress him. Then more students will write ten-page papers, and a few will raise the ante to fifteen. Pity the poor student who is still just doing the assignment.

I have painted too drab a portrait of today's students, making them seem a solemn lot. That is only half of their story; if they were so dreary I wouldn't so thoroughly enjoy their company. The other half is that they are easy to like. They are quick to laugh and to offer friendship. They are not introverts. They are usually kind and are more considerate of one another than any student generation I have known.

If I have described the modern undergraduate primarily as a driven creature who is largely ignoring the blithe spirit inside who keeps trying to come out and play, it's because that's where the crunch is, throughout American education. It's why I think we should all be worried about the values that are nurturing a generation so fearful of risk and so goal-obsessed at such an early age.

INTRODUCTION TO HIGHER EDUCATION
Dr. Irwin S. Polishook

Two conflicting developments have characterized higher education in the past decade. First, more people than ever before have taken the opportunity to attend college — more underprivileged people, more women, more minority members, more adults, more workers. It is an exciting step in the history of American progress, and it is uniquely American. We have hardly begun to appreciate its great significance to society as a whole: The growth in educational opportunity means the realization of social justice, of economic mobility, of democracy itself.

Our appreciation of this epochal advance has been marked, however, by a contrary development. As more and more people go to college, they are being told that it isn't really worth it: It does not "pay off." Or, one widespread variation goes, the colleges you can gain admission to are not all that good. The only colleges worth attending, it is said, are the ones that continue to be inaccessible to most students.

Somehow, we are told, higher education is good for society but superfluous for the individual.

It is no wonder that many students feel cheated. Here at last they have the chance to obtain an invaluable benefit, and it turns out to be tarnished.

We believe that higher education is being slandered by selfish interests that have nothing to do with democracy and for reasons that have nothing to do with the facts.

WHY GO TO COLLEGE IN THE FIRST PLACE?   Helen Vines and Aaron Alexander

Jobs! Jobs! Jobs! That's what college is all about, as far as most freshmen are concerned. By the time they're seniors, though, they've discovered there's much more to it.[1]

Of course college may prepare you for a career. First it helps expand your view of yourself and of what's out there, so that you can make an intelligent career choice. Then it develops your resources to succeed in your chosen field. It builds your knowledge and, more important than what you learn, the ability to keep on learning long after you're out of college.

These advantages will give you a better chance of getting a job. And they'll give you a better chance of getting a good job, no matter how you define "good job." Is it job satisfaction, work that is challenging and varied (rather than monotonous), security (staying employed), status, the opportunity to get ahead, earning potential? All of these job qualities are made more possible by college attendance.

What's more, a good college education will give you the depth to progress in your career and the flexibility to change careers later if you choose to, as many people do.

Most freshmen assume these things when they first set foot on campus. What they find out later is that work, vital as it is, represents only one aspect of their lives. They discover new territories of knowledge and art to explore, for their own sake. And they realize that the whole of their future, not just their careers, may be enriched by higher education.

How does this happen? It happens through a wide range of experiences with people you meet inside and outside the classroom. It happens through extracurricular activities. It happens through your career-related studies, which have uses beyond your occupation. And it happens through the liberal arts.

Liberal arts are such subjects as literature, languages, history, philosophy and surveys of science that are your general education rather than your narrow career training. Who needs them? Liberal arts are useless to cogs in an occupational machine. But if you want to be a whole person and to understand who you are and how you relate to the rest of your world, they're essential. That's why the liberal arts are required in college.

Vocational schools advertise that they dispense with all that stuff, and they're not lying. Only college can give you the total experience, and its benefits — in self-discovery, independence, individuality, self-confidence, the ability to cope and the capacity to participate in the general culture.

If you approach college with the tunnel vision that sees nothing but a job or a degree at the end, you'll miss these vital points of collegiate life:

- Why the basic skills are so important, even if you get no "credit" for them. Writing, reading, and mathematics are "basic" because they're at the basis of everything else in college and beyond. Only by mastering them will you be able to cope with your other studies, your work and other activities.
- Why you should do well in liberal arts and other required courses that may not seem clearly related to your occupational field. They may very well be related to your career. And they are certainly related — and necessary — to the rest of your existence.
- What college has to offer you outside the classroom, what is not mandatory but highly profitable if you want to get your full money's worth out of college.

Between what your college has to offer and what you get out of it there is some distance.

THE STUDENT AND THE UNIVERSITY: LIBERAL EDUCATION
Professor Allan Bloom

What image does a first-rank college or university present to-day to a teen-ager leaving home for the first time, off to the adventure of a liberal education? He has four years of freedom to discover himself — a space between the intellectual wasteland he has left behind and the inevitable dreary professional training that awaits him after the baccalaureate. In this short time he must learn that there is a great world beyond the little one he knows, experience the exhilaration of it and digest enough of it to sustain himself in the intellectual deserts he is destined to traverse. He must do this, that is, if he is to have any hope of a higher life. These are the charmed years when he can, if he so chooses, become anything he wishes and when he has the opportunity to survey his alternatives, not merely those current in his time or provided by careers, but those available to him as a human being. The importance of these years for an American cannot be overestimated. They are civilization's only chance to get to him.

In looking at him we are forced to reflect on what he should learn if he is to be called educated; we must speculate on what the human potential to be fulfilled is. In the specialties we can avoid such speculation, and the avoidance of them is one of specialization's charms. But here it is a simple duty. What are we to teach this person? The answer may not be evident, but to attempt to answer the question is already to philosophize and to begin to educate. . . .

The real problem is those students who come hoping to find out what career they want to have, or are simply looking for an adventure with themselves. There are plenty of things for them to do — courses and disciplines enough to spend many a lifetime on. Each department or great division of the university makes a pitch for itself, and each offers a course of study that will make the student an initiate. But how to choose among them? How do they relate to one another? The fact is they do not address one another. They are competing and contradictory, without being aware of it. The problem of the whole is urgently indicated by the very existence of the specialties, but it is never systematically posed. The net effect of the student's encounter with the college catalogue is bewilderment and very often demoralization. It is just a matter of chance whether he finds one or two professors who can give him an insight into one of the great visions of education that have been the distinguishing part of every civilized nation. Most professors are specialists, concerned only with their own fields, interested in the advancement of those fields in their own terms, or in their own personal advancement in a world where all the rewards are on the side of professional distinction. They have been entirely emancipated from the old structure of the university, which at least helped to indicate that they are incomplete, only parts of an unexamined and undiscovered whole. So the student must navigate among a collection of carnival barkers, each trying to lure him into a particular sideshow. This undecided student is an embarrassment to most universities, because he seems to be saying, "I am a whole human being. Help me to form myself in my wholeness and let me develop my real potential," and he is the one to whom they have nothing to say.

Discussion

1. Thinking over these readings, what points did you note that might make you consider altering the direction of your flow chart?
2. Which of the four pressures Zinsser names creates the most difficulty for you? Why?
3. Were Dr. Polishook and Professor Bloom to sit down to discuss the role of the student in university life, would they be likely to agree or disagree with one another?

IN-CLASS WRITING

Writing What You're Thinking as Fast as You're Thinking It. Especially about your college, about you, and your role in it. Your question, rightly enough, may just be, "But how do you expect me to write about all that in one class period?" No one in his or her right mind would expect that of a writer. But this chapter has been raising some rather large issues and asking some vital questions, enough to send your head swirling with what to answer, what to consider. Quite probably freewriting is your best strategy when you're trying to find out what it is you really think. You may not come up with answers or solutions, but you will begin to discover what you think. Why you are in college may begin to make sense to you.

The activity at the beginning of this chapter raises some very personal questions regarding self and survival in college now and a job and career in the future. The readings raise troubling questions about things that you say are beyond your control, yet they pervade everything you're doing now.

It is time now to start getting down on paper some of the outer layers of that thinking. You can begin with questions for which you have no ready answers, assertions you don't have to back up, and demands and protests made with no planned agenda. After all, you're writing only what you're thinking at the moment. But you will find that what you write reveals ideas and opinions that are in the process of forming.

READINGS

HOW I DISCOVERED WORDS: A HOMEMADE EDUCATION
Malcolm X

It was because of my letters that I happened to stumble upon starting to acquire some kind of a homemade education.

I became increasingly frustrated at not being able to express what I wanted to convey in letters that I wrote, especially those to Mr. Elijah Muhammad. In the street, I had been the most articulate hustler out there — I had commanded attention when I said something. But now, trying to write simple English, I not only wasn't articulate, I wasn't even functional. How would I sound writing in slang, the way I would *say* it, something such as, "Look, daddy, let me pull your coat about a cat. Elijah Muhammad — "

Many who today hear me somewhere in person, or on television, or those who read something I've said, will think I went to school far beyond the eighth grade. This impression is due entirely to my prison studies.

It had really begun back in the Charlestown Prison, when Bimbi first made me feel envy of his stock of knowledge. Bimbi had always taken charge of any conversation he was in, and I had tried to emulate him. But every book I picked up had few sentences which didn't contain anywhere from one to nearly all of the words that might as well have been in Chinese. When I just skipped those words, of course, I really ended up with little idea of what the book said. So I had come to the Norfolk Prison Colony still going through only book-reading motions. Pretty soon, I would have quit even these motions, unless I had received the motivation that I did.

I saw that the best thing I could do was get hold of a dictionary —to study, to learn some words. I was lucky enough to reason also that I should try to improve my penmanship. It was sad. I couldn't even write in a straight line. It was both ideas together that moved me to request a dictionary along with some tablets and pencils from the Norfolk Prison Colony school.

I spent two days just riffling uncertainly through the dictionary's pages. I'd never realized so many words existed! I didn't know *which* words I needed to learn. Finally, just to start some kind of action, I began copying.

In my slow, painstaking, ragged handwriting, I copied into my tablet everything printed on that first page, down to the punctuation marks.

I believe it took me a day. Then, aloud, I read back, to myself, everything I'd written on the tablet. Over and over, aloud, to myself, I read my own handwriting.

I woke up the next morning, thinking about those words —immensely proud to realize that not only had I written so much at one time, but I'd written words that I never knew were in the world. Moreover, with a little effort, I also could remember what many of these words meant. I reviewed the words whose meanings I didn't remember. Funny thing, from the dictionary first page right now, that "aardvark" springs to my mind. The dictionary had a picture of it, a long-tailed, long-eared, burrowing African mammal, which lives off termites caught by sticking out its tongue as an anteater does for ants.

I was so fascinated that I went on — I copied the dictionary's next page. And the same experience came when I studied that. With every succeeding page, I also learned of people and places and events from history. Actually the dictionary is like a miniature encyclopedia. Finally the dictionary's A section had filled a whole tablet — and I went on into the B's. That was the way I started copying what eventually became the entire dictionary. It went a lot faster after so much practice helped me pick up handwriting speed. Between what I wrote in my tablet, and writing letters, during the rest of my time in prison I would guess I wrote a million words.

I suppose it was inevitable that as my word-base broadened, I could for the first time pick up a book and read and now begin to understand what the book was saying. Anyone who has read a great deal can imagine the new world that opened. Let me tell you something: from then until I left that prison, in every free moment I had, if I was not reading in the library, I was reading on my bunk. You couldn't have gotten me out of books with a wedge. Between Mr. Muhammad's teachings, my correspondence, my visitors — usually Ella and Reginald — and my reading of books, months passed without my even thinking about being imprisoned. In fact, up to then, I never had been so truly free in my life.

Discussion

1. Which seems more self-restricting to you, prison or illiteracy?
2. In the last line of the reading, does the adverb *truly* add a particular dimension of meaning to *free* that otherwise might not be present? In other words, how does *truly* modify *free*?
3. Would you say that had Malcolm X not been in jail, he would never have understood what it means to be free?

This excerpt from V. S. Naipaul's "Prologue to an Autobiography" tells the story of how a story came to be written; it was his first published work, three thousand words, a turning point in his life.

From PROLOGUE TO AN AUTOBIOGRAPHY   V. S. Naipaul

It is now nearly thirty years since, in a BBC room in London, on an old BBC typewriter, and on smooth, "non-rustle" BBC script paper, I wrote the first sentence of my first publishable book. I was some three months short of my twenty-third birthday.

It was in that Victorian-Edwardian gloom, and at one of those typewriters late one afternoon, without having any idea where I was going, and not perhaps intending to type to the end of the page, I wrote: *Every morning when he got up Hat would sit on the banister of his back verandah and shout across, "What happening there, Bogart?"*

That was a Port of Spain memory. It seemed to come from far back, but it was only eleven or twelve years old.

Hat was our neighbor on the street. He wasn't negro or mulatto. But we thought of him as halfway there. He was a Port of Spain Indian.

That shout of "Bogart!" was in more than one way a shout from the street. And, to add to the incongruity, it was addressed to someone in our yard: a young man, very quiet, yet another person connected in some way with my mother's family. He had come not long before from the country and was living in the separate one-room building at the back of our yard. We called this room the servant room.

As diarists and letter writers repeatedly prove, any attempt at narrative can give value to an experience which might otherwise evaporate away. When I began to write about Bogart's street I began to sink into a tract of experience I hadn't before contemplated as a writer. This blindness might seem extraordinary in someone who wanted so much to be a writer. Half a writer's work, though, is the discovery of his subject. . . .

Every morning when he got up Hat would sit on the banister of his back verandah and shout across, "What happening there, Bogart?" That was a good place to begin. But I couldn't stay there. My anxiety constantly to prove myself as a writer, the need to write another book and then another, led me away.

There was much in that call of "Bogart!" that had to be examined. Luck was with me, because that first sentence was so direct, so uncluttered, so without complications, that it provoked the sentence that was to follow. *Bogart would turn in his bed and mumble softly, so that no one heard, "What happening there, Hat?"*

The first sentence was true. The second was invention. But together — to me, the writer — they had done something extraordinary. Though they had left out everything — the setting, the historical time, the racial and social complexities of the people concerned — they had suggested it all; they had created the world of the street. And together, as sentences, words, they had set up a rhythm, a speed, which dictated all that was to follow.

The story developed a first-person narrator. And for the sake of speed, to avoid complications, to match the rhythm of what had gone before, this narrator could not be myself. My narrator lived alone with his mother in a house on the street. He had no father, he had no other family. so, very simply, all the crowd of my mother's extended family, as cumbersome in real life as it would have been to a writer, was abolished; and, again out of my wish to simplify, I had a narrator more in tune with the life of the street than I had been.

The speed of the narrative — that was the speed of the writer. And everything that was later to look like considered literary devices came only from the anxiety of the writer. I wanted above all to take the story to the end. I feared that if I stopped too long anywhere I might lose faith in what I was doing, give up once more, and be left with nothing.

The story was short, three thousand words, two foolscap sheets and a bit. I had — a conscious piece of magic that afternoon — set the typewriter at single space, to get as much as possible on the first sheet and also to create the effect of the printed page.

Reflecting on the meaning of the story to himself, Naipaul summarizes its meaning:

To write was to learn. Beginning a book, I always felt I was in possession of all the facts about myself; at the end I was always surprised. The book before always turned out to have been written by a man with incomplete knowledge. And the very first, the one begun in the freelances' room, seemed to have been written by an innocent, a man at the beginning of knowledge both about himself and about the writing career that had been his ambition from childhood.

Discussion

1. Naipaul says, "Half a writer's work, though, is the discovery of his subject." What does this statement mean to you? Can you make it work for you?
2. "To write was to learn," Naipaul writes. The past tense verb indicates the statement was true for him. If he had written "To write is to learn," he would mean that the statement is a true statement at all times, for all people. From your own experience so far, would you agree that the statement is true?

LANGUAGE LEARNING	**Using Verbs to Express Action.** When writing anecdotes or any narrative, the action words, or verbs, provide much of the force of your sentences. A writer may say, *He walked into the room.* Yet this sentence does not give clear indication of how the man entered.

It is much more effective if you can find a substitute for *walk.* If you cannot think of an alternate, you can consult a *thesaurus,* a kind of dictionary that lists together words of similar meaning. For example, if you look up the word *walk* in the thesaurus, you will find, among the many words listed, the following suggestions:

amble	prance	stagger
saunter	stalk	reel
stroll	hobble	stumble
stride	shamble	trudge
strut	shuffle	
swagger	slough	

These are just some of the entries given!

Rewrite the following sentence five times, using another word for *talk* in each one:

The teacher talked to the class.

If you cannot think of good substitutes for *talk,* consult a thesaurus.

How does the difference in verb affect the meaning of the sentence?

Using Verbs as Modifiers

There are forms of verbs, however, that you can use as modifiers much in the same way you use the adjectives *blue, cold,* and *gloomy.* One of these forms is the present participle, the form of the verb ending in *-ing.* You can use present participles both as a single adjective *(smouldering, pounding, towering)* and a compound adjective *(blood-freezing).*

In addition to the present participle, there is the past participle, which is a little more difficult to recognize immediately. Past participles may be used to achieve as many adjectival effects as you want: *Beaten and caught, shaken by fear, and strung out on his own broken promises, he came back, finally, to his old neighborhood.* As you notice, the past participle, just like the present, may be used (a) as coordinates *(Beaten and caught);* (b) in phrases *(shaken by fear, strung out on);* or (c) as single adjectives *(broken promises).* When used with linking verbs, past and present participles describe; for example, *The old house on the corner looks haunted, but its architecture is so fascinating that people are amazed that nobody buys it.* One word of caution is needed here. We tend to write what we hear, but in past participles like *amazed, surprised, prejudiced,* and *determined,* the final *-d* is seldom heard in speech, so that when writing, many people often omit it.

When you use past participles as modifiers, remember that there are two distinct groups of verbs: *regular* and *irregular.* When using *regular* verbs in both the past and past participle forms, you simply add *-d* or *-ed,* as in the following:

Present	Past	Past Participle
dance	danced	danced
look	looked	looked
determine	determined	determined

With irregular verbs, all three forms may be the same:

Present	Past	Past Participle
hit	hit	hit
cut	cut	cut
hurt	hurt	hurt
burst	burst	burst

or past and past participle may be the same but different from the present:

Present	Past	Past Participle
say	said	said
tell	told	told
hear	heard	heard
spend	spent	spent
catch	caught	caught

or all three forms may be different:

Present	Past	Past Participle
fly	flew	flown
drink	drank	drunk
ride	rode	ridden
slay	slew	slain

The past and past participle forms of verbs are listed in the dictionary. If you are uncertain of the correct verb form, be sure to check the dictionary. Also, there is a list of irregular verbs in the Appendix, on pages 225–257.

Using Verbs to Express Tense

Probably you are most familiar with this use of verb—letting the readers know whether the action is taking place right now, whether it took place some time in the past, or whether it will take place some time in the future. In Chapter 2 we talked about the various forms of the present tense of verbs; here we want to explain some of the special features of the past tense forms.

You can recognize the past tense of most English verbs by noting that they end with either *-d* or *-ed*.

I traded my old car for a motorcycle.
We talked to our coach for two hours.

If you removed the *-d* or *-ed* from the verbs in the examples, you will see that the sentences, although clumsy, are in the present tense. When you speak, you rarely pronounce the *-d* or *-ed* very clearly, and if your listeners are confused, they can always ask you what you meant. In writing, however, your reader cannot ask any questions, and so you have to be particularly careful to include these endings.

The problem is further complicated by the fact that (instead of just adding the *-d* or *-ed)* some of the most commonly used verbs in English completely change their form for the past tense. A few examples are listed below:

Present	Past
am, is	was
are	were
begin	began
can	could
dig	dug
get	got
has, have	had
know	knew
make	made
stink	stank
study	studied
take	took

A fuller list of these verbs appears in the Appendix. If you have any difficulties with them, make a special effort to memorize them.

Exercise

Here is a section from Piri Thomas's *Down These Mean Streets*. Although originally written in the past tense, here the passage has been rewritten in the present tense. In the blank spaces, fill in the proper form of the past tense of the verbs printed in italics.

When you're a kid, everything has some kind of special meaning. I always *can* _____ find something to do, even if it *is* _____ doing nothing. But going to school *is* _____ something else. School *stinks* _____. I *hate* _____ school and all its teachers. I *hate* _____ the crispy look of the teachers and the draggy-long hours they *take* _____ out of my life from nine to three-thirty. I *dig* _____ being outside no matter what kind of weather. Only chumps *work* _____ and *study* _____.

Every day *begins* _____ with a fight to get me out of bed for school. Momma *plays* _____ the same record over an' over every day: "Piri, get up, it's time to go to school." And I *play* _____ mine: "Aw, Momma, I don't feel so good. I think I got a fever or something."

Always it *ends* _____ up the same old way. I *get* _____ up and *go* _____ to school. But I *don't* _____ always stay there. Sometimes, I *report* _____ for class, let my teacher see me and then *begin* _____ the game of sneaking out of the room. It *is* _____ like escaping from some kind of prison. I *wait* _____ for the teacher to turn her back, then I *slip* _____ out of my seat and hugging the floor, *crawl* _____ on my belly toward the door. The other kids *know* _____ what I *am* _____ doing; they *are* _____ trying not to burst out laughing. Sometimes a wise guy near me *makes* _____ a noise to bring the teacher's attention my way. When this *happens* _____, I lay still between the row of desks until the teacher *returns* _____ to whatever he or she *has* _____ been doing.

RHETORIC LEARNING

Writing a Narrative. The number of the gathering doesn't seem to matter, nor does the time of day, nor does the seating arrangement. There may be thirty or fifteen or two, but before the gathering breaks, someone tells a story and the others listen. This has happened under the stars, before a fireplace, around an anniversary table, and over the telephone. Few can resist the impulse to tell — or listen to — a story.

Writing is not the spontaneous event that talking is; for one thing, it is considerably more recent, and it is a far more deliberate and planned event.

You are still in the early weeks of a writing course, and you've begun writing stories for this course and writing notes for another that you will eventually organize into a lab report or an essay exam. And mostly you will use a narrative structure for these separate kinds of information, just as, later on as a nursing or medical student, you would prepare a patient's progress report.

But how exactly does a narrative happen? There is no one "correct" way, but one of the most frequently used approaches relies on the sequence of events in time. With this approach, you describe each part of the incident in the order in which it occurred — in other words, you begin at the beginning and describe each segment in chronological order until you come to the point you consider the end and stop there. This approach is, obviously, much easier to describe than to do, for as you probably already know, it is no simple matter to say when an event actually began or even when it really ended. Nevertheless, it is one of the responsibilities and privileges you have as a writer to make these decisions.

Keep in mind a few considerations. First, make sure that your readers know who you are talking about and that they have some understanding of where and when the events took place and exactly what happened. You also need to pay special attention to that part of your story which is the moment of greatest excitement. Usually this is the most difficult part to describe, and many writers fail to spend enough time on it so that their readers can really understand the reason for their excitement. You should also supply, either at the beginning or the end, a sentence or two that indicates what you feel the incident meant to you.

IN-CLASS WRITING   **Writing a Draft as Getting Started.** At this point, freewriting might prove the most useful strategy for getting started with the Formal Writing that follows. Read the assignment over a couple of times to make sure you understand what you're expected to write about and how you're asked to write it. In a classroom, bolstered by the presence of your classmates, you may use freewriting as a way of trying out other voices or other personas, and then read them back as a way of both hearing yourself and evaluating how others hear you when you take on the challenge of being someone else. In this freewriting episode, let the first ideas that come to you take charge and direct you as they will. Then, it is time to read your piece, listen to it to see if it can't serve as a first draft of the letter you will write.

FORMAL
WRITING **A Letter to a Friend: A Narrative.** This Formal Writing assignment is the final written work for Part One of this book. It takes the form of a letter that you write to a friend of rather recent acquaintance, someone who, like yourself, recently went off to college and is full of tales of new discoveries about life and learning and of the flips you turn when meeting change.

As writer of the letter, you are free to write a story of an event that you yourself experienced, or you may, as Naipaul did in writing his first story, invent a first-person narrator who tells the story. Often when we tell a story of something that happened to us, the more we tell it, the less it seems actually to have happened; we are telling it, but it seems as though it happened to someone else.

Whether you write fact or fiction, using your own persona or that of another, your responsibilities are the same. Tell a story about what it's like to be in college at this moment. Is it like being in heaven? in hell? or in some space and time between the two?

Part Two

FINDING AND DEVELOPING IDEAS — WHO WE WERE

One of a writer's tasks is to inform an audience. But for beginning writers, an overwhelming consideration is deciding first what to write about and then where to find the information and what details to include. In Part Two we focus primarily on those issues, paying special attention to tapping one of the great resources available — memory.

In the first part of this book we discussed one major source of information from which you could find material to write about — the information we receive through our senses. Developing an awareness of the world around us and discovering the vocabulary with which to express it led naturally to a focus on our present lives. Tapping the resources of memory will lead us to a consideration of the past.

In Chapter 4 we present two strategies for tapping memory — the memory chain and focusing — and the area of the past on which we focus is the family. In Chapter 5 we introduce another strategy — listing — and concentrate on memories of school, paying special attention to the varying perspectives that different people can have on the same incident. And in Chapter 6 we consider ways of combining information from a number of sources and of separating significant detail from the trivial.

In Part Two we also introduce you to two approaches that can appreciably improve the quality of your finished compositions. Working with a group of students in a reading/writing group will give you a sense of what others experience as they listen to your work and will enable you to revise your papers to compensate for any difficulties your listeners identify. Keeping a writer's log will give you the chance to experiment with ideas related to the main topic of the Final Writing assignment without the pressure of other people's judgments.

CHAPTER 4

Discovery, Memory, and the Family

All of us have experienced the depressing situation in which we are called upon to recall some information only to have our minds go completely blank. Whether it was the dates of a war for a history quiz or the items on this week's shopping list, the experience left us feeling annoyed with ourselves at the least.

The problem becomes more serious for student writers who, when asked to write a composition, feel as if they have nothing to say. Although their memories are vast treasure troves filled with the richness of experience, they do not know how to tap their resources. The two strategies presented in this chapter will provide just such access. The memory chain is designed to help you survey your memory and then select one experience to write about, and the focusing activity that follows provides an additional chance to recapture the details of that experience. Throughout this chapter, you will be working on a single piece of writing, writing and revising it, revising it and writing it, until it seems complete.

But revising is itself a specialized technique, one for which you will be given help through participation in a reading/writing group. Your fellow students, who thus far have served as an informal audience, will now be assigned a more formal role. Their responses to a given set of questions will provide a valuable guide to the changes that you can make to improve your paper.

In the same way, the writer's log presented in this chapter will also give you a chance to improve your fluency, as well as work out ideas on your own, without the interference of the eyes of others.

ACTIVITY   **Memory Chain.** Every so often we notice an object or occurrence that reminds us of something from our past. And sometimes that first remembrance leads us back to another moment in our lives, to another memory. Similar to this kind of experience is writing a memory chain, an activity introduced to us by James Moffett. It is one of the techniques adapted by the New York City Writing Project.

In this activity you will select any object you can see and use it as a memory trigger. Then you will use each memory that follows as the trigger for the next memory, thereby creating a string, or chain, of memories. As a result, many memories will be called forth, and you will have a wealth of material from which to select as a writing topic an experience with your family.

There are several ways to write a memory chain. Some chains are unpunctuated, merely listing each memory, one after the other; some are written in whole sentences; and some include short paragraphs that provide a bit of detail about each particular memory. Following is an example of an unpunctuated memory chain that uses the words *reminds me of*. Notice that each memory in this chain is named and that occasionally some detail is provided. But since the point here is to amass as many memories as possible, reflection and extensive detail are not yet necessary.

An Example of a Memory Chain

BROKEN PENCIL   Carol Schoen

Broken pencil reminds me of school reminds me of first grade reminds me of Miss Hopkins reminds me of schoolmate Jean reminds me of walking to school reminds me of crossing Seventh Street reminds me of the traffic reminds me of the bus that almost ran me over reminds me of walking to school alone reminds me of my brothers who walked with their friends reminds me of my mother reminds me of the kitchen reminds me of my grandmother who stayed with us for a while reminds me of Friday night supper reminds me of the chicken soup that spilled reminds me of how fat my grandmother was reminds me of how she insisted on helping reminds me of my mother trying to work around her reminds me of how small the kitchen was reminds me of fights with my brother reminds me of the applecake we had for dessert reminds me of the apple trees in the backyard reminds me of climbing the trees reminds me of the clubhouse my brothers made among the trees.

Writing a Memory Chain

Step 1.   Select something you can see and write down the name of that object.

Step 2.   Ask yourself, "What from my past does this remind me of?" and write down that memory.

Step 3.   Look to see what this memory reminds you of and write that down.

Step 4.   Continue to let each memory remind you of another memory or of another part of the memory that precedes it. Continue to write down each memory as it comes to you.

Try not to censor your words and thoughts. Sometimes you will remember a series of events or things all related to the same memory and sometimes you will move rapidly from one memory to the next, following no particular time sequence. All of that is acceptable in a memory chain.

Remember, this chain is just a series of notes to yourself, so use whatever form works best for you. Just try to get hold of as many memories as you can. You may get stuck. If you do, select another object in the room and begin another chain.

Step 5.   At this point you might want to hear some of the chains read aloud. In what ways do the chains differ? Are there any moods or themes that recur in a person's memory chain?

Step 6.   Now go back over your own memory chain and read it again, paying special attention to those experiences which involve your relationship with your family. (You may have come up with some interesting memories about your school and work experiences, or concerning friends. Don't discard those notes, for they will be helpful for other writing experiences.) Consider which memory about your family interests you most and is one you could write about. Make sure it is a specific experience, one that happened at a particular moment in time. For instance, the author of the memory chain above might want to write about the time her mother and grandmother were cooking together in the kitchen and had an accident with the soup.

In selecting a memory to write about, don't worry if you are not clear about all the details. As you write about this experience you will have additional opportunities to recall and recreate these details.

<table>
<tr>
<td>

IN-CLASS WRITING

</td>
<td>

First Draft. Spend the next fifteen or twenty minutes writing about the personal experience you have selected. Try in writing to recall all that you can about the experience. To accomplish this, it might be helpful *not* to let anything get in the way of your writing and remembering. For example, it is not necessary at this point to worry about the order or form or correctness of things, especially since you will have many chances to work on those matters as you continue to revise the piece. In this initial experience, you may discover that very often it is through the actual writing of something that the feelings, events, and details of that experience are more completely and vividly recalled.

Here again, you might want to read to your classmates what you have written.

</td>
</tr>
<tr>
<td>

ACTIVITY

</td>
<td>

Focusing. Writing is one way to recall the particulars of an experience, to open the door to your memory of that experience. Another way to do this is through focusing. Here we use the term *focusing* in its most general sense. By it we mean concentrating on the pictures in your mind or your emotional responses to past experiences. You have probably already done some focusing, for it is a common feature of the writing process. Often when you pause during the process of writing, it is because you are recalling some aspect of your subject, attempting to express in words what you have just sensed.

In the activity that follows, you will use focusing to recall more about the experience you have chosen to write about. You will use it to look back at that experience in order more fully to express what occurred.

Directions

The object of this focusing activity is to recreate, in as much detail as possible, the experience you are writing about. You will want to pay full attention to this experience. To accomplish this, it might be useful either to close your eyes or to stare at a blank sheet of paper.

Before you begin this exercise, read through all the directions. Then, during each phase of the activity, reread the directions for

</td>
</tr>
</table>

that step or have someone slowly read them aloud to the entire class.

Take notes on what you observe; you may do so during the activity or after each phase of the activity is completed.

Step 1.   Focus on the experience you are writing about. Try to picture the experience, to imagine yourself in that space. Notice all that surrounds you — the colors and shapes, the room or hall or car or class, the field or hill or path, the street or bridge or river. Take your time, and look at everything, large and small, that is there. Then look again at everything there, at all that is a part of the setting. Whenever you are ready, describe what you have just observed.

Step 2.   Now focus on the experience once again. Go back to the space where the incident took place, and this time recall who was there. Recall how each person looked, what each person was wearing, how people were standing or sitting. Observe the expressions on their faces, the attitudes and personalities behind those expressions, the stance of their bodies. Then look at everyone once again and take notes on what you see.

Step 3.   This time, recall the event in action. Return to the space where the incident took place, and add sound and motion to the scene you have just recreated. Recall the experience in full detail from start to finish, omitting nothing. Observe all that is taking place; listen to all that is being said. Take notes on what you are witnessing.

READINGS   Family memories have inspired many people to write in many forms. Here are two poems that might interest you.

NIKKI-ROSA   Nikki Giovanni

childhood remembrances are always a drag
if you're Black
you always remember things like living in Woodlawn
with no inside toilet
and if you become famous or something
they never talk about how happy you were to have
your mother
all to yourself and
how good the water felt when you got your bath

from one of those
big tubs that folk in chicago barbecue in
and somehow when you talk about home
it never gets across how much you
understood their feelings
as the whole family attended meetings about Hollydale
and even though you remember
your biographers never understand
your father's pain as he sells his stock
and another dream goes
And though you're poor it isn't poverty that
concerns you
and though they fought a lot
it isn't your father's drinking that makes any difference
but only that everybody is together and you
and your sister have happy birthdays and very good
christmasses and I really hope no white person ever has
cause to write about me because they never understand
Black love is Black wealth and they'll probably talk
about my hard childhood and never understand that all
the while I was quite happy.

MY PAPA'S WALTZ   Theodore Roethke

The whiskey on your breath
Could make a small boy dizzy;
But I hung on like death;
Such waltzing was not easy.

He stomped until the pans
Slid from the kitchen shelf.
My mother's countenance
Could not unfrown itself.

The hand that held my wrist
Was battered on one knuckle.
At every step you missed
My right ear scraped a buckle.

You beat time on my head
With a palm caked hard by dirt.
Then waltzed me off to bed
Still clinging to your shirt.

Discussion

1. Do you consider Nikki Giovanni's description of her childhood
   depressing? Why or why not?

2. What emotions do you think the child in "My Papa's Waltz" is feeling?

3. In what ways have the poets' choice of words enabled them to express the mixture of feelings they have?

WRITER'S LOG   One technique that many professional, as well as amateur, writers use is to record their thoughts regularly in some form of permanent file or book, sometimes called a journal or, as we name it here, a writer's log. Although such a tool can be used to reflect any event or idea that interests you, we are suggesting it here as a way of experimenting with the subjects treated in the various chapters of this book. Each chapter after this one will include a list of possible topics related to the subject of the Formal Writing for that chapter; writing about these topics will give you a chance to explore your reflections and memories. Because in this chapter the theme has been family events, the topics here will concern that area of your life.

You are not, of course, restricted to the topics we suggest but are free to select your own. Keep in mind, however, that a writer's log is not a diary — that is, it is not simply a record of each day's events. Rather, it is a record of your ideas written in order to fill out your impressions and provide material for your final essay. For the most part, your writer's log is a private document, written for your eyes alone, and you can therefore create your own rules about what you wish to include in it. Some teachers, however, may want to look at your journals, and in that event, you might want to limit what you write about. The time spent doing your entries for the writer's log can be moments when you are free to enjoy your own thoughts and memories. At the same time you can enhance your writing skills and add to your supply of information for your college writing assignments.

The following topics may be useful, or you may write on others that you have thought of yourself.

The morning the alarm didn't go off
The family Christmas that was special
A birthday to remember
The time my mother (father, brother, sister, grandmother, and so on) got sick
The time I got sick
The fight I had with my brother (sister, father, mother, and so on)

The joys and sorrows of having brothers and/or sisters
Why families are a problem
A special family vacation

You should write in your journal at least three times a week on topics related to the theme presented in each chapter.

RHETORIC LEARNING	**Selecting Significant Details.** By now you will have accumulated a mass of information about your relationships with your family over many years. In fact, you will have so much information that, as in Chapter 2, it may be difficult to decide which details to include and which to leave out. You will, of course, want to make sure that you establish the basic elements needed for your readers to understand your composition. Your readers need to know who the people that you are discussing are, where and when the event took place, and what happened and why. These elements — who, where, when, what, and why — are what journalists call the five W's, and they are necessary elements for all kinds of writing besides newspapers. If, for example, the writer of the memory chain on page 72 decided to write about the preparation of a Friday night dinner, she would want to mention the flowered curtains at the kitchen window, the cramped space that caused her mother and grandmother to bump into each other, and the steaming pot of soup on the stove. She would pay special attention to acquainting readers with the looks and personalities of her mother and grandmother, so that their basic love for, but growing irritation with, each other could be understood. Probably most significant would be the action of the event, the spilling of the soup with the resultant mess, the fear of injury, the flare-up of anger, and, finally, the explosion of laughter.

Another important factor in selecting significant details is what overall theme you want to convey through your narrative. In part, this theme involves the underlying emotions you want to stress, whether fear or love, anger or warmth, loneliness or any of the other myriad feelings that people have. Although the writer of the narrative about the Friday night dinner might want to accentuate the momentary anger and fear caused by the event, she would also want to show how the underlying love between the two women overcame the temporary upset in their relationship.

An equally important aspect of theme involves establishing the message, or meaning of the event to the writer. One possible message for the above event might be:

I realized that a strong family relationship can overcome minor tragedies.

In selecting details to include in her story, the writer might want to mention her mother's quick temper and her grandmother's nervousness; she would probably want to let readers know that her grandmother's ample body made it difficult for anyone to work with her in the tiny kitchen. But the writer would leave out such facts as how long her mother had been married, why the grandmother was living with the family, what the dinner menu was, and who the guests were.

READING   As you read the following passage from *The Big Sea*, by Langston Hughes, pay particular attention to the way the author achieves the effects of intimacy and intensity.

SALVATION   Langston Hughes

I was saved from sin when I was going on thirteen. But not really saved. It happened like this. There was a big revival at my Auntie Reed's church. Every night for weeks there had been much preaching, singing, praying, and shouting, and some very hardened sinners had been brought to Christ, and the membership of the church had grown by leaps and bounds. Then just before the revival ended, they held a special meeting for children, "to bring the young lambs to the fold." My aunt spoke of it for days ahead. That night I was escorted to the front row and placed on the mourners' bench with all the other young sinners, who had not yet been brought to Jesus.

My aunt told me that when you were saved you saw a light, and something happened to you inside! And Jesus came into your life! And God was with you from then on! She said you could see and hear and feel Jesus in your soul. I believed her. I had heard a great many old people say the same thing and it seemed to me they ought to know. So I sat there calmly in the hot, crowded church, waiting for Jesus to come to me.

The preacher preached a wonderful rhythmical sermon, all moans and shouts and lonely cries and dire pictures of hell, and then he sang a song about the ninety and nine safe in the fold, but one little lamb was left out in the cold. Then he said: "Won't you come? Won't you come to Jesus? Young lambs, won't you come?" And he held out his arms to all us young sinners there on the mourners' bench. And the little girls cried. And some of them jumped up and went to Jesus right away. But most of us just sat there.

A great many old people came and knelt around us and prayed, old women with jet-black faces and braided hair, old men with work-gnarled hands. And the church sang a song about the lower lights are burning, some poor sinners to be saved. And the whole building rocked with prayer and song.

Still I kept waiting to see Jesus.

Finally all the young people had gone to the altar and were saved, but one boy and me. He was a rounder's son named Westley. Westley and I were surrounded by sisters and deacons praying. It was very hot in the church, and getting late now. Finally Westley said to me in a whisper: "God damn! I'm tired o' sitting here. Let's get up and be saved." So he got up and was saved.

Then I was left all alone on the mourners' bench. My aunt came and knelt at my knees and cried, while prayers and songs swirled all around me in the little church. The whole congregation prayed for me alone, in a mighty wail of moans and voices. And I kept waiting serenely for Jesus, waiting, waiting — but he didn't come. I wanted to see him, but nothing happened to me. Nothing! I wanted something to happen to me, but nothing happened.

I heard the songs and the minister saying: "Why don't you come? My dear child, why don't you come to Jesus? Jesus is waiting for you. He wants you. Why don't you come? Sister Reed, what is this child's name?"

"Langston," my aunt sobbed.

"Langston, why don't you come? Why don't you come and be saved? Oh, Lamb of God! Why don't you come?"

Now it was really getting late. I began to be ashamed of myself, holding everything up so long. I began to wonder what God thought about Westley, who certainly hadn't seen Jesus either, but who was now sitting proudly on the platform, swinging his knickerbockered legs and grinning down at me, surrounded by deacons and old women on their knees praying. God had not struck Westley dead for taking his name in vain or for lying in the temple. So I decided that maybe to save further trouble, I'd better lie, too, and say that Jesus had come, and get up and be saved.

So I got up.

Suddenly the whole room broke into a sea of shouting, as they saw me rise. Waves of rejoicing swept the place. Women leaped in the air. My aunt threw her arms around me. The minister took me by the hand and led me to the platform.

When things quieted down, in a hushed silence, punctuated by a few ecstatic "Amens," all the new young lambs were blessed in the name of God. Then joyous singing filled the room.

That night, for the last time in my life but one — for I was a big boy twelve years old — I cried, I cried, in bed alone, and couldn't stop. I buried my head under the quilts, but my aunt heard me. She woke up and told my uncle I was crying because the Holy Ghost had come into my life, and because I had seen Jesus. But I was really crying because I couldn't bear to tell her that I had lied, that I had deceived everybody in the church, and I hadn't seen Jesus, and that now I didn't believe there was a Jesus any more, since he didn't come to help me.

Discussion

1. Can you spot the beginning, the middle, and the end of the story?
2. How does the description of the various places in the story help you to grasp the author's theme?
3. What other effects in this story do you feel are important in a personal narrative?

LANGUAGE LEARNING

Using Pronouns. Since you will not want to repeat the name of the characters in your story over and over again, you will frequently make use of pronouns. A problem might arise, however, if your readers are not sure to whom a pronoun is referring. Look at the following passage:

> Maria, Joe, James, and Cheryl went to Burger King to buy lunch. *She* wanted a Junior Whopper, but *they* wanted Whoppers. He wanted *his* with lettuce and pickles, while *she* wanted *hers* with onion and ketchup. *They*, however, wanted *theirs* with "the works."

Which person got which hamburger? Rewrite the passage and put in names in place of the italicized words. Compare your version with your classmates'. How many different ways were there to distribute the hamburgers?

Words like *he, she,* and *they* — called pronouns — are used to prevent the monotony caused by having to say the name of a person, place, or thing over and over again. The most frequently used forms are usually listed in the following way:

First person (used to substitute for the *speaker*):

Singular	Plural
I	we
my, mine	our, ours
me	us

Second person (used to substitute for the *person being spoken to):*

Singular and plural (the same form is used for both)
you
your, yours
you

Third person (used to substitute for a *person, place, or thing being talked about):*

Singular

Masculine	Feminine	Neuter
he	she	it
his	her, hers	its
him	her	it

Plural

Masculine	Feminine	Neuter
	they	
	their, theirs	
	them	

(the same form is used for all)

(Notice that *its* does *not* have an apostrophe. *It's* is used to mean *it is.)*

If you were the waiter or waitress at Burger King, you could tell who wanted the hamburgers by watching the faces or gestures. But when you are reading, you have no such clues. That is why you have to be careful when you use pronouns. As a general rule, a pronoun refers to the last-named person or thing.

Exercise

Read the following sentences and then rewrite them in as many ways as you can to cover all possible meanings.

1. James gave Bill a book he liked.
2. Mary and JoAnn helped Sue and Carol into their car.
3. Elaine told Nila that she was going to win the game.
4. We decided to hold an election. That caused trouble.

Read the paragraphs below. They sound peculiar because we have not used any pronouns. In place of *students* in the first sentence, use *John and Mary.* In the remaining sentences, substitute *John, Mary,* or the proper pronoun for *the student.* In some cases, you may have to rewrite the whole sentence.

Two students feel very uncomfortable in the freshman composition class. One student dislikes English, while the other student likes to read but thinks writing involves some mysterious process.

One student told the other student that the student has nothing to say and the student does not know what the student can write about. The other student said that the student has many ideas but the student's thoughts seem to get confused when the student has to put the words on paper. Both students hope that the instructor will help solve the problems of the students.

IN-CLASS WRITING

Second Draft. Read over your first draft, the notes you accumulated during the focusing exercise, and any entries from your writer's log that might be relevant.

Step 1.   List the emotions you want to convey through your story. Then select the ones you think are most important.

Step 2.   Write a sentence that expresses the meaning that this story has for you. You may not yet be able to condense the meaning into a single sentence, but do try to express the reason that the experience made an indelible impression on you.

Step 3.   Look again at your draft and your notes. Underline all those sentences which you think are valuable for your narrative.

Step 4.   Establish the sequence of events as you want them to appear in your paper. Determine which ones are the most significant and what details you will want to supply in order to emphasize them.

GROUP READING AND REVISION

In the first few chapters of this book, you were asked frequently to share your writings with your fellow students, and you undoubtedly watched their faces and listened carefully to their comments in order to understand how they were affected by your words. You were, in fact, using them as an audience and getting feedback. This sense of an audience is one of the most important aspects of writing. In this and later chapters we will put this procedure of testing out your writings with an audience into a more formal structure, so that this audience response can provide concrete information to guide your revisions of a composition.

Each student will now become part of a reading/writing group. Your instructor may assign you to a group of four or five classmates, or you might choose to form your own group. Each group member should supply all other members with a copy of his or her paper, and each writer should then read his or her piece aloud while the others read along silently. It is important to read your piece aloud, for the process serves to heighten any details in your writing that might in a silent reading be sloughed over. Even though you are still working on your composition, you should get some feedback from your fellow students.

The members of the group need to listen very closely and to respect each author's efforts and goals. Sharp criticism based on a limited understanding not only does not help a writer but can be extremely destructive, thoroughly discouraging a person's efforts to improve. For that reason, your group's efforts should be limited to the following three activities:

1. Each listener should repeat back to the writer what he or she has heard.
2. Each listener should note all the words and phrases he or she thinks are particularly effective.
3. Each listener should state what he or she believes is the main idea of the piece — the meaning or message he or she got from it.

With your second draft in hand, you are now ready to consult with your writing group to see where you have been successful in conveying your meaning to your readers, where you need to clarify events, and what additional details you need to sharpen your picture. As a participant in the group, you will do the same for your fellow students.

RHETORIC LEARNING

How to Revise. It is one thing to get feedback from others about your writing; but it is quite another to know what to do with it. No aspect of writing is quite so complex as revision, and no writer, not even the most professional of authors, does not struggle with the task. Although the suggestions given below may make the process less difficult, you should resign yourself to the fact that revision will never be a simple task.

First, keep in mind that the word *revision* literally means "seeing again." You need to look at your writing with fresh eyes, as if you were seeing it for the first time. But how do you separate yourself from something over which you have struggled and into which you have poured the very best you have to offer on the subject? You need to stop seeing the writing as if it were a part of yourself, and start seeing it for what it in fact is — a sample of your thoughts on a topic at a particular moment, as separate from you as last year's winter coat. If you wanted to lengthen or shorten that coat, let out the seams or change the color or even discard it, you might complain about the time and trouble those changes entail but you would not feel personally endangered. The same attitude should be applied to your writing.

This separation of yourself from your work is termed *distancing*. In part, it can be achieved by putting a certain amount of time between the writing of the piece and the start of the revising process. Sometimes a few hours are enough; frequently you need a day or two. Another way of distancing yourself is to pretend, as you reread your work, to be someone else. You might imagine that you are a friend, a parent, or a teacher. The person you choose, however, should be someone whom you like and whose intelligence you respect, someone who you believe likes you and would not be deliberately cruel.

As important as it is to distance yourself, it is equally important not to block out any thoughts about your paper just because you have finished a draft. Mulling over the subject as you are traveling to and from class may yield ideas that you want to add or facts that you forgot to include. It will surely give you a sense that the draft is capable of being changed.

Getting Down to Work on Your Revision

Although the members of your reading/writing group have given you some important information about your paper, it is you who must listen closely to what they are saying and then decide how you can apply it. Each of the three kinds of responses your classmates gave you offers a different opportunity for improving your paper.

For instance, as you listened to your fellow students repeat the points of your story, did you notice that some facts were misinterpreted while others were omitted entirely? You will have to underline those sections of your text and decide how to reword some facts and put others in a place where they will not be missed.

You should also mark, perhaps with a star, those words and phrases that your readers noted as being most effective, to indicate passages that should be retained whenever possible.

You need to pay special attention to the message, or meaning your readers received from your paper. Is it the same as you intended? If not, you will have to reread your paper to see how you can emphasize the meaning you intended to convey and eliminate or rephrase the parts that caused confusion. You should also give some thought to the possibility that there is a second meaning to your story that might be as important or even more important than the one you began with. The writer of the story about the spilled soup, for example, might discover that her group was more impressed by the danger in the situation than she had intended. Accordingly, she could either tone down the language she used in that section or she might revise her aim to emphasize this new aspect of the event.

If your readers were unable to state a clear message from your composition, you will have to reread your entire paper to find ways to clarify it. Keep in mind, though, that it is your paper and all changes should reflect your point of view.

Before you start rereading your paper, look at the notes you made from your group members' comments or at the notes your teacher made in the margin or at the end of your paper. What seem to be the key problems? Are there places where readers wanted more detail? If so, reread such sections and see what you can add. One simple way to identify additional details is to review the five senses. Are there further facts of sight, sound, smell, taste, or touch that you might insert?

Were your readers confused by the order? Since most of the writing for this text thus far has been in narrative form, you need to check your list of events against the way they are presented in your paper. Have you omitted some key event or misplaced an event?

Did your readers feel that a certain part of your paper seems unrelated to the main direction? If so, you may need to add some sentence or sentences that explain why this information is necessary to a full understanding. If not, you may have to cut that portion out.

Were your readers unclear about the main point or theme of your paper? You need to find the sentence or two that states the point and then place it where it will stand out, usually in the first, or sometimes in the last, paragraph. Frequently you will find that you have to write these sentences and insert them.

These are the major areas of problems in student papers. Handling each one separately may mean going over your paper a number of times, yet it does break the task down into small workable units, which is usually easier to deal with than trying to do everything at once. As you spend more and more time on revision, you will find that the task becomes more manageable, even though few writers ever find the process particularly enjoyable.

FORMAL WRITING

The Final Draft. You are now ready to begin your final draft — although you are also free, if you wish, to abandon your original draft and begin again with an entirely new piece. If you do so, however, you must go through all the steps outlined above — selecting an incident from your memory chain, focusing on that event, examining your writer's log entries, preparing your drafts, and consulting with your writing group. By now you are aware that a first draft is only a first step, not a finished product.

Many instructors, while appreciating the value of narrative writing, feel that the college composition classroom should be used exclusively for the kinds of writings demanded by other college courses. You may therefore be asked to write an objective piece rather than a personal narrative. Although the final product will be quite different from a personal narrative, you will find that the beginning processes are surprisingly similar. The memory chain and focusing activities are necessary to clarify your thinking and to provide examples to support your ideas. You need to decide what the main point of your paper will be, that is, what answer you would give to the questions suggested below as topics. If you create your own topics, phrase them as questions so that your one- or two-sentence answer can supply a main point for your paper. The material from your writer's log and your memory chain will supply the specific details to support your position, and the particular event you want to describe can become the evidence to explain what you mean. In Part Four of this book are many more suggestions about this kind of writing.

Possible topics that you might choose to write about are as follows:

Why do some families fail?
What are the values found in a good family life?
How are families changing?

CHAPTER 5

Developing Objectivity
Memories of School

A major concern in college writing is the fair presentation of an issue or problem from the various points of view of the different participants. Whether your assignment involves a case study for sociology or consideration of an economic theory, you will need to include a reasonable explanation of opposing attitudes. To help you develop the objectivity and rhetorical strategies necessary for this kind of writing, we focus in this chapter on seeing events from other people's perspective. You will be asked to write about an event that happened to you as it might have been experienced by another person. Once more you will be asked to tap your memory, this time paying special attention to your recollections of school.

Most of the writing you have done thus far has concerned events as seen from your own point of view and has even involved writing in the first person, that is, using "I" as the subject of your sentences. When you wrote about your family, it was as you remembered them; when you described your neighborhood, it was as you saw it. But, of course, there were other people involved and they probably viewed the event from their own perspective. This difference might account for the way they behaved, and noting that fact could add to your understanding of the event itself. You might have had an inkling of the difference if in Chapter 3 you had created, rather than related, an incident for your letter.

Paying attention to these differences will broaden your writing skills in a number of ways: It will expand the information at your disposal to include in your writing; it will introduce you to the conventions of the third-person narrative; and it will help you achieve the degree of objectivity that is a necessary part of good college writing. The activities and writings in this chapter give you a chance to practice this technique.

WRITER'S LOG   Since the Formal Writing assignment at the end of this chapter deals with memories of school, you should use your writer's log to focus on events from that aspect of your life. The list below provides some suggestions for your entries.

> The exam I didn't expect to pass
> The day at school when something wonderful (or awful) happened
> Playing on the team
> A teacher to remember
> My first day at _____ school

READING   In the excerpt below, Edward Rivera describes a fight he had with a fellow student at the tender age of six. As you read, try to imagine what Antonio was thinking as he was being attacked or what Chuito had in mind when he was instigating the fight.

From FAMILY INSTALLMENTS   Edward Rivera

I spent the first grade of school under Luisa Lugones ("Mees Lugones"), the first-grade teacher of Bautabarro, who never laid a hand on anybody. She might hug one of her thirty-something students for standing out in class, but hit one of her neighbors' children for whatever infraction, never. "That's not what I get paid to do," she used to say. (She earned a couple of dollars a week, maybe less.) She took any complaints against you to your father and mother, or your guardians if you were an orphan, and let them handle the situation, which she explained, in front of you, briefly and honestly. If your parents wanted details, she gave them the details, in a serious but not morbid way and without dramatics or sermons. If they wanted to make a big deal out of it, that was their business, and your misfortune, part of the price you had to pay for disturbing her class. It was a well-run class.

I was doubly lucky, because Papi had taken off for New York years before I started school, so I escaped getting it from him during that year I spent in the first grade. Not that I gave Mees Lugones much reason to complain about me. She chose to do it only once, the time I got into a fight with Antonio Carretas. My adopted brother, Chuito, had instigated it when I told him Antonio had stolen a piece of buttered bread Chuito had bought me that morning for lunch. As usual whenever he could get away from his peon's job, Chuito had waited for me outside the schoolhouse — the same site my father and uncle Mito had tried turning into a general store — and walked home with me.

"You look a little hungry today, Santos," he told me. "Anemic. Tomorrow I'll buy you a two-cents piece of bread. I'll tell Arsenio to smear extra butter on it." He was on good terms with Arsenio Pagán, the eight-fingered grocer.

"I didn't eat that bread you gave me, Chuito," I confessed. "That's why I'm anemic today."

"You lost it? A serpent got to it before you did?"

"Antonio Carretas took it. He stole it."

He threw up his hands. "Jesus Christ! It runs in his family, that little punk. They're all crooks. *Ladrones maricones.* Even the grandfather. He's still stealing chickens when you turn your back on them." And one of the Carretas brothers had stolen a good-looking girl from under Chuito's nose. He couldn't come right out and hit the thief for that kind of theft, but he had it in for him; he was waiting for any excuse to get him. "And you didn't grab that piece of bread back from that little cowshit?" he asked me.

"I couldn't. He ate it all up right away. In one swallow. You should have seen his mouth."

"I'll tell you how I want to see his mouth tomorrow, Santos. Without teeth. All gums. And you're going to be his dentist. Let me see your right fist." I made a tight fist and showed it to him. "Fine," he said. "Maybe it's not as big as Antonio's mouth, but it's big enough to destroy it. No?"

Under the circumstances, yes. I should have kept my mouth shut about that piece of bread. Too late. I'd have to fight Antonio for it, and for Chuito's grievance over that stolen anonymous girl.

He took the rest of that afternoon off to give me "special lessons" on how to destroy Antonio Carretas next morning. We had to do it a good distance from the house, because Mami wanted nothing to do with violence and would have given us no end of hell, and no dinner that night, if she had caught us working out (situps, pushups, side-to-side twists, squats, chinning from branches, jogging up and down hills, swinging the arms windmill fashion to, as he put it, "loosen up your muscles, Santos"), and sparring. He cautioned me against leading with my right — or maybe my left; I couldn't remember which next morning, after a night of uneasy dreams, and too much breakfast "for stamina" — and when I walked up to Antonio Carretas outside the schoolshack, tapped him on the shoulder, and took a good swing at his mouth when he turned around, I missed. Not by much, but with someone like Antonio you didn't have to miss by much to lose the fight. He caught me on the nose right away — if his big mouth was an "easy" target, so was my oversized nose — and drew blood. He hadn't needed a

workout or an extra serving of breakfast to put me out of conten-
tion. And he took the two-cents piece of extra-buttered bread
Chuito had bought me that morning. He ran off with it before Mees
Lugones arrived on the scene of my defeat, my second in two days.

She told one of the other students to go pick a handful of medicinal grass for my nose and took me inside the shack, where I had
to lie on her two-plank desk, flat on my back and feeling pretty
demolished, circled by about twenty-eight fellow students of both
sexes, for about thirty minutes. It took the medicinal grass that long
to stop the flow of blood from my swollen nose. She and a couple
of students had taken turns chewing the grass into compresses, one
to a nostril, with frequent changes of compress, before the flow let
up and finally stopped.

"I wouldn't go into boxing if I were you, Santos," Chuito was
to tell me that night (our beds adjoined). "I think you're the kind
that's going to need a friend or a weapon when you get into trouble
with the Antonio Carretases of this shitty world." The day before
my defeat, he had called it "the greatest world ever invented" and
even gave God some credit for it. Now it was a shitty world all of a
sudden. He had some confusions to straighten out.

And Mees Lugones, without giving me a sermon on decent behavior and other moralities, took me home after class let out for
that day. "By swinging at Antonio first, you put yourself in the
wrong, Santos," was all she told me on the walk home, trailed by
all my fellow students except Antonio Carretas, who had made
himself scarce.

Chuito had been spying on us from behind the bushes all
along. He had seen me get it in the nose and failed to show himself
all morning; and unknown to any of us, he followed us all the way
home and stayed within easy reach, hiding until it was time for
him to come back from "work" in my grandfather's fields. Papa-
gante reported his absence to Mami next day, and he had to make
up a quick lie to get out of it. I don't think they were taken in by it
— he wasn't a good liar; his lips always shook when he wasn't
being honest — but there was nothing they could do about it. He
was on his own.

So I was the one who ended up paying the price for his unsuc-
cessful revenge on the Carretas brother who had swiped his sweet-
heart. "I don't think it was all Santos's fault, Doña Lilia," Mees Lugones told Mami (she was older than Mami). "But — well, I don't
want to preach, but just take a look at him. His poor nose."

"Poor nose nothing," Mami said. She must have been trying to
sound as Papi would have if he had been there to take charge. "If it
stays swollen like that, he may keep out of trouble the rest of his
life and live longer." Then she thanked Mees Lugones and walked
out with her as far as our chicken coop, where four hens were
keeping our breakfast eggs warm.

She was applying a damp rag to my nose when Chuito got back from his labors, put on a startled look to disguise his guilt —taking it for granted I wasn't going to rat on him — and said, after shaking his head, "It'll come off by itself, Mami." He was talking about the blood that had caked in my nostrils. "It's *dry* blood. Let him suffer a little." He couldn't hold back a big grin.

"Get out!" she told him. "I'll call you when it's time to eat." But when she stepped out and called him, about an hour later, he was gone off somewhere.

Discussion

1. In what ways does the author provide a sense of Chuito's anger?
2. What kind of details does Rivera use to create the character of the teacher?
3. If this story has a moral, what might that be?

ACTIVITY   **Building a Character.** In order to present another person's viewpoint, you need to be able to recreate that person fully, not only how he or she behaves in the situation about which you are writing, but also how the person behaves in other situations, even what he or she looks like and what the person might do in his or her spare time. With two or three of your fellow students, discuss the character of either Antonio or Chuito in the reading above. Answering the following questions may help you to visualize these boys.

1. What does Antonio look like? Chuito?
2. What kind of games do they like to play?
3. What are their ambitions and dreams for the future?

Your answers do not have to agree with your classmates'. In fact, seeing the variations may help you to appreciate the way different ideas occur to different people.

IN-CLASS   **Internal Monologue.** Imagine that you are either Antonio or
WRITING   Chuito in Edward Rivera's story. Write out the thoughts that you think are going on in either character's head during the incident described. For example, Chuito might be thinking: "Now I'm going to get even with the Carretas family. That little pipsqueak

Antonio stole Santos' breakfast and his brother stole my girl. Just wait till Santos beats him up in the fight. Of course, Santos isn't much of a fighter; he's awfully skinny . . . "

This form of writing, called an internal monologue, is one of the major ways of creating a character. When you have completed your monologue, share it with others in your class.

READINGS   Below are two readings about different sorts of school experiences. They will give you a sense of how other people feel about their school experiences and may remind you of incidents in your own life that you had forgotten.

THE CHANCE   Harold Bond

First grade. I am the skinny
one with the foreign accent. I am
so scared I think I will wee
in my pants. Miss Breen is teaching us
colors. We are cutting out
strips of paper in the fashion of
Indian feathers. We must

order them in descending hues on
a black headband. I cannot
understand Miss Breen. It is not done
the way it should be: blue with
yellow and black with white. Unless I
do something soon Miss Breen will
say I am a dumb Armenian. So

without looking I shuffle
my feathers in my hand. I paste them
over my headband. I spill
my pastepot, and I know I will wee
now because here comes Miss Breen,
only Miss Breen says, Good, Harold, good,
blue after purple and green

after blue. It happened, it happened
like a rainbow, like a swatch
of oil on water, eight feathers thieved
in perfect succession one
on the other. Miss Breen did not say
I am a dumb Armenian,
and I do not even have to wee.

From THE PRIME OF MISS JEAN BRODIE   Muriel Spark

Six years previously, Miss Brodie had led her new class into the garden for a history lesson underneath the big elm. On the way through the school corridors they passed the headmistress's study. The door was wide open, the room was empty.

"Little girls," said Miss Brodie, "come and observe this."

They clustered round the open door while she pointed to a large poster pinned with drawing-pins on the opposite wall within the room. It depicted a man's big face. Underneath were the words "Safety First."

"This is Stanley Baldwin who got in as Prime Minister and got out again ere long," said Miss Brodie. "Miss Mackay retains him on the wall because she believes in the slogan 'Safety First.' But Safety does not come first. Goodness, Truth and Beauty come first. Follow me."

This was the first intimation, to the girls, of an odds between Miss Brodie and the rest of the teaching staff. Indeed, to some of them, it was the first time they had realised it was possible for people glued together in grown-up authority to differ at all. Taking inward note of this, and with the exhilarating feeling of being in on the faint smell of row, without being endangered by it, they followed dangerous Miss Brodie into the secure shade of the elm.

Often, that sunny autumn, when the weather permitted, the small girls took their lessons seated on three benches arranged about the elm.

"Hold up your books," said Miss Brodie quite often that autumn, "prop them up in your hands, in case of intruders. If there are any intruders, we are doing our history lesson . . . our poetry . . . English grammar."

The small girls held up their books with their eyes not on them, but on Miss Brodie.

"Meantime I will tell you about my last summer holiday in Egypt . . . I will tell you about care of the skin, and of the hands . . . about the Frenchman I met in the train to Biarritz . . . and I must tell you about the Italian painting I saw. Who is the greatest Italian painter?"

"Leonardo da Vinci, Miss Brodie."

"That is incorrect. The answer is Giotto, he is my favourite."

Some days it seemed to Sandy that Miss Brodie's chest was flat, no bulges at all, but straight as her back. On other days her chest was breast-shaped and large, very noticeable, something for Sandy to sit and peer at through her tiny eyes while Miss Brodie on a day of lessons indoors stood erect, with her brown head held high, staring out of the window like Joan of Arc as she spoke.

"I have frequently told you, and the holidays just past have convinced me, that my prime has truly begun. One's prime is elusive. You little girls, when you grow up, must be on the alert to recognize your prime at which-ever time of your life it may occur. You must then live it to the full. Mary, what have you got under your desk; what are you looking at?"

Mary sat lump-like and too stupid to invent something. She was too stupid ever to tell a lie, she didn't know how to cover up.

"A comic, Miss Brodie," she said.

"Do you mean a comedian, a droll?"

Everyone tittered.

"A comic paper," said Mary.

"A comic paper, forsooth. How old are you?"

"Ten, ma'am."

"You are too old for comic papers at ten. Give it to me."

Miss Brodie looked at the coloured sheets. "*Tiger Tim's* forsooth," she said, and threw it into the wastepaper basket. Perceiving all eyes upon it she lifted it out of the basket, tore it up beyond redemption and put it back again.

"Attend to me, girls. One's prime is the moment one was born for. Now that my prime has begun — Students, your attention is wandering. What have I been talking about?"

"Your prime, Miss Brodie."

"If anyone comes along," said Miss Brodie, "in the course of the following lesson, remember that it is the hour for English grammar. Meantime I will tell you a little of my life when I was younger than I am now, though six years older than the man himself."

She leaned against the elm. It was one of the last autumn days when the leaves were falling in little gusts. They fell on the children who were thankful for this excuse to wriggle and for the allowable movements in brushing the leaves from their hair and laps.

"Season of mists and mellow fruitfulness. I was engaged to a young man at the beginning of the War but he fell on Flanders Field," said Miss Brodie. "Are you thinking, Sandy, of doing a day's washing?"

"No, Miss Brodie."

"Because you have got your sleeves rolled up. I won't have to do with girls who roll up the sleeves of their blouses, however fine the weather. Roll them down at once, we are civilized beings. He fell the week before Armistice was declared. He fell like an autumn leaf, although he was only twenty-two years of age. When we go indoors we shall look on the map at Flanders, and the spot where my lover was laid before you were born. He was poor. He came from Ayrshire, a countryman, but a hard-working and clever scholar. He said, when he asked me to marry him, "We shall have to drink water and walk slow." That was Hugh's country way of expressing that we would live quietly. We shall drink water and walk slow. What does the saying signify, Rose?"

"That you would live quietly, Miss Brodie," said Rose Stanley who six years later had a great reputation for sex.

The story of Miss Brodie's felled fiancé was well on its way when the headmistress, Miss Mackay, was seen to approach across the lawn. Tears had already started to drop from Sandy's little pig-like eyes and Sandy's tears now affected her friend Jenny, later famous in the school for her beauty, who gave a sob and groped up the leg of her knickers for her handkerchief. "Hugh was killed," said Miss Brodie, "a week before the Armistice. After that there was a general election and people were saying, 'Hang the Kaiser!' Hugh was one of the Flowers of the Forest, lying in his grave." Rose Stanley had now begun to weep. Sandy slid her wet eyes sideways, watching the advance of Miss Mackay, head and shoulders forward, across the lawn.

"I am come to see you and I have to be off," she said. "What are you little girls crying for?"

"They are moved by a story I have been telling them. We are having a history lesson," said Miss Brodie, catching a falling leaf neatly in her hand as she spoke.

"Crying over a story at ten years of age!" said Miss Mackay to the girls who had stragglingly risen from the benches, still dazed with Hugh the warrior. "I am only come to see you and I must be off. Well, girls, the new term has begun. I hope you all had a splendid summer holiday and I look forward to seeing your splendid essays on how you spent them. You shouldn't be crying over history at the age of ten. My word!"

"You did well," said Miss Brodie to the class, when Miss Mackay had gone, "not to answer the question put to you. It is well, when in difficulties, to say never a word, neither black nor white. Speech is silver but silence is golden. Mary, are you listening? What was I saying?"

Mary Macgregor, lumpy, with merely two eyes, a nose and a mouth like a snowman, who was later famous for being stupid and always to blame and who, at the age of twenty-three, lost her life in a hotel fire, ventured, "Golden."

"What did I say was golden?"

Mary cast her eyes around her and up above. Sandy whispered, "The falling leaves."

"The falling leaves," said Mary.

"Plainly," said Miss Brodie, "you were not listening to me. If only you small girls would listen to me I would make you the crème de la crème."

Discussion

1. What sense of the teacher do we get from each of these selections?

2. If you were a student in either of these classrooms, how would you describe the scene?

ACTIVITY   **Listing.** When in Chapter 4 you created the memory chain, you may have noted a school experience that you would now be interested in writing about. Reread your memory chain to see what it has to offer.

Another way of jogging your memory is to make a list of all the people and places you remember about school. Begin by making a column that lists all the grades from kindergarten through senior year in high school. Next, in a second column, fill in the name of the school and where it was located, even the classroom if you can recall it. Then, in a third column, put in the name of the teacher and of any classmates you remember. Your paper might look like the one below.

Kindergarten	Hubbard School Plainfield, N.J.	Miss Stebbins
First grade	Hubbard School 2nd floor	Miss Hopkins Jean Weider Herbie Smith

As you start to create your list, you might be amazed at how much information comes flooding back from your memory. As the author of this part of the text set down the words "Hubbard School," she immediately saw, as if some slide projector in her brain had been activated and a picture flashed on a screen, the red-brick, colonial-style building with its small red and white tower; the slim metal flagpole with its huge American flag; and the broad expanse of white cement sidewalk leading up to the main entrance in the center of the building — an entrance the students were never permitted to use. As each new item was added to the list, more and more pictures appeared. For this writer, memories come back mainly as pictures; for others, sounds or smells may be equally evocative.

Sometimes asking yourself questions as you create your list can bring forth more and more detail. As this writer set down the words "First grade," vague outlines of a classroom formed. Asking, "Where are the windows? the blackboard? the teacher's desk?" helped her to see a wall of windows along one length of the room, and a line of blackboards, with a beautifully printed frieze of the alphabet above them, running along the other three walls. The teacher's desk materialized in a corner of the room where the window met the front blackboard wall.

Setting down the teacher's name, "Miss Hopkins," produced a picture of a tall, stocky, gray-haired lady. With unexpected suddenness, the still picture became a movie, the scene took on life, and Miss Hopkins was looking down sternly at a classmate, Jean Weider, and the writer, now a small child, and was accusing them of cheating. That incident had not been thought about for decades, yet there it was, waiting to be called forth. The sense of shame, humiliation, and anger that suffuses the scene testifies to the strong emotions that are still connected to the incident. In our memories, emotions do not dim with time.

IN-CLASS WRITING	**Point of View.** Write an account of what you think the teacher, Miss Hopkins, might have been thinking in the scene above. What led her to suspect cheating? Why was she speaking so sternly to those six-year-old girls? What was the expression on the teacher's face? on the faces of the little girls? You can add to your account by imagining whether the day was sunny or cloudy, winter or spring, early morning or late afternoon. Since you are writing this story from Miss Hopkins' point of view, you need to try to understand how she felt at that moment. It would not do to turn her into a mean old woman, since clearly she would not see herself that way. Was she concerned about her students' honesty? Did she believe that an important part of her role was to develop their moral values? What other explanations might she have given for her actions? The story now is yours; you can add any details you want, so long as you retain the basic facts of the situation.
RHETORIC LEARNING	**Third-Person Narrative.** The assignment for this chapter is to write about an event from your days at school as if it were being told by someone who is outside the action. Until now, the narratives you have written for this text have been seen from your own viewpoint, that is, with yourself as the hero or heroine and the bulk of the explanation based on what you thought, what you said, and what you felt. As you wrote, you used the words, "I said," and "I did." For a third-person narrative, you need to stand back

from the scene. No longer are your emotions and perceptions the only ones to consider; you need to give equal weight to those of the other people involved in the incident. And instead of using "I," you will have to use your name — "Mary said" or "Mary did."

As you can see, a third-person narrative makes new demands on you. The chief requirement is that you need to separate yourself as writer from the person you are in the situation you are writing about. It is as if there are now two people who are "you" — the young person to whom the event happened and the more mature person who is looking back and telling the story. The more mature "you," the writer, needs to be aware of the fact that all of the participants in the situation had reasons for behaving as they did and that their versions of the story need to be presented as well as your own. Your sympathies may still go out to the younger "you," the person in the story who is an earlier version of yourself, and your writing can and should reflect that feeling. But you must be careful not to go overboard in your concern for your own version of the story. You need to limit your subjective view and develop a more objective stance.

IN-CLASS WRITING

First Draft of Formal Writing Assignment. You are now ready to write a first draft, as a third-person narrative, of an event that happened to you during your schooldays. Read over the list you made of your school years, the memory chain you did for the previous chapter, and the entries in your writer's log. Find an event that interests you and that you would enjoy writing about. While your emotional ties to an important event may make it more difficult to distance yourself from the situation, you would only bore yourself and your readers if you chose to write about an event that meant nothing to you.

Before you start, create a sentence that states the meaning, the message, the theme of your paper. This statement is useful as a tentative guide for your writing, providing the controlling idea of what you want to accomplish by your composition. It is also helpful for your readers to have such a sentence, for it will cue them in to an understanding of what is to come. A possible message for the incident involving Miss Hopkins and the cheating first-graders might be "Teachers sometimes are overly strict when they want to teach their students important moral values." Remember, the message you choose is only tentative; as you get involved in the story, you may find that other, more important meanings come to the surface. Don't be afraid to follow your intuition, for you can always change your opening statement. This draft is, after all, only a first draft — a first working out of your ideas. It will be revised at least once, if not more often, before it is considered finished.

Another consideration in writing your draft is to give sufficient emphasis to the climax of the story. One way to do so is to stretch out the moments before the final resolution by recreating, through memory or imagination, the words that the characters said to one another. This use of dialogue produces an intensity of emotion that helps your reader feel the full force of the moment.

LANGUAGE
LEARNING

Writing and Punctuating Dialogue. When you write about an event, one of the best ways to make the experience come alive for your readers is to record what was actually said.

If you look back at the various readings, you will see how the use of dialogue gives you a sense of actually being on the scene. The authors probably did not remember the specific words that were spoken, but by combining their memory with their imagination, they were able to recreate what might have been said. When you write about an experience, you too will find that you don't remember the exact language that was used. By using your general impression as a starting point, however, you can probably make up sentences that fit the situation.

If you remember a co-worker who was always yelling but don't remember precisely what he or she said, you might make up a speech like this: "I want the order book, and I want it NOW!" screamed Mr. Simpson.

There is a particular form that all writers use when they include dialogue. This form is useful; it lets the reader know exactly what words were spoken. The rules for the form are quite simple.

1. Quotation marks ("/") go in front of the first word of the speech you are quoting and after the last word of that speech. As long as there is no interruption, it does not matter if the speech is one word or a hundred words in several sentences; you need quotation marks only at the beginning and end of the speech.

    Quoth the Raven, "Nevermore!"

    "We were on the bus when this funny old lady got on. She had four shopping bags and when she tried to get her fare out of her handbag, she dropped one of the shopping bags and all her groceries spilled out," said Jane.

2. The first word of the quotation is capitalized and all end punctuation marks — commas, periods, question marks, exclamation points — are included inside the quotation marks.

"Didn't you see that stop sign?" asked the cop.

Kate shouted up the stairs, "You'd better get up now, Eric, or you'll be late."

3. The speaker's manner of talking is usually indicated, but this is done outside the quotation marks. Dialogue tags, as they are called, are easy to handle when they come at the beginning or end of the quotation. They are separated from the quotation by a comma.

"Tomorrow night? I'd love to," said Jane.

The coach said quietly, "We are going to win."

When the dialogue tag comes in the middle of the quotation, the speech is interrupted. Quotation marks must be used after the last word actually spoken and before the first word of the quote following the tag. Commas, too, must be used to separate the tag from the quote.

"I rewrote this essay four times," said Mary proudly, "and I finally got an A!"

Remember, these marks can often change the meaning of a sentence. Look at the way the meaning changes in the following example:

The alligator said Mary ate the frog.

"The alligator," said Mary, "ate the frog."

The alligator said, "Mary ate the frog."

GROUP READING AND REVISION

New Questions. The feedback that you receive from your reading/writing group can help you to go over your draft and make it better. As noted in the previous chapter, the group members' comments should point up the positive qualities of your paper, and it is up to you, the writer, to note that the areas where readers could not make such positive comments are the areas you need to work on.

In the previous chapter, you learned the following guidelines for members of a reading/writing group:

1. Repeat back to the writer what has been heard.
2. Mention all words and phrases that were particularly effective.
3. State the main point of the paper.

Now the following should be added:

4. State the reasons given in the story for each character behaving the way he or she did.
5. Point out all the ways the climax was strengthened.
6. Point out aspects of the story that enhanced the main theme.

FORMAL WRITING

The Final Draft. The story on which you have been working should now be revised so that it can serve as your Formal Writing assignment. As in the past, you may want to discard your initial story and begin again, using another incident from another time in your life. If you do so, however, you will need to go through all the steps outlined in this chapter to produce a different story.

Alternate Assignment

If you would rather not write a narrative, or if your teacher prefers that you work on a different kind of composition, you might want either to create a character sketch about a teacher or a schoolmate or to write on one of the following topics:

What is a good way to teach reading (writing)?

What changes should be made in high school?

What qualities distinguish a good teacher?

What do children learn that is not in books?

What should schools teach that they don't?

Remember, though, that you will need to have specific examples to support your ideas, and so the techniques for jogging your memory will still be useful. You will also find it necessary to create a sentence that expresses the message or theme of your paper.

CHAPTER 6

Combining Information from Different Sources
Who Am I?

A major challenge for all writers is finding ways to combine information from a number of different sources into one coherent piece of writing. Such a skill is particularly useful in college, where you are frequently asked to write research papers based on readings from several books and periodicals. (In Chapter 9 you will get a chance to practice this skill using articles and books.) In this chapter your task is somewhat different, in that the subject of your research will be yourself and the readings you consult will be your own — the entries in your writer's log, the memory chains you have created, the lists of events you have made, and the papers you have written for Formal Writing assignments.

Although there is still much more that you could uncover by continuing to explore your memories, you now have more than enough material to look back and reflect on all those experiences and feelings. As you have done in previous chapters, you need now to formulate a sentence or two that sums up the ideas you will want to express in your paper. Can you come to some tentative conclusion about who you are at this particular moment in time? Who are you — the person who has grown up in the places where you have lived, attended the schools you did, lived with the members of your family, known just those moments of joy and sorrow? Can you begin to say who you are?

In order to answer such a question, you will need to bring together some of the various bits of information you have collected thus far. You will also have to decide, as you have done several times before in this book, which details are significant and which are trivial. You may also find that you need to search your memory to find details whose significance you had not previously appreciated. Combining ideas that you have already written with newly discovered thoughts is like filling in the pieces of an immense jig-saw puzzle, a puzzle that will produce a picture of the "real you." Writing this paper will be no simple task, nor will you be able to produce a simple answer, for like all human beings, you are far too complex to be explained in a single paper. However tentative your self-definition may be, it is a necessary step to creating a unified paper as well as to deciding what you would like to do with your future.

WRITER'S LOG   Since the material in this chapter continues to focus on you, your writer's log entries might concentrate on aspects of your life not covered in the previous two chapters. Areas that you might want to consider include:

> Jobs I have held
>
> My favorite music
>
> My goals for the future
>
> When I am lonely, I _____.

Remember, the topics above are no more than suggestions; you are free to write on any topic you wish. It is your writer's log; only you can decide what should be included.

READING   The following selection presents one of the dilemmas people face when trying to decide who they are. In it, the poet gives her read-ers not only some sense of who she is but also an awareness of how contradictory her attitudes can be.

ON THE WAY TO BEING REAL   Barry Stevens

In the beginning, I was one person, knowing nothing but my own experience.

Then I was told things, and I became two people: the little girl who said how terrible it was that the boys had a fire going in the lot next door where they were roasting apples (which was what the women said) — and the little girl who, when the boys were called by their mothers to go to the store, ran out and tended the fire and the apples because she loved doing it.

So then there were two of I.

One I always doing something the other I disapproved of. Or

other I said what I disapproved of. All this argument in me so much.

In the beginning was I, and I was good.

Then came in other I. Outside authority. This was confusing. And then other I became very confused because there were so many different outside authorities.

Sit nicely. Leave the room to blow your nose. Don't do that, that's silly. Why, the poor child doesn't even know how to pick a bone! Flush the toilet at night because if you don't it makes it harder to clean. Don't flush the toilet at night — you wake people up! Always be nice to people. Even if you don't like them, you mustn't hurt their feelings. Be frank and honest. If you don't tell people what you think of them, that's cowardly. Butter knives. It is important to use butter knives. Butter knives? What foolishness! Speak nicely. Sissy! Kipling is wonderful! Ugh! Kipling (turning away).

The most important thing is to have a career. The most important thing is to get married. The hell with everyone. Be nice to everyone. The most important thing is sex. The most important thing is to have money in the bank. The most important thing is to have everyone like you. The most important thing is to dress well. The most important thing is to be sophisticated and say what you don't mean and don't let anyone know what you feel. The most important thing is to be ahead of everyone else. The most important thing is a black seal coat and china and silver. The most important thing is to be clean. The most important thing is to always pay your debts. The most important thing is not to be taken in by anyone else. The most important thing is to love your parents. The most important thing is to work. The most important thing is to be independent. The most important thing is to speak correct English. The most important thing is to be dutiful to your husband. The most important thing is to see that your children behave well. The most important thing is to go to the right plays and read the right books. The most important thing is to do what others say. And others say all these things.

All the time, I is saying, live with life. That is what is important.

But when I lives with life, other I says no, that's bad. All the different other I's say this. It's dangerous. It isn't practical. You'll come to a bad end. Of course . . . everyone felt that way once, the way you do, but *you'll learn!*

Out of all the other I's some are chosen as a pattern that is me. But there are all the other possibilities of patterns within what all the others say which come into me and become other I which is not myself, and sometimes these take over. Then who am I?

I does not bother about who am I. I *is*, and is happy being. But when I is happy being, other I says get to work, do something, do something worthwhile. I is happy doing dishes. "You're weird!" I is happy being with people saying nothing. Other I says talk. Talk, talk, talk. I gets lost.

I knows that things are to be played with, not possessed. I likes putting things together, lightly. Taking things apart, lightly. "You'll never have anything!" Making things of things in a way that the things themselves take part in, putting themselves together with surprise and delight to I. "There's no money in that!"

I is human. If someone needs, I gives. "You can't do that! You'll never have anything for yourself! We'll have to support you!"

I loves. I loves in a way that other I does not know. I loves. "That's too warm for friends!" "That's too cool for lovers!" "Don't feel so bad, he's just a friend. It's not as though you loved him." "How can you let him go? I thought you loved him?" So cool the warm for friends and hot up the love for lovers, and I gets lost.

So both I's have a house and a husband and children and all that, and friends and respectability and all that, and security and all that, but both I's are confused because other I says, "You see? You're lucky," while I goes on crying. "What are you crying about? Why are you so ungrateful?" I doesn't know gratitude or ingratitude, and cannot argue. I goes on crying. Other I pushes it out, says "I am happy! I am very lucky to have such a fine family and a nice house and good neighbors and lots of friends who want me to do this, do that." I is not reasonable, either. I goes on crying.

Other I gets tired, and goes on smiling, because that is the thing to do. Smile, and you will be rewarded. Like the seal who gets tossed a piece of fish. Be nice to everyone and you will be rewarded. People will be nice to you, and you can be happy with that. You know they like you. Like a dog who gets patted on the head for good behavior. Tell funny stories. Be gay. Smile, smile, smile. . . . I is crying. . . . "Don't be sorry for yourself! Go out and do things for people!" "Go out and be with people!" I is still crying, but now that is not heard and felt so much.

Suddenly: "What am I doing?" "Am I to go through life playing the clown?" "What am I doing, going to parties that I do not enjoy?" "What am I doing, being with people who bore me?" "Why am I so hollow and the hollowness filled with emptiness?" A shell. How has this shell grown around me? Why am I proud of my children and unhappy about their lives which are not good enough? Why am I disappointed? Why do I feel so much waste?

I comes through, a little. In moments. And gets pushed back by other I.

I refuses to play the clown any more. Which I is that? "She used to be fun, but now she thinks too much about herself." I lets friends drop away. Which I is that? "She's being too much by herself. That's bad. She's losing her mind." Which mind?

Discussion

1. What is the effect for you of the author's use of "I" as the name of a person in the poem?
2. What are the characteristics the author associates with each of the two "selves"? Do you think the separation is accurate?
3. Some people have said that this is not a poem. Do you agree? Why or why not?

ACTIVITY   **Reviewing the Data.** A first step in preparing your paper for this chapter is to review the material you have already accumulated. Reread your writer's log, memory chains, materials from focusing, lists of events, and papers that you have written thus far. Try to organize your ideas. What characteristics emerge? What seem to be your chief interests? What are your particular hates? What people seem to have played the most significant role in your life? What places seem to have been important in your development? What events seem to have made the deepest impression on you?

To develop an overall sense of what you have said about yourself thus far, you may have to read through your material several times. As you read, highlight those parts of your materials that could become part of your Formal Writing for this chapter. If you underline a passage, be sure to write a note in the margin indicating why you have marked it.

After you have reread your materials at least once and marked all the passages that might be important, you will begin to develop an overall sense of yourself. Rarely will this sense of yourself be something that you could put into words right now, but you will have some sense of an overall impression. The following steps will help you turn that impression into words.

Step 1.   Make a list of all the characteristics that have been displayed in your papers. Are you impulsive or cautious? patient or assertive? outgoing or thoughtful? optimistic or pessimistic? Try to make your list as complete as possible, even if you find you are including characteristics that contradict each other.

Step 2.   Make a list of all the people and places you have mentioned who you feel have made an important contribution to your development.

Step 3.   Make a list of all the events you have mentioned that you feel are crucial in displaying who you are.

Step 4.   Now see if you can connect any of the characteristics in Step 1 with any of the people and places in Step 2 or with any of the events in Step 3.

When you have finished, share your lists with your classmates. See if they agree with your assessment.

IN-CLASS WRITING

Freewriting. For a few people, the steps outlined above will be sufficient to produce a worthwhile paper. For most writers, though, the materials collected thus far will seem superficial and incomplete. Once again you will need to look into your storehouse of thoughts and memories to discover further ideas that will make your own understanding of yourself more complete.

But you now have jumping-off points that will make the task easier, and there are a number of ways you can approach this freewriting. You can select one of the characteristics you have identified as important and, through focused freewriting, see what more you want to say about it. Or you can select an event and, through freewriting, mull over the sense you have of who you were at the time. Another way to begin is to focus on a significant person in your life and consider more deeply who that person is and how he or she has influenced you.

RHETORIC LEARNING

Finding a Central Idea. When you build a paper out of bits and pieces from other writings, you need to create some central idea that will unify the various elements into a coherent whole. For the present composition, the unifying idea might be the characteristics you wish to stress. The sentences that name those characteristics would then provide the central idea and would be placed at the beginning of your composition.

Below are two entries from a writer's log kept by Trish Wiggins. Trish wants to write about her sister Frances as the person who has influenced her the most, and about her own high school graduation day as an event that was significant. The characteristics she wants to stress are generosity and independence.

Entry #1. My sister is a very pretty young lady. She stands about 5 feet and 4 inches high. My sister Frances can't walk down the street without getting compliments from people.

Frances is a pretty brown complextion. Now I understand the phrase brown sugar. She has an oval shaped face with black eyes, that's complimented with a small jet black mole that is right underneath her left eye. Frances has long wavy jet black hair that stops right in the center of her back. She has a button shaped nose that sits right in the center of her face, and small lips with a mole on her bottom lip.

Frances was never a selfish person. I guess she left that up to me. She shares her knowledge, her kindness and whatever she feels you need to have. If she has something that you want, you could bet your last dollar my sister would give it to you without a second thought.

Frances is a very easygoing person. I guess she inherited that from my mother. She hardly ever argues with anyone — you would have to work to really make her mad. Frances is easy to get along with. My sister has a lot of friends because she is so easygoing, but she stays to herself a lot of the time.

Entry #2. My high school graduation was an event that I was looking forward to. I was excited by the fact that I was finally finishing high school. I always thought that a high school graduation should be one event that you always would remember. I was kind of impatient for it to take place.

The graduation was to be held in Davis Hall in City College. This was a place where there were no windows. Our rehearsals were always held in our high school auditorium and not where we were going to graduate. When I first found out that there were no windows in this building I was already having second thoughts about going to this event.

Our rehearsals were always full of fun and games — no one took the rehearsals seriously. The students laughed and joked. No one paid any attention to what the teachers were saying. That was when I decided I was not going to go. My mother and the rest of my family were the reason why I was going to go. But then I decided not to go.

In a way I felt bad because I wasn't going because my mother spent a lot of money on the things I had needed. My mother has a habit of telling her friends and the rest of my family whatever goes on in our household. Later on that day some of my relatives and friends of my mother dropped over. They tried to change my mind, but my mind was made up. All I wanted to do was to save myself and my family some embarrassment.

On the day of graduation I waited until I was certain that it was over. Then I got dressed in the clothes that were originally intended for graduation. I went down to City College to find out what went on. As people came out of Davis Hall I didn't see a lot of smiles. In fact, everyone looked mad and they were talking about how awful the graduation had been. I was glad I wasn't there.

But now would I have made the same decision? I think I would've gone through with it because I had a feeling of loneliness because I wasn't with all my friends as a class for those last moments.

The opening sentence of Trish's composition might read as follows:

I am a very independent person who is learning to be more generous because of my sister's example.

With this sentence as a guide, Trish could then tell, in the first section of her paper, the story of her high school graduation in order to show her independence. Following that, she could go on to talk about how her sister Frances' example has helped her to become more generous.

READINGS   The selection below will show you how some writers have used brief descriptions of persons, places, and events in their works.

From THE HOMEWOOD TRILOGY   John Widemen

That's when I saw her. When my grandmother, Freeda, came to me. She is wearing a thin, gray cardigan, buttonless, perhaps another color once, mauve perhaps as I look more closely or perhaps the purplish blue of the housedress beneath the worn threads gives the wool its suggestion of color. The sleeves of the sweater are pushed back from her wrists. One long hand rests in her lap. The skin on the back of her hand seems dry and loose. If she tried to lift anything heavier than the hand to which it was attached, her fragile wrist protruding from the cuffed and frayed sweater sleeve would snap. She sits in her wooden rocker in front of the fireplace which has been covered over with simulated-brick Contact paper. Just over her head is the mantelpiece crowded with all of our pictures. The television set is muttering a few feet away. Bursts of laughter and applause. Dull flickers of light as the image twitches and rolls. She reaches inside the front of her dress and fumbles with a safety pin which secures the handkerchief cached there against her underclothes. Lilies hidden beneath her dress. Lilies spreading in her lap as she unties the knotted corners of the flowered handkerchief. In the center of the handkerchief a few coins and two or three bills folded into neat squares, one of which she opens as slowly as she had opened the silk. When she learned to talk again after her second stroke, she could only manage a minimal movement of her lips. Her head moves from side to side with the effort of producing the strange, nasal, tonal language of rhythms and grunts. If you listened closely, you could detect the risings and fallings of familiar sentence patterns. The words blurred and elided but you could get the message if you listened.

Take it. Take it. Take it, Spanky. I am leaving home. The first one in the family to go off to college. She thrusts the money in my hand. *Take it. Go on, boy.* A five-dollar bill as wrinkled and crisscrossed as the skin at the corners of her eyes.

From A WALKER IN THE CITY   Alfred Kazin

The block: *my* block. It was on the Chester Street side of our house, between the grocery and the back wall of the old drugstore, that I was hammered into the shape of the streets. Everything beginning at Blake Avenue would always wear for me some delightful strangeness and mildness, simply because it was not of my block, *the* block, where the clang of your head sounded against the pavement when you fell in a fist fight, and the rows of storelights on each side were pitiless, watching you. Anything away from the block was good: even a school you never went to, two blocks away: there were vegetable gardens in the park across the street. Returning from "New York," I would take the longest routes home from the subway, get off a station ahead of our own, only for the unexpectedness of walking through Betsy Head Park and hearing the gravel crunch under my feet as I went beyond the vegetable gardens, smelling the sweaty sweet dampness from the pool in summer and the dust on the leaves as I passed under the ailanthus trees. On the block itself everything rose up only to test me.

We worked every inch of it, from the cellars and the backyards to the sickening space between the roofs. Any wall, any stoop, any curving metal edge on a billboard sign made a place against which to knock a ball; any bottom rung of a fire escape ladder a goal in basketball; any sewer cover a base; any crack in the pavement a "net" for the tense sharp tennis that we played by beating a soft ball back and forth with our hands between the squares. Betsy Head Park two blocks away would always feel slightly foreign, for it belonged to the Amboys and the Bristols and the Hopkinsons as much as it did to us. Our life every day was fought out on the pavement and in the gutter, up against the walls of the houses and the glass fronts of the drugstore and the grocery, in and out of the fresh steaming piles of horse manure, the wheels of passing carts and automobiles, along the iron spikes of the stairway to the cellar, the jagged edge of the open garbage cans, the crumbly steps of the old farmhouses still left on one side of the street.

As I go back to the block now, and for a moment fold my body up again in its narrow arena — there, just there, between the black of the asphalt and the old women in their kerchiefs and flowered housedresses sitting on the tawny kitchen chairs — the back wall of the drugstore still rises up to test me. Every day we smashed a small black viciously hard regulation handball against it with fanatical cuts and drives and slams, beating and slashing at it almost in hatred for the blind strength of the wall itself. I was never good enough at handball, was always practicing some trick shot that might earn me esteem, and when I was weary of trying, would often bat a ball down Chester Street just to get myself to Blake Avenue. I have this memory of playing one-o'-cat by myself in the sleepy twilight, at a moment when everyone else had left the block. The sparrows floated down from the telephone wires to peck at every fresh pile of horse manure, and there was a smell of brine from the delicatessen store, of egg crates and of the milk scum left in the great metal cans outside the grocery, of the thick white paste oozing out from behind the fresh Hecker's Flour ad on the metal signboard. I would throw the ball in the air, hit it with my bat, then with perfect satisfaction drop the bat to the ground and run to the next sewer cover. Over and over I did this, from sewer cover to sewer cover, until I had worked my way to Blake Avenue and could see the park.

From THE WOMAN WARRIOR   Maxine Hong Kingston

"Improve that voice," she had instructed my mother, "or else you'll never marry her off. Even the fool half ghosts won't have her." So I discovered the next plan to get rid of us: marry us off here without waiting until China. The villagers' peasant minds converged on marriage. Late at night when we walked home from the laundry, they should have been sleeping behind locked doors, not overflowing into the streets in front of the benevolent associations, all alit. We stood on tiptoes and on one another's shoulders, and through the door we saw spotlights open on tall singers afire with sequins. An opera from San Francisco! An opera from Hong Kong! Usually I did not understand the words in operas, whether because of our obscure dialect or theirs I didn't know, but I heard one line sung out into the night air in a woman's voice high and clear as ice. She was standing on a chair, and she sang, "Beat me, then, beat me." The crowd laughed until the tears rolled down their cheeks while the cymbals clashed — the dragon's copper laugh — and the drums banged like firecrackers. "She is playing the part of a new daughter-in-law," my mother explained. "Beat me, then, beat me," she sang again and again. It must have been a refrain; each time she

sang it, the audience broke up laughing. Men laughed; women
laughed. They were having a great time.

"Chinese smeared bad daughters-in-law with honey and tied
them naked on top of ant nests," my father said. "A husband may
kill a wife who disobeys him. Confucius said that." Confucius, the
rational man.

The singer, I thought, sounded like me talking, yet everyone
said, "Oh, beautiful. Beautiful," when she sang high.

Walking home, the noisy women shook their old heads and
sang a folk song that made them laugh uproariously:

> "Marry a rooster, follow a rooster.
> Marry a dog, follow a dog.
> Married to a cudgel, married to a pestle,
> Be faithful to it. Follow it."

I learned that young men were placing ads in the *Gold Moun-
tain News* to find wives when my mother and father started answering them. Suddenly a series of new workers showed up at the
laundry; they each worked for a week before they disappeared.
They ate with us. They talked Chinese with my parents. They did
not talk to us. We were to call them "Elder Brother" although they
were not related to us. They were all funny-looking FOB's, Fresh-
off-the-Boat's, as the Chinese-American kids at school called the
young immigrants. FOB's wear high-riding gray slacks and white
shirts with the sleeves rolled up. Their eyes do not focus correctly
— shifty-eyed — and they hold their mouths slack, not tight-jawed
masculine. They shave off their sideburns. The girls said *they'd*
never date an FOB. My mother took one home from the laundry,
and I saw him looking over our photographs. "This one," he said,
picking up my sister's picture.

"No. No," said my mother. "This one," my picture.

"The oldest first," she said. Good. I was an obstacle. I would
protect my sister and myself at the same time. As my parents and
the FOB sat talking at the kitchen table, I dropped two dishes. I
found my walking stick and limped across the floor. I twisted my
mouth and caught my hand in the knots of my hair. I spilled soup
on the FOB when I handed him his bowl. "She can sew, though," I
heard my mother say, "and sweep." I raised dust swirls sweeping
around and under the FOB's chair — very bad luck because spirits
live inside the broom. I put on my shoes with the open flaps and
flapped about like a Wino Ghost. From then on, I wore those shoes
to parties, whenever the mothers gathered to talk about marriages.
The FOB and my parents paid me no attention, half ghosts, half invisible, but when he left, my mother yelled at me about the dried-
duck voice, the bad temper, the laziness, the clumsiness, the stu-
pidity that comes from reading too much. The young men stopped

visiting; not one came back. "Couldn't you just stop rubbing your nose?" she scolded. "All the village ladies are talking about your nose. They're afraid to eat our pastries because you might have kneaded the dough." But I couldn't stop at will anymore, and a crease developed across the bridge. My parents would not give up, though. "Though you can't see it," my mother said, "a red string around your ankle ties you to the person you'll marry. He's already born, and he's on the other end of the string."

Discussion

1. Each of these authors has selected a particular group of details to include in his or her description. What similarities do you find? what differences?
2. In what ways do these physical details enhance the sense of person and place the authors are describing?
3. What emotions do you feel from these selections? What words can you pick out that add to those emotions?

RHETORIC LEARNING

Revising Your Own Material for Use in a Different Context.

When you want to present material from your writer's log or other papers in a new context, you will usually need to revise it so that it fits the new situation. Your writer's log, for example, may contain a description of a person, written when you were experimenting with presenting physical detail. Although some of that detail would be useful for your new paper, much of it would probably be unnecessary. At the same time, your entry might make only scant mention of that person's effect on your personality, so that you would have to add information for this new purpose.

Look at Trish's description of her sister Frances (page 108). What should Trish omit? What parts should she expand?

Look at the materials you would be using in your paper. What parts would you want to leave out? Where would you want to add more information? Check with your reading/writing group to see if its members agree with your decisions. The feedback you receive from the group can be especially helpful in creating a paper of this sort. You may want to consult with group members even before you begin your first draft, showing them the characteristics you want to discuss and the material you want to use from your previous writings. The group members could tell you what kinds of information they would like to see added to your original material to bring out the characteristics you wish to emphasize.

Now start your first draft.

LANGUAGE LEARNING **Recognizing and Avoiding Run-on Sentences.** With the constant practice in writing you have had since you began this course, you have probably developed greater fluency and are using more complex sentence structures. These gains are to be applauded, but they do bring with them some trouble areas that need to be avoided. One potential problem is the run-on sentence. (Some teachers make a distinction between run-on sentences and comma splices, but we are treating them together here.) The run-on sentence occurs when two subject-verb units, or sentence cores, are put together without establishing a suitable connection, or alternatively, supplying a suitable separation. For example, a sentence with a single sentence core might read as follows:

Nila waited an hour for Elaine.

As a more skilled writer, you might want to add one or two additional ideas to that basic unit. The result of the additions might be:

Nila waited an hour for Elaine, she left, she had to go to class.

You probably know that a comma is insufficient to separate two sentence cores, so you might try to correct the sentence by adding periods. The result would be:

Nila waited an hour for Elaine. She left. She had to go to class.

Although this change is technically correct, it is hardly an improvement, for the resulting sentences are choppy and staccato. Far better would be using joining words that establish the necessary connections among these ideas. The sentence might be rephrased in the following way:

Nila waited an hour for Elaine, *but* she left because she had to go to class.

As you can see, using joining words not only avoids run-ons, but also gives an easy flow to your writing.

The correction of a run-on sentence can be challenging, and it is often difficult to catch run-ons before you hand in your paper. Count the subject-verb cores in each sentence and make sure you have a joining word if there is more than one core.

Exercise

Part I. Punctuate the following sentences.

1. Joe had a good time he went to the movies.
2. Mary has a B+ average she works hard on her assignments.
3. There's a big sale at the record shop I bought five tapes for $10.
4. The twins went to each other's classes on April Fool's Day they completely fooled all their teachers.
5. We painted the car a beautiful deep purple we hoped our father would like it but he didn't.

Part II. The punctuation has been omitted from the following paragraph. Read it through and add the words and/or punctuation marks that will make it correct.

> It had been seven years since I graduated from high school college seemed very strange as I stood in line at the bookstore to buy my texts I was shocked at how young my classmates appeared they seemed so carefree they didn't have a worry in the world I thought of my wife and children my job in the post office I couldn't neglect them even though I had added this new responsibility then in the freshman composition class I felt even more different here the boys talked about the basketball team the girls giggled and flirted with the boys the first assignment was the toughest I was asked to describe myself to the class I tried to describe the years of dull frustrating jobs I tried to explain how much I hoped that college would improve my chances finally I tried to tell them how old I felt when I read my paper to the class I felt they still didn't understand what I was trying to say later a man came over to me I hadn't noticed him in the class before he said he had been out of school for five years and knew just what I meant suddenly I felt more relaxed I had found a friend.

GROUP READING AND REVISION   Once you have finished your first draft, you will want to read it to your group and in turn listen to group members' papers. In addition to asking the questions outlined in the preceding chapters, group members should now ask the following:

1. Does the central idea in the opening sentence cover the main ideas in the paper?

2. What methods are used to illustrate the characteristics in each of the main sections of the paper?

FORMAL WRITING	**Final Draft.** With the comments from your reading group, you are now ready to revise your first draft. One advantage of writing this sort of paper is that you can change whole parts of it but still keep the overall frame. If you are dissatisfied with a section of your paper, you might want to change one of the characteristics you discuss, or you might want to use another example to explain and illustrate a characteristic if you and your reading group feel that the example you now use does not make the characteristic clear.

Alternate Assignment

If you prefer to write a less personal paper, you might consider one of the following topics:

What characteristics are necessary for success in college?
What is the true meaning of courage (loyalty, honesty, generosity, and the like)?

For this kind of paper, the strategies you use will be slightly different, although the basic pattern of your approach will remain the same. You will still have to review all your previous writings in order to find those sections which you can use for your paper. You will need to isolate events and people who can best illustrate the points you want to make. And, of course, you will need to formulate a sentence that indicates what your paper will be about. Instead of focusing on yourself, however, your paper will concentrate on the general situation. For example, instead of having a sentence that talks about the characteristic you found most valuable for your present situation, such as

I found that my determination and perseverance were most valuable for getting and keeping myself in college.

You might write

Determination and perseverance are important for getting into college and for staying there.

You would use your own experience as your supporting information.

Part Three

THE WHOLE ESSAY — WHAT DOES THE FUTURE HOLD?

The compositions you have written thus far have all had a sense of wholeness and completeness, even though we have not made any conscious effort to stress those factors. Now, however, in Part Three of this text, we will introduce you to several of the basic concepts for providing unity and coherence in your college essays. By the time you complete the assignments in these three chapters, you will know how to produce an essay that contains (a) an introduction setting forth a thesis, (b) a body of well-developed paragraphs with topic sentences, and (c) a thought-out conclusion.

In the course of learning about this kind of writing, you will focus on visions of the future. In some ways, adult considerations of the future are no different from children's responses to fairy tales. Children listen with wonder and amazement at the exploits of handsome princes, wicked witches, fairy godmothers, and mischievous goblins; they wait with bated breath for the inevitable "they lived happily ever after" of fairy-tale endings. Even though adults pride themselves on their realistic outlook on life borne from experience, they, too, have their dream stories. The only difference between the child and the adult is that the child's fairy tales people his or her present, whereas the adult's fairy tales are fantasies about the future. How many of us can say that we do not gaze into the crystal ball of our future with wonder and fascination? Doesn't the thought of what the future holds often fill the entirety of our minds, our hearts? Sometimes our fairy-tale fantasies do come true and sometimes they don't, but we hope, dream, and plan for that future all our lives.

In the next three chapters the rhetorical concerns of the college essay are combined with the issues connected with your plans for the future. In Chapter 7 you will study the basic organization of the paragraph as you consider the issue of what career choice you might make. In Chapter 8 you will learn to develop thesis statements as you ponder the pros and cons of future relationships. And in Chapter 9 you will learn about introductions and conclusions as you consider major issues in society at large. In all three chapters you will continue to use your writer's log to explore ideas, will continue to use reading/writing groups to increase your ability to learn from and help your fellow students, and will refresh your knowledge about several basic points of grammar.

CHAPTER 7

Sorting and Organizing
Choosing a Career

One of the difficulties of writing is achieving a smooth flow of information and ideas. Essential to this flow is organization. As a writer, you have to decide what to put first and then what to put next. Even more important, you have to determine what bits of information belong together.

Organizing, however, is not only a problem of writing; it is a matter of thinking as well. How you group ideas and information grows out of your thinking and, in turn, affects how you further think about a topic. This is particularly true when you consider what is a major issue for college students — choice of career. Some of you are making decisions about a career for the first time, while others are considering which career to change to as a result of current educational pursuits. Therefore, throughout this chapter the focus is on career choices and the process of planning for and getting a job.

As you explore the opportunities available to you, you will be gathering quantities of information that you will need to sort and organize into coherent units. The activities in this chapter will help you to see how both purpose and content affect the groupings you create. The activities will guide you in deciding when and why you should shift from paragraph to paragraph and will show you how key sentences within each paragraph alert readers to your objective.

Since the Formal Writing assignment asks you to combine information from a number of sources, you will be shown the "cut and paste" method of creating and revising a paper. Finally, we will discuss the use of transitional words in order to help you achieve that smooth flow of language which marks good writing.

121

ACTIVITY   **Sorting Careers.** Below is a random list of some careers for the 1980s and 1990s. To make sense of this list, you need to come up with several ways of categorizing the careers. One way to group them is by areas of knowledge, such as health care or education.

List of Careers for the 1980s and 1990s

Physician	Hotel manager
Airline pilot	Advertising account
Dentist	executive
Lawyer	Political scientist
Optometrist	Geologist
Chiropractor	Mathematician
Veterinarian	Oceanographer
Astronomer	Food technologist
Podiatrist	Statistician
Product manager	Real estate broker
Physicist	Sociologist
Economist	Historian
Health services	Agricultural/Biological
administrator	scientist
Anthropologist	Architect
Chemist	Pharmacist
Meteorologist	Geographer
FBI agent	Photographer
Psychologist	Biochemist
Personnel specialist	Land surveyor
Accountant	Insurance agent/Broker
Bank officer	Dietitian
Optician	Physical therapist
Computer programmer	Speech pathologist/
Urban/Regional planner	Audiologist
Forester	Librarian
Landscape architect	Social worker
Editor	Commercial artist/Graphic
Credit manager	designer
Soil conservationist	Medical lab technologist
Vocational rehabilitation	Computer service
counselor	technician
Engineer	Interior designer
Air traffic controller	TV industry technician

When you have grouped the careers by areas of knowledge, consider what you have learned about them. For instance, what category offers the most varied occupations or professions? What category appeals to you most?

Now consider other ways of looking at the careers. Are there some careers that require creativity and others that require mechanical nimbleness? Which careers require working alone, and which ones entail working with people? Then again, do some careers call for working outdoors while others necessitate working indoors? And yet again, which ones involve working with your hands and which with your head, as with figures, words, or pictures?

Now try to sort the careers a second time according to the new categories you have come up with. As you sort them for different purposes, you will notice that many of the careers you sorted by areas of knowledge are no longer together — for example, careers involving indoor work versus those involving outdoor work.

Discussion

1. How did the categorizing help you to make sense out of the list of occupations?
2. Were any of your approaches to categorizing more useful or more interesting than others? Which approach(es)? Why?

WRITER'S LOG
As you proceed with this chapter, you may wish to use some of the following career-related topics for entries in your writer's log.

Topics
1. When I grow up, I want to be _____ . (a childhood dream)
2. Smells and sounds inside a working place. (hospital, office, auto repair shop)
3. The most important goal in my life.
4. What am I particularly good at.
5. A day in my life fifteen years from now.
6. The most successful person I know.
7. What I want from my job.
8. How I manage my time.
9. How I am preparing myself for the career of my choice.

IN-CLASS WRITING	**Writing About Careers.** You have just completed grouping careers according to several different purposes. Now write about (a) one career that appeals to you and why, (b) another that you wish to know more about, and (c) one more that you would never choose. You may also wish to write about a career that interests you but is not on the list.

Notice that these instructions ask that you write about at least three careers and your reactions to each of them. In other words, there is a clear shift in both content (career) and purpose (reaction). Be sure to start a new paragraph when you move from discussing one career to another, for doing so will signal the change in focus for your reader.

RHETORIC LEARNING	**Writing Within a Paragraph.** In the career-sorting activity, you made sense out of a random list of careers by grouping them according to several specific purposes. The same activity occurs when you arrange sentences within each paragraph in an essay.

Paragraphs are not merely a random list of sentences; they do not just happen. The sentences that are joined together in a paragraph are there because a writer deliberately grouped them together. Usually it is the writer's purpose (that is, what the writer is trying to communicate), as well as the information itself, that determines which ideas should be grouped together and therefore what each paragraph should include.

Once information has been sorted and organized into groups, it is then possible to consider where one paragraph should end and another begin. In your reading and writing you have most likely noticed that the thoughts that are grouped together into paragraphs focus on one particular aspect of the subject. Thus, knowing where to begin and end a paragraph has to do with shifting from one aspect of a subject to another.

In this section you will sort, group, and organize sentences into paragraphs. What follows is an article entitled "The Fast Food Blues." The introduction and conclusion have been fully reproduced as in the original. However, the sentences in the three body paragraphs have been jumbled.

Step 1.   Read the introductory paragraph carefully.
Step 2.   Determine what three groups of ideas the article treats.
Step 3.   Draw up your paper with columns as shown following

the opening paragraphs. Label each column according to the three ideas the column discusses.

Step 4.   Now go over the jumbled list of sentences and fit each sentence into the category in which it belongs.

Step 5.   Once you have separated the sentences into the three categories, try to order the sentences within each category so that the paragraphs makes sense.

READING   THE FAST FOOD BLUES   Roy Pierce

To millions of people, rushing here and there, the gaudy, neon signs of fast food restaurants are a beacon, a place to rest their feet and have a quick, hot meal. But to the thousands of people who work in them, these restaurants are simply a means to an end — survival. At seventeen, fresh out of high school, I was one of the hundreds of students who was overjoyed to find a job as cook in a fast food restaurant. However, I was totally unprepared for the gruelling work, the low pay, and the dangerous working conditions. Working in a fast food restaurant was the worst experience I have ever had.

Column 1	**Column 2**	**Column 3**
_____	_____	_____
_____	_____	_____
_____	_____	_____

. . . Till then, I had felt that in spite of the exhausting work, paltry wages, and intolerable working conditions, having a job was better than no job at all. But that was the last straw. I gave in my notice and walked out. That evening as I counted the scars from burns and cuts on my body, some of which I still have to this day, I made a decision. I resolved to go to college and acquire an education, so I would never have to work at a dangerous, degrading job again.

List of Jumbled Sentences
1. Being late meant being fired.
2. Despite these drawbacks, I worked on a double shift on Fridays and Saturdays to fatten my meagre salary.
3. For eight hours a day, I rushed back and forth between vats of boiling oil, fire hot ovens, sharp-edged steel tables.
4. Within 15 minutes, I turned on the grills and vats, beat 5 to 6 dozen eggs, cut and placed pounds of bacon strips on the grill,

and stood ready to cook and serve breakfast to the deluge of workers who swarmed in at 6:30 A.M.

5. First of all, the physical demands of the work tested my body to its limit.

6. Although most were nothing more than minor cuts and burns, there was one accident I will never forget.

7. In addition to the strenuous work, the pay was a mere pittance.

8. From the rapid and abrupt changes in temperature, he got dizzy and slipped on the floor, spilling a vat of boiling oil all over his hands and chest.

9. Every morning I dragged myself out of bed at 4:30 A.M., so I could be at work by 6:00 A.M.

10. But far worse than the backbreaking work and the poor pay, the most degrading aspect of the job was the working environment.

11. Add nine other workers jostling around me in the close, cramped kitchen area without the benefit of air conditioning in the middle of a busy lunch hour in summer, and you have a situation in which accidents were almost a daily occurrence.

12. However, after taxes and other deductions, I was lucky if I took home $85 a week.

13. One day a young exchange student, who had been working for two hours in the 100° kitchen, was told to arrange some stock in the 0° freezer.

14. For three hours I carried ice cold, rock hard cases of frozen chicken, hamburger meat, and french fries down a flight of steps, across a basement and into a freezer that was bigger than my bedroom.

15. If I wasn't satisfied with my earnings, I knew there were many others just waiting to take my place.

16. This took him an hour, after which he resumed work in the kitchen.

17. And I had to finish within three hours before the next rush of customers came, or I was in trouble.

18. Within an hour, his blistering body was taken away before our horror stricken eyes and we were told to resume work as usual.

19. I worked for the minimum wage of that time: $2.15 an hour.

20. I once figured out that on an average, I was carrying about 150 cases weighing approximately 75 lbs. each, in those three hours each day.

21. Then the deliveries arrived.

22. There was no extra pay for overtime, no tips, no benefits.
23. Thus every week, I put in 56 hours of work for which I earned $120.40.

LANGUAGE LEARNING

Using Transitional Words. When sorting and organizing jumbled sentences in the previous exercise, you may have noticed certain key words and phrases such as *first of all, then, in addition, thus,* and *however* that signaled a particular relationship of thoughts between two sentences.

Thoughts, like human beings, do not exist by themselves; like human beings, they are related to other thoughts, and as with human beings, the relationship may vary. No matter what kind of writing you do, you will need to make clear the connection between one thought and another, whether the connection is (a) between parts of a sentence, (b) between sentences, or (c) between paragraphs. Words that signal these connections are called transitions; without them, it can be quite difficult to achieve coherency and a smooth flow of ideas in your writing.

Some of the more frequently used transitions give the following signals:

1. Result: *therefore, then, thus, hence, consequently, as a result*

   Tom worked hard all summer. He was able to pay his tuition fees for the fall semester.

   Tom worked hard all summer. *Therefore,* he was able to pay his tuition fees for the fall semester.

   In the second version the transition *therefore* makes clear the connection between the first idea and the second.

2. Contrast: *however, on the contrary, nevertheless, on the other hand*

   Hazel was feeling unwell. She decided to go to work.

   Hazel was feeling unwell. *Nevertheless,* she decided to go to work.

3. Adding or amplifying: *in addition, moreover, furthermore, further*

   Marilyn was offered a bigger salary than she expected. She got fringe benefits such as an annual vacation with full pay and health insurance for herself and her family.

   Marilyn was offered a bigger salary than she expected. *Moreover,* she got fringe benefits such as an annual vacation with full pay and health insurance for herself and her family.

4. Time: *sometimes, frequently, often, seldom, never, at the same time, before, after, now, by now, until now*

> Tim is determined to move up in his firm. He works in his office late into the night.

> Tim is determined to move up in his firm. *Frequently*, he works in his office late into the night.

5. Place: *here, there, above, below, farther on, elsewhere*

> Exhausted and hungry, Tom stood outside the last place he had interviewed at. He saw the yellow neon *M* of McDonald's down the street.

> Exhausted and hungry, Tom stood outside the last place he had interviewed at. *Farther on* down the street, he saw the yellow neon *M* of McDonald's.

6. Time sequence: *first, second, next, then, last, finally*

> Sally worked on her resume into the early hours of the morning. At 6:00 A.M. she went to bed satisfied.

> Sally worked on her resume into the early hours of the morning. *Finally*, at 6:00 A.M., she went to bed satisfied.

RHETORIC LEARNING

Topic Sentence: What It Does. You can probably best visualize the relationship between the topic sentence and the paragraph by mentally picturing the two basic motions of the body's muscular system — contraction and expansion. Think of the paragraph as representing the expansion of your ideas and information, including all the detail you need in order to present, support, and clarify your position or point of view. Then think of the topic sentence as the contraction of your thought, abridging it to a single sentence, yet adequately and accurately reflecting the main idea of your paragraph. Like many of the conventions you must observe when you write, the topic sentence functions primarily as a convenience for your reader, but it is also an aid for you, the writer, in that it provides, almost at a glance, the path of thought your composition takes from the first paragraph to the last.

Although it may be true that most often you speak in neither paragraphs nor topic sentences, both are more than just conventions you use when you write. When you have an idea and you want to speak it out, even to your best friend, you first need to organize your thoughts. At some point, you'll verbalize your main idea and then proceed to support it. Just as forcefully, you may reverse the process, in which, detail by detail, you build gradually toward the main idea you want to communicate. In writing, the topic sentence most frequently occurs at or near the opening of the paragraph; occasionally it appears in the middle, but quite often it comes at the end.

The three paragraphs that follow have been excerpted from a magazine essay. After you have read the paragraphs, find the topic sentence in each and justify your choice. In addition, explain how all the other sentences in the paragraphs support, justify, and further expand on each topic sentence.

HOW TO MAKE PEOPLE SMALLER THAN THEY ARE
Norman Cousins

The irony of the emphasis being placed on careers is that nothing is more valuable for anyone who has had a professional or vocational education than to be able to deal with abstractions or complexities, or to feel comfortable with subtleties of thought or language, or to think sequentially. The doctor who knows only disease is at a disadvantage alongside the doctor who knows at least as much about people as he does about pathological organisms. The lawyer who argues in court from a narrow legal base is no match for the lawyer who can connect legal precedents to historical experience and who employs wide-ranging intellectual resources. The business executive whose competence in general management is bolstered by an artistic ability to deal with people is of prime value to his company. For the technologist, the engineering of consent can be just as important as the engineering of moving parts. In all these respects, the liberal arts have much to offer. Just in terms of career preparation, therefore, a student is shortchanging himself by shortcutting the humanities.

But even if it could be demonstrated that the humanities contribute nothing directly to a job, they would still be an essential part of the educational equipment of any person who wants to come to terms with life. The humanities would be expendable only if human beings didn't have to make decisions that affect their lives and lives of others; if the human past never existed or had nothing to tell us about the present; if thought processes were irrelevant to the achievement of purpose; if creativity was beyond the human mind and had nothing to do with the joy of living; if human relationships were random aspects of life; if human beings never had to cope with panic or pain, or if they never had to anticipate the connection between cause and effect; if all the mysteries of mind and nature were fully plumbed; and if no special demands arose from the accident of being born a human being instead of hen or a hog.

Finally, there would be good reason to eliminate the humanities if a free society were not absolutely dependent on a functioning citizenry. If the main purpose of a university is job training, then the underlying philosophy of our government has little meaning. The debates that went into the making of American society concerned not just institutions or governing principles but the capacity of humans to sustain those institutions. Whatever the disagreements were over other issues at the American Constitutional Convention, the fundamental question sensed by everyone, a question that lay over the entire assembly, was whether the people themselves would understand what it meant to hold the ultimate power of society, and whether they had enough of a sense of history and destiny to know where they had been and where they ought to be going.

Discussion

1. Identify the topic sentence in each paragraph.
2. Has the author presented supporting details in each paragraph in a way that unity is achieved?
3. Is there any information or comment in any of the paragraphs that seems not to issue from the topic sentence? Explain.
4. In what way would you say that the author achieves coherence?

ACTIVITY   **Placing Topic Sentences in Paragraphs.** Using the following topic sentences, experiment with where to place them in the paragraphs you write — at the beginning, in the middle, or at the end.

1. I learned from that experience not to quit a job unless I already had another.
2. The amount of money you earn is not as important as enjoying the work you do.
3. Punching someone else's time card can really cause a lot of problems.

READINGS   Although the following reading selections are valuable as sources of information, their inclusion here is primarily to heighten your awareness of how work dominates our lives.

CAREER PLANNING: A SYSTEMATIZED APPROACH FOR
SENIORS   Selbourne G. Brown

> If you want to find suitable work, don't just look for a job. Pre-
> pare yourself for employment. . . .

What Businesses Need

After years of hiring and supervising for an insurance company, I have learned this: Employers do not *give* jobs to anyone. . . .
Corporations have business problems and they need people who
can come up with solutions. Smart managers hire on that premise.
However, each person hired out of college represents a major risk
on the part of the hiring manager. Without a track record in business, how that person will perform a given job is anybody's guess. I
have seen "A" students fizzle when confronted with the problems
of the workplace. If [you] are to compete successfully in the job
market [you] must gear your preparation to the needs of business.

In the past few years, it seems a whole industry has grown up
around preparing people for the job search. It rightfully assumes
that a great deal rests on the interview. Unfortunately, with so
much emphasis, the interview has become a high-stakes game of
Twenty Questions, an end in itself. The candidates are "prepped"
to anticipate the interviewer's every question and to respond with a
litany of stock answers. The hiring manager has had to learn to spot
the employee he needs from among the "professional" applicants.
When he fails, he ends up with a mismatch that is unproductive to
his company, and damaging to the individual who must be fired. To
avoid this, some hiring supervisors tend to dismiss the obviously
professionally coached applicant simply because it is so difficult to
tell what's behind the facade.

A New Strategy

What is needed is a strategy based on preparation for work instead of preparation for interviews. One rule of thumb that employers follow in selecting employees is this: What a person has done in
the past is a far better indication of what he will do in the future
than a college degree or anything he says. The most successful
strategy will, therefore, necessarily consist of two major components: learning the skills that employers need, and recording your
accomplishments to be used as proof of your capabilities.

Learning Workplace Skills

It is safe to assume that your classes will teach you the techni-
cal skills of your chosen profession. However, some of the skills of
the workplace can only be learned in a work environment. With a
little effort, the jobs you take while a student can prove invaluable
in this respect.

Seek work that will develop and test the skills you will need.
Two broad categories on which you might concentrate are problem-
solving and planning.

Stay away from the cafeteria and athletic center jobs unless you have career interests in those fields. Try the Library, the Office of the President, or the Admissions Office. Don't forget Student Government. If possible, try to find part-time work with a company in which you are truly interested. If all else fails, and you can afford to do so, volunteer. This is the most effective and risk-free method of developing a credible track record. It also provides the perfect answer to the inevitable question about how you spent your spare time.

Whatever position you take, take it seriously. *Don't just do the work.* Improve the job if possible. Is there a more efficient way to do your duties? Are there any problems on the job? If there are, tackle them. Don't wait for someone to ask you. If the problem is a major one, document your involvement. Describe the problem as best you understand it. What are its consequences? How would the job be improved if the problem were solved? Plan and write out your solution. Discuss it with your superior. If he does not implement it, don't be discouraged. He might have good reasons.

Your Personal Achievement File (PAF)

The second component of your strategy is the recording of your achievements in the workplace.

Set up a Personal Achievement File. This will become a permanent record of your work experience. It should contain a description of each job you've held. List the duties and responsibilities of each. Clearly show the manner in which you performed those duties. Include any documentation that supports your position.

Let your employer know that you keep this file. If you are careful, you will not only remove any suspicion from his mind, you will probably impress him quite favorably. If he keeps complete records, ask for copies of anything that will serve as proof of the way you did the job. If he does not, as is usually the case with campus jobs, ask him to write a note verifying the accuracy of your file. For the same reason, you need to have him initial future entries.

When you begin to seek permanent employment, this file will serve as a tangible account of your performance. It will save you from having to remember, on short notice, all you did on previous jobs. Its importance cannot be overstated. A friend of mine who is an executive at Xerox puts it this way: "Everybody is in business for himself. Don't allow anyone to keep score for you." This does not necessarily imply that anyone is out to cheat you. It simply means leave nothing to chance. If someone forgets to record your achievements, the result to you is the same as sabotage.

The Resume

Much has been written about the resume; most of it true and reliable. The basic rules: Keep it short — no more than two pages (both sides of the same sheet). It should be impeccably neat. Check the library or placement office for a book of samples. Choose a format that best exhibits your achievements. Follow the instructions for gathering your background information. Don't forget to draw from your PAF. If your typing is not of professional quality, have someone more qualified type it for you.

Cashing in the Preparation

If you follow these procedures throughout college, by your senior year you will be more prepared for the job market than most of your classmates. Stay ahead of the pack. If you have not already done so, begin making serious contact with the companies for which you wish to work. Make a list and target them one at a time. Find out all you can about each.

Use the Career Counseling Office

Take advantage of the placement office. Its main function is to act as a liaison to the business world. Use it as such. Alumni in business often give preference to applicants from their alma mater. Placement officers know these people. Your instructors are other possible sources of business contacts. Your chemistry professor might know of a former student who is now a vice-president in a chemical company. He will probably not tell you unless you ask him.

It is up to you to work creatively with these people to maximize the payoff on all your preparation. Start making your contacts now. Don't wait for the annual job fair where you will find yourself competing with the other soon-to-be graduates.

Visit the Company

Once you have identified your first choice of possible employers, discuss it with your Career Counselor. Show her your PAF. Ask her to make contact with the company for you. If possible, have her arrange a visit for you. She might not succeed at this. But if you convince her that you are worth it, she might be able to convince them of the same. Try to get a tour of the actual department in which you are interested. Don't let your efforts die in the company's personnel office if you can help it.

Prepare for the Visit

If you were not fortunate enough to get the personal introduction, you will have to go through the employment office like everyone else. On the other hand, if you got lucky, you still have your work cut out for you.

Find out all you can about the company. If they haven't left introductory material in the placement office, ask the office to write for some. Review whatever material you get and make note of any question you have. Research your PAF and identify any records that appear to be related to the type of business the company does. Scan your resume. Is it up-to-date? If not, have a new one typed.

Dress for the Visit

Let the workplace dictate your style. Don't outdress your host. Don't wear a black suit, white shirt and black tie, and carry a clipboard to see a factory foreman. He is likely to think you are the efficiency expert he's been dodging, and treat you accordingly. By the same token, avoid the Saturday night duds unless the office is a nightclub. If you really have no idea what to wear, ask.

Bring Pen and Paper

Few things convince people of your seriousness as does writing things down. Some years ago when I lived in California I spent many Sunday afternoons wine-tasting in the vineyards north of San Francisco. After a while I discovered that the servers spent more time, and wine, with the taster who carried a discrete note-pad and pencil. On my next visit I carried a professional-looking notebook labeled "Wine Catalog." The benefits were immediate and two-fold: better attention at the wineries, and a neat, up-to-date listing and description of my favorite wines — and those to avoid! Apply the same formula to your upcoming interview.

The Interview

These guidelines apply to any job interview you might have. Bring your PAF and the latest version of your resume. *Be yourself.* Take a matter-of-fact approach to the whole affair. You are interviewing them as much as they are interviewing you. You too have a list of questions you want answered. Ask them clearly and listen to the answers. What are the responsibilities of the job? What kind of training is provided? For how long? Will you have people reporting to you? When you ask about advancement, focus on the job, not yourself. Are there any changes planned for the job in the future? Will they require classroom training, or will on-the-job training suffice? Listen to the questions and answer them honestly. Don't try to second-guess the interviewer.

When he asks about your qualifications, discuss your academic achievements, then produce your PAF. Point out your outstanding accomplishments. Highlight those that lend themselves to the position in question. Even if he is not impressed with the jobs you have had, I guarantee he will be impressed with the records you have kept. This is the kind of thing that separates you from the pack.

Compensation

Finally, there is the question of salary; and this should be the final question. Managers take a dim view of the candidate whose driving motive is the dollar sign. Don't discuss "money" in a vacuum. Think in terms of "compensation." This shows you acknowledge that your pay is for work done, and that it is usually more than what shows on your paycheck. It normally includes the life insurance, medical insurance and whatever other inducements the company offers its employees. Ask for an outline of the compensation package. You can then decide if the cash portion meets your needs.

Summary

Even though this strategy calls for hard work, it is really quite simple when you think about it: Rather than preparing for interviewing, you prepare for working. Try to find meaningful work that will teach you valuable skills such as planning and problem-solving. Keep a neat record of your accomplishments. Stay clear of the pack by working creatively with the people who can help you. Take a matter-of-fact approach to the interview. Show your capabilities by showing your accomplishments. Your systematic approach will impress potential employers, and make you a much more attractive candidate. Try it. You may never have to look for a job.

Discussion

1. What do you think is the difference between looking for a job and preparing for employment?
2. What careers are you interested in? As students, what kinds of jobs should you find to best prepare you for these careers?
3. According to Selbourne Brown, one rule of thumb that employers follow in selecting employees is this: "What a person has done in the past is a far better indication of what he will do in the future than a college degree or anything he says." Do you think this is an effective method of hiring a person? Why?

MANAGING YOUR TIME   Edwin Bliss

I first became interested in the effective use of time when I was an assistant to a U.S. Senator. Members of Congress are faced with urgent and conflicting demands on their time — for committee work, floor votes, speeches, interviews, briefings, correspondence, investigations, constituents' problems, and the need to be informed on a wide range of subjects. The more successful Congressmen develop techniques for getting maximum benefit from minimum investments of time. If they don't, they don't return.

Realizing that I was not one of those who use time effectively, I began to apply in my own life some of the techniques I had observed. Here are ten I have found most helpful.

Plan. You need a game plan for your day. Otherwise, you'll allocate your time according to whatever happens to land on your desk. And you will find yourself making the fatal mistake of dealing primarily with problems rather than opportunities. Start each day by making a general schedule, with particular emphasis on the two or three major things you would like to accomplish — including things that will achieve long-term goals. Remember, studies prove what common sense tells us: the more time we spend planning a project, the less total time is required for it. Don't let today's busywork crowd planning-time out of your schedule.

Concentrate. Of all the principles of time management, none is more basic than concentration. People who have serious time-management problems invariably are trying to do too many things at once. The amount of time spent on a project is not what counts: it's the amount of *uninterrupted* time. Few problems can resist an all-out attack; few can be solved piecemeal.

Take Breaks. To work for long periods without taking a break is not an effective use of time. Energy decreases, boredom sets in, and physical stress and tension accumulate. Switching for a few minutes from a mental task to something physical — isometric exercises, walking around the office, even changing from a sitting position to a standing position for a while — can provide relief.

Merely resting, however, is often the best course, and you should not think of a "rest" break as poor use of time. Not only will being refreshed increase your efficiency, but relieving tension will benefit your health. Anything that contributes to health is good time management.

Avoid Clutter. Some people have a constant swirl of papers on their desks and assume that somehow the most important matters will float to the top. In most cases, however, clutter hinders concentration and can create tension and frustration — a feeling of being "snowed under."

Whenever you find your desk becoming chaotic, take time out to reorganize. Go through all your papers (making generous use of the wastebasket) and divide them into categories: (1) Immediate action, (2) Low priority, (3) Pending, (4) Reading material. Put the highest priority item from your first pile in the center of your desk, then put everything else out of sight. Remember, you can think of only one thing at a time, and you can work on only one task at a time, so focus all your attention on the most important one. A final point: clearing the desk completely, or at least organizing it, each evening should be standard practice. It gets the next day off to a good start.

Don't Be a Perfectionist. There is a difference between striving for excellence and striving for perfection. The first is attainable, gratifying and healthy. The second is often unattainable, frustrating and neurotic. It's also a terrible waste of time. The stenographer who retypes a lengthy letter because of a trivial error, or the boss who demands such retyping, might profit from examining the Declaration of Independence. When the inscriber of that document made two errors of omission, he inserted the missing letters between the lines. If this is acceptable in the document that gave birth to American freedom, surely it would be acceptable in a letter that will be briefly glanced at en route to someone's file cabinet or wastebasket!

Don't Be Afraid to Say No. Of all the time-saving techniques ever developed, perhaps the most effective is frequent use of the word *no*. Learn to decline, tactfully but firmly, every request that does not contribute to your goals. If you point out that your motivation is not to get out of work but to save your time to do a better job on the really important things, you'll have a good chance of avoiding unproductive tasks. Remember, many people who worry about offending others wind up living according to other people's priorities.

Don't Procrastinate. Procrastination is usually a deeply rooted habit. But we can change our habits provided we use the right system. William James, the father of American psychology, discussed such a system in his famous *Principles of Psychology*, published in 1890. It works as follows:

1. Decide to start changing as soon as you finish reading this article, while you are motivated. Taking that first step promptly is important.
2. Don't try to do too much too quickly. Just force yourself right now to do one thing you have been putting off. Then, beginning tomorrow morning, start each day by doing the most unpleasant thing on your schedule. Often it will be a small matter: an overdue apology; a confrontation with a fellow worker; an annoying chore you know you should tackle. Whatever it is, do it before you begin your usual morning routine. This simple procedure can well set the tone for your day. You will get a feeling of exhilaration from knowing that although the day is only 15 minutes old, you have already accomplished the most unpleasant thing you have to do all day.

There is one caution, however: Do not permit any exceptions. William James compared it to rolling up a ball of string; a single slip can undo more than many turns can wind up. Be tough with yourself, for the first few minutes of each day, for the next two weeks, and I promise you a new habit of priceless value.

Apply Radical Surgery. Time-wasting activities are like cancers. They drain off vitality and have a tendency to grow. The only cure is radical surgery. If you are wasting your time in activities that bore you, divert you from your real goals and sap your energy, cut them out, once and for all.

The principle applies to personal habits, routines and activities as much as to ones associated with your work. Check your appointment calendar, your extracurricular activities, your reading list, your television viewing habits, and ax everything that doesn't give you a feeling of accomplishment or satisfaction.

Delegate. An early example of failure to delegate is found in the Bible. Moses, having led his people out of Egypt, was so impressed with his own knowledge and authority that he insisted on ruling personally on every controversy that arose in Israel. His wise father-in-law, Jethro, recognizing that this was poor use of a leader's time, recommended a two-phase approach: first, educate the people concerning the laws; second, select capable leaders and give them full authority over routine matters, freeing Moses to concentrate on major decisions. The advice is still sound.

You don't have to be a national leader or a corporate executive to delegate, either. Parents who don't delegate household chores are doing a disservice to themselves and their children. Running a Boy Scout troop can be as time-consuming as running General Motors if you try to do everything yourself. One caution: giving subordinates jobs that neither you nor anyone else wants to do isn't delegating, it's assigning. Learn to delegate the challenging and rewarding tasks, along with sufficient authority to make necessary decisions. It can help to free your time.

Don't Be a "Workaholic." Most successful executives I know work long hours, but they don't let work interfere with the really important things in life, such as friends, family and fly fishing. This differentiates them from the workaholic who becomes addicted to work just as people become addicted to alcohol. Symptoms of work addiction include refusal to take a vacation, inability to put the office out of the mind on weekends, a bulging briefcase, and a wife, son or daughter who is practically a stranger.

Counseling can help people cope with such problems. But for starters, do a bit of self-counseling. Ask yourself whether the midnight oil you are burning is adversely affecting your health. Ask where your family comes in your list of priorities, whether you are giving enough of yourself to your children and spouse, and whether you are deceiving yourself by pretending that the sacrifices you are making are really for them.

Above all else, good time management involves an awareness that today is all we ever have to work with. The past is irretrievably gone, the future is only a concept. British art critic John Ruskin had the word "TODAY" carved into a small marble block that he kept on his desk as a constant reminder to "Do It Now." But my favorite quotation is by an anonymous philosopher:

> Yesterday is a canceled check.
> Tomorrow is a promissory note.
> Today is ready cash. Use it!

Discussion

1. Bliss offers ten steps for effective time management. Taking into consideration your lives as students with other responsibilities, what steps would you add or delete? Why?
2. As individuals, specify which steps you need to get "maximum benefit." How can you incorporate them into your day?
3. What does Bliss mean by "There is a difference between striving for excellence and striving for perfection"? Which one does Bliss believe to be more productive? Do you agree? Why or why not?

FORMAL WRITING

Writing About a Career. For your past assignments you gathered information by concentrating on what goes on inside you and around you and by delving into the deep recesses of your memory. For this assignment, however, you will need to get information from sources outside yourself. What we ask you to write is a description of the career you plan to prepare for.

Furthermore, this assignment has two parts: (a) gathering information from two persons you will interview and (b) sorting and presenting your information in yet another way, the "cut and paste" method of writing and revising.

Gathering Information

The first person you need to speak with is a counselor at your college. He or she will provide you with information about the nature of work and the employment outlook for your chosen career, as well as the courses, grades, summer jobs, and extracurricular activities that will prepare you for it.

Another important source of information is a person who is currently working in that field and can provide you with the living experience of what it is like — its highs and lows, its unexpected rewards and disappointing setbacks. If you do not know such a person, your family, friends, teachers, or counselors may know someone you can interview.

Here are a few questions to help you get the kind of information you may want.

1. How many years have you been working, and how would you sum up what you think you've learned in those years?

2. How would you rate your present (or last) job for salary, relationships with employer and fellow employees, and personal satisfaction and fulfillment compared with previous jobs you've had?
3. What do you think employers want from employees and vice versa?
4. Since you began working, in what ways have you noticed people's attitudes changing about working and earning a living?
5. Considering all you believe you've learned, what kind of advice would you offer someone who is just entering the job market?

You may notice that the last two questions suggest you are talking to an older person who's been working quite a long time. You may want to keep this in mind when you make your choice as to whom you'll interview.

Revising — Cut and Paste

Here is another method for writing and revising your paper.

First Draft. You should write up your first draft as soon as you have interviewed both a counselor and a professional, while the information, thoughts, and impressions are still fresh in your mind. At this point, don't concern yourself with how to organize your piece; it is enough to concentrate on recording every piece of information you can remember.

You should write on only one side of the sheet, so that when you need to reorganize your information for greater clarity and coherence you will be free to shift the ideas by cutting parts in order to arrange and rearrange your material.

Second Draft. In writing your second draft, you will want to concentrate most of your efforts on sorting and organizing your information so that you can find a clear pattern of presentation and establish a frame of reference. To find such a pattern, you will need to stand at some distance from your material so as to act as an objective commentator or narrator.

One way to do this is called cut and paste, a particularly useful method when you are not sure how to make a coherent whole out of a pile of information; some important, some not; some interesting, some not. Here is how the method works.

Step 1. Find all the important pieces of information and, with scissors, cut them away from the rest.

Step 2. Group the information into categories — for example, nature of work experience, training and qualifications required, employment outlook, earnings, and working conditions.

Step 3. Now put your groups in the best order you can devise. Remember that you want not only to inform readers about the nature of the job but also to entertain them, arouse their curiosity and interest. You may want to begin or end with a humorous anecdote from the professional you interviewed; you may want to use some of his or her on-the-job experiences to clarify your explanation of the kind of work required; or you may want to highlight the challenges he or she faced in acquiring the necessary qualifications. Paste the items on a blank sheet of paper in the order that you think would be most interesting and informative.

Step 4. Review your arrangement to be sure that separate ideas are treated in separate paragraphs. You should have combined into separate paragraphs all references to salary, promotions, friendships cemented at work, and so on.

Third Draft. When all your pieces are in the right order, do what writing is necessary to connect them into complete, coherent sentences and paragraphs.

In this draft, you'll need to call forth just about everything you've learned about writing, for here you give the final shape, texture, and meaning to what you've been writing. Besides just polishing your language, checking your grammar, and examining your sentences for structure and thought, you must now pay careful attention to accuracy of statement as well.

GROUP READING AND REVISION

In college, at work, and, to a lesser extent, during our leisure time, much of what we read or write is informational. If the information is not, above all, clearly and fully presented, we lose interest if we are readers and we lose our audience if we are writers. Unlike what you have written thus far, this paper is far more objective and informational. Therefore, before you write your final draft you should consult with your reading/writing group to find out whether you have conveyed your information fully, whether you have focused on each aspect of your subject clearly, and whether you will need to add or delete certain details.

In addition to the steps you have previously followed in giving and receiving group feedback, you may want to ask the following questions:

1. Does each paragraph develop only one idea?
2. Does each paragraph have a topic sentence that supplies the controlling idea of the paragraph?
3. Are appropriate transitional words used to make the relationship between ideas clear?

CHAPTER 8

Unifying the Essay
Social Relationships

A key ingredient of a college essay is the sentence that expresses your point of view, that tells your reader what you think about the subject of your composition. Before you can create such a sentence, however, you need to discover precisely what it is you think about that subject, a task that can prove surprisingly difficult. For example, you may have a general notion of your views but find, as you start writing, that there are large areas of confusing and contradictory ideas. How to work through this confusion and create the unifying sentence and the essay that goes with it is the main work of this chapter.

Your writing topic will be one about which there always has been and probably always will be some confusion. If one side of the coin of adulthood is choosing a career and making a living, then the other side, for most of us, is getting married and raising a family. Although it may vary in its form and context, marriage is the central social institution in cultures around the globe; it is the one universally recognized bond that is best suited for the bearing and rearing of children, hence the propagation of the human race.

In our society, with its stress on individual endeavors, achievement, and fulfillment, we look to marriage and the raising of children as a source of emotional satisfaction and stability. If it is the world of work that demands the constant assertion of the "I", then it is the spouse and child who satisfy the hunger in each of us for merging and being part of a "we."

In this chapter, then, you will be addressing the issue of marriage, its role in society and in the lives of individuals. But before you do so, look around the classroom. Among you are some who are single, others who are married, and perhaps still others who are divorced, remarried, or single parents. It is inevitable that your expectations, concepts, and ideals will be as varied as your experiences. Yet because of the variety of your views, you will need to be especially careful to present your position clearly and precisely.

ACTIVITY	**Brainstorming.** Thunderstorms and brainstorms have one thing in common: they both create a turbulence in energy, one in the atmosphere and the other in the brain. However, what remains in the wake of these storms is an entirely different matter. Thunderstorms may leave behind them chaos and destruction, but brainstorms leave behind a wealth of ideas, bits of information and experience from which a work of writing can be created. The more powerful the thunderstorm, the greater the disaster; the more vigorous the brainstorm, the richer the hoard of ideas.

I. Working with a few others, list on the board (or jot down on a piece of paper) anything and everything you can think of about marriage. Don't eliminate any of your thoughts; write down anything that pops into your mind about the topic. Don't worry about being messy or putting down unrelated ideas. Include what you think marriage offers — its promises, its good points, its bad points, its responsibilities, its rewards, and anything else that comes to mind.

You now have a large body of material. What can you do to make some sense out of it?

II. Observe what happens to this body of material when you organize it according to a specific purpose.

A1. Imagine that you are on a panel of experts that has been asked to present its views at a high school forum on teen marriages. You want to warn students against marrying at a young age but at the same time point out the benefits of marrying at a mature age.

A2. Regroup the ideas you have related to this purpose.

A3. Eliminate any ideas that do not suit this purpose.

B1. Now shift gears and imagine that you live in a society that is in danger of being overwhelmed by an increasing number of parentless children. Your goal is to produce a pamphlet that will convince the entire population to select marriage over single life.

B2. Regroup your ideas related to this purpose.

B3. Eliminate any ideas that do not fit your goal.

C1. Try to come up with other situations for which you would need to group your ideas to suit your purpose.

C2. Follow steps 2 and 3 as in A and B above.

The following are, first, the results of one brainstorming session and, second, one attempt to organize the information.

Marriage
love
companionship
share troubles and joys
worry about paying bills
bring up children
sleepless nights
doctors' bills
clothes
toys
come home to cook, clean, help with housework
safe sexual fulfillment
work, study, and take care of house and family
working overtime
frustration
in-laws — interference, influence

Marrying at a Young Age
1. work
   study   } too much pressure
   take care of house and family
2. bring up children
   medical problems
   clothes
   toys   } too much worry
   entertainment (parks, shows, games)
   sleepless nights
   homework
3. worry about bills
   rent
   food   } too little income
   doctors' bills
   transportation
4. in-laws -- interfere with children
             create friction   } additional pressure
             give too much advice

| WRITER'S LOG | Now that you have done some thinking on the subject of marriage and raising a family, you may want to use your writer's log to consider certain aspects of the subject. You might use some of the topics below; whether you do or not, feel free to explore any additional aspects that you come up with. |

Topics

1. What is marriage?
2. My idea of an ideal mate.
3. The responsibilities of marriage.
4. People I know who are married/divorced.
5. Will I have children? Why?
6. Will I get married or remain single?
7. The way it happened (recollections of my wedding day).
8. How important is being married to my present or future career?
9. What kinds of conversations do I have with my husband/wife?
10. Why I will/will not marry.

| IN-CLASS WRITING | **Writing and Organizing Ideas.** Refer again to the several groupings of ideas according to specific purposes you created from your brainstorming, and choose one that you'd like to explore further. |

1. Now take that topic and write it down on a blank sheet of paper.
2. Put your pen or pencil down for a moment and try to clear your mind of anything that might be in the way of your writing today. Then ask yourself, "What are all the parts I can say about this topic right now?" Spend about fifteen or twenty minutes writing down your responses.
3. Now ask yourself, "What's this topic about for me — what's important about this that I haven't said yet?" Spend another fifteen minutes or so responding on paper to this question.
4. If at any point you get stuck, either repeat the question to yourself or just ask yourself, "What's missing?"
5. Finally, ask yourself, "What's the point I'm trying to make?"
6. Once you can say what your point is, look back over what you have written and add anything else that comes to mind. Also note those places where you might need additional information or support.

Now share this piece of writing with a few of your classmates, making note of anything in their comments that is of interest to you.

RHETORIC LEARNING

The Thesis Statement. You have just written a great deal about one aspect of the topic "Marriage" but you have by no means created a finished product. The draft you just wrote is likely to be quite disorganized and still in need of additional information. But you should now be clear about what you intend to communicate as well as very much in control of what your paper will include. Creating the thesis statement for your piece of writing can now be a simple matter.

In the following space, write the statement from your draft that represents the point you are trying to make.

_____

_____

_____

_____

Look over the thesis statements that follow. Note that although each statement makes clear one main idea the writer has chosen to focus on, each statement also further restricts this idea to one or two aspects of it.

1. Many teenage marriages end in divorce because teenagers find themselves unable to manage their finances, unable to cope with interference from in-laws, and unable to deal with the responsibility of raising children.
2. Today, as more and more women join the work force either out of necessity or for personal fulfillment, they are often faced with the dilemma of conflicting priorities between their families and their careers.
3. Although living together without the formality of marriage may have given a sense of freedom to couples of the 1960s and 1970s, young people today are returning to the institution of marriage as they rediscover the rewards of sharing work, responsibility, and commitment.

The thesis is an important part of your essay. It tells your readers what the purpose of your paper is, what point you are going to prove, and what they may expect to gain from reading your essay. And it gives you a focus for organizing your thoughts. You might think of your thesis as if it were a judge's decision in a court case. The decision is the point of the judge's report; everything else to be said on the subject has to supply reasons supporting that decision. Your thesis should provide a similar focus for the rest of your essay.

Return now to the statement you wrote a few moments ago. Use the space provided here to revise this statement, making sure that your thesis clearly communicates the single issue your paper is going to be about and the aspects of that issue you plan to focus on.

If your thesis works, a reader will know on reading it what the purpose of your paper is and what point you are making. Read the thesis statement you have just rewritten to several of your class-mates. Ask them to tell you what the central issue of your paper will be, what you are intending to get across about this issue, and what aspects of this issue you will be covering. If your readers can answer these questions correctly, then you have developed a thesis that effectively communicates to your audience what you intend to do in your paper.

Notice also that besides informing your readers about the content and direction of your paper, the thesis statement offers you a way of organizing this piece of writing. For example, in the first thesis statement about teenage marriages ending in divorce, three reasons are mentioned: inability to deal with money problems, interference from in-laws, and the responsibility of children. Each of these reasons is one subdivision of the writer's paper. Therefore, the piece might be organized as follows:

- a paragraph of introduction that includes the thesis
- a paragraph explaining the financial problems that confront the teen couple
- a paragraph about how in-laws interfere
- a paragraph that tells why a teenage cannot deal with raising a child
- a paragraph of conclusion that reaffirms the point the author has made in the thesis

Spend the next few minutes considering the organization suggested by your thesis statement. Use this space to list the focal point of each paragraph that your essay will include:

_____

_____

_____

_____

_____

Exercise

Below are a number of topics to be discussed in an essay, followed by supporting ideas. Compose a thesis sentence for each essay.

1. "The Value of a College Education"
   to earn more money in the future
   to develop interests that bring lifelong satisfaction
   to improve one's ability to serve the community
   Thesis sentence: _____

2. "The Pleasure of Motorcycles"
   test skills and reflexes
   gives a sense of personal freedom
   teaches the user basic mechanics
   Thesis sentence: _____

3. "The Advantages of Marriage"
   provides security
   ensures a safe way to raise children
   provides companionship
   Thesis sentence: _____

LANGUAGE LEARNING

Building Sentences with Clauses. As you have developed as a writer, you have discovered that your complex thoughts require more complex sentence structures to express your ideas adequately. That is, you have found that you need to join ideas together to show the relationship between them. Of course, you have been using a wide variety of sentence patterns all your life, quite automatically. In presenting this discussion here, we aim to explain some of the principles that underlie sentence combinations so that you can become more aware of the choices available to you and can thus select the one that best suits your purposes.

The most common way to join ideas is to connect two subject-verb units with either the word *and* or the word *but.* You could say, for example:

The boy cried, *but* his sister laughed.
The baby took her first step, *and* the whole family clapped with joy.

In examples like these, both parts of the sentence — on either side of the connecting words *but* and *and* — are given equal importance, and either part could stand on its own. It is possible, in fact, for each section, even the one that begins with *but* or *and,* to be a sentence by itself. Sentences of this sort rarely cause any major problems. Just make sure that you have made the proper choice between the two words. *And* indicates that the added idea follows in the same direction as the first one, whereas *but* indicates that the addition is unexpected or goes off in a different direction. Compare the meanings of the following two sentences:

She was bright and she was pretty.

She was bright, but she was pretty.

Very often, though, when you want to add information to your sentence, you want to show that one of your thoughts is the dominant one while a second one supplies a reason or explains the timing or the conditions under which the main idea occurred.
When you want to join an idea in order to show under what condition something occurred, you can use words like *unless, although,* and *if.*

Unless two people feel that they can trust each other, they should not get married.

When you want to join ideas to show a time relationship, you can use words like *after, before, until, when,* and *while.*

Before a couple decide to have a child, they should be financially stable.

When you want to join ideas to indicate a place relationship, you can use words like *where* and *wherever.*

John and Phyllis got married in New York, *where* they had first met.

And when you want to show a causal relationship, words like *because, since,* and *so that* supply the means.

Grace wants to have a traditional wedding *because* she respects Old World values.

Then there are times when you want to add information about a subject you are discussing in your sentence. You could do so by adding a second sentence:

Luisa was married at sixteen.
She has two children.

Or you could combine the two sentences in one:

Luisa, who has two children, was married at sixteen.

The difference between the two methods is that in the second version the word *who* has been substituted for *she.* Thus, the word *who* acts both as a pronoun serving to substitute for Luisa (as *she* did) and as a joining word to join the two thoughts into one sentence. Other words that work in the same way are *whom; whose* when used about people; and *which,* used for objects. *That,* as you probably know, can be used for either people or objects.

The advantage of using *who, which,* and *that* in your writing is that you can eliminate the many short sentences that give a choppy effect. The smooth flow of ideas from one category to another that you have achieved by good paragraphing will be further enhanced by the smooth flow of each sentence within the paragraph.

Exercise

Part I. Below are several groups, each with two sentences. Join the two sentences together with the word in parentheses.

1. Joan washed all the dirty dishes. She finished her supper of fish and chips. *(as soon as)*
2. Maria and Yvonne went ice-skating at the local rink. George and Victor played basketball in the schoolyard. *(while)*
3. The mountains were covered with a dusky glow. The sun had set. *(after)*
4. Bob could not repair the broken bicycle behind the garage. He could not find the proper tools. *(because)*
5. Loretta wanted to go to the movies. She could not get tickets for the rock concert. *(since)*

Part II. Below are groups of "sentences." In each group, two of the three units can be joined. Depending on which of the two units you join, the emphasis of the sentence will be different. Rewrite each of the five groups so that there will be just two complete sentences in each one. Then rewrite each of the groups a second time, making a new combination. What is the difference in emphasis?

1. The boys will finish the job. When they get back from class. They will have enough time.
2. John failed chemistry. Although he studied all last night. He didn't understand the directions.
3. The movie was terrific. Although the actors weren't very good. We enjoyed the story.
4. Joe's girl friend walked out on him. After he danced with her best friend all evening. She told him she wasn't interested in him anymore.
5. Billy and Maria are going to the Pizza Hut. Unless you speak to them first. They will not know you are waiting for them at McDonald's.

Part III. Finish the following sentences by adding a second complete sentence unit. Notice that the joining word can come at the beginning or in the middle of the sentence.

1. When I am lonely
2. I feel sad when
3. After I have finished my homework
4. I drove the red Escort after
5. My father cheered enthusiastically because
6. Because our school chorus gave a concert

Part IV. Each of the following groups of words has one thought plus a joining word. Finish the sentence any way you wish, making sure you have added a thought that completes the sentence.

1. Tony who was coming down the ski slope at a dangerously high speed
2. The two puppies that nipped each other playfully
3. The crowd that milled through the streets
4. The ten-speed bicycle that Joe wanted for Christmas
5. The little girl who raced noisily through the supermarket aisles

READINGS   The short story and two articles that follow explore the relationship between men and women as spouses and as parents. As you read the selections, be aware of how the issues covered reflect, relate to, or shed new light on your own views and experiences.

THE STORY OF AN HOUR   Kate Chopin

Knowing that Mrs. Mallard was afflicted with a heart trouble, great care was taken to break to her as gently as possible the news of her husband's death.

It was her sister Josephine who told her, in broken sentences, veiled hints that revealed in half concealing. Her husband's friend Richards was there, too, near her. It was he who had been in the newspaper office when intelligence of the railroad disaster was received, with Brently Mallard's name leading the list of "killed." He had only taken the time to assure himself of its truth by a second telegram, and had hastened to forestall any less careful, less tender friend in bearing the sad message.

She did not hear the story as many women have heard the same, with a paralyzed inability to accept its significance. She wept at once, with sudden, wild abandonment, in her sister's arms. When the storm of grief had spent itself she went away to her room alone. She would have no one follow her.

There stood, facing the open window, a comfortable, roomy armchair. Into this she sank, pressed down by a physical exhaustion that haunted her body and seemed to reach into her soul.

She could see in the open square before her house the tops of trees that were all aquiver with the new spring life. The delicious breath of rain was in the air. In the street below a peddler was crying his wares. The notes of a distant song which some one was singing reached her faintly, and countless sparrows were twittering in the eaves.

There were patches of blue sky showing here and there through the clouds that had met and piled above the other in the west facing her window.

She sat with her head thrown back upon the cushion of the chair quite motionless, except when a sob came up into her throat and shook her, as a child who has cried itself to sleep continues to sob in its dreams.

She was young, with a fair, calm face, whose lines bespoke repression and even a certain strength. But now there was a dull stare in her eyes, whose gaze was fixed away off yonder on one of those patches of blue sky. It was not a glance of reflection, but rather indicated a suspension of intelligent thought.

There was something coming to her and she was waiting for it, fearfully. What was it? She did not know; it was too subtle and elusive to name. But she felt it, creeping out of the sky, reaching toward her through the sounds, the scents, the color that filled the air.

Now her bosom rose and fell tumultuously. She was beginning to recognize this thing that was approaching to possess her, and she was striving to beat it back with all her will — as powerless as her two white slender hands would have been.

When she abandoned herself a little whispered word escaped her slightly parted lips. She said it over and over under her breath: "Free, free, free!" The vacant stare and the look of terror that had followed it went from her eyes. They stayed keen and bright. Her pulses beat fast, and the coursing blood warmed and relaxed every inch of her body.

She did not stop to ask if it were not a monstrous joy that held her. A clear and exalted perception enabled her to dismiss the suggestion as trivial.

She knew that she would weep again when she saw the kind, tender hands folded in death; the face that had never looked save with love upon her, fixed and gray and dead. But she saw beyond that bitter moment a long procession of years to come that would belong to her absolutely. And she opened and spread her arms out to them in welcome.

There would be no one to live for during those coming years; she would live for herself. There would be no powerful will bending her in that blind persistence with which men and women believe they have a right to impose a private will upon a fellow-creature. A kind intention or a cruel intention made the act seem no less a crime as she looked upon it in that brief moment of illumination.

And yet she had loved him — sometimes. Often she had not. What did it matter! What could love, the unsolved mystery, count for in face of this possession of self-assertion which she suddenly recognized as the strongest impulse of her being!

"Free! Body and soul free!" she kept whispering.

Josephine was kneeling before the closed door with her lips to the keyhole, imploring for admission. "Louise, open the door! I beg; open the door — you will make yourself ill. What are you doing, Louise? For heaven's sake open the door."

"Go away. I am not making myself ill." No: she was drinking in a very elixir of life through that open window.

Her fancy was running riot along those days ahead of her. Spring days, and summer days, and all sorts of days that would be her own. She breathed a quick prayer that life might be long. It was only yesterday she had thought with a shudder that life might be long.

She arose at length and opened the door to her sister's importunities. There was a feverish triumph in her eyes, and she carried herself unwittingly like a goddess of Victory. She clasped her sister's waist, and together they descended the stairs. Richards stood waiting for them at the bottom.

Some one was opening the front door with a latchkey. It was Brently Mallard who entered, a little travel-stained, composedly carrying his grip-sack and umbrella. He had been far from the scene of accident, and did not even know there had been one. He stood amazed at Josephine's piercing cry; at Richards' quick motion to screen him from the view of his wife.

But Richards was too late.

When the doctors came they said she had died of heart disease — of joy that kills.

Discussion

1. Why does Mrs. Mallard — unlike many women, who go into shock when they hear tragic news — weep at once when she is told of her husband's death?
2. What discovery does Mrs. Mallard make when she is alone in her room? How does she react?
3. Why does Mrs. Mallard die when she sees her husband?
4. What insight into the relationship between husband and wife does this story give you?

MAN TO MAN, WOMAN TO WOMAN   Sherman and Haas

When it comes to conversation, husbands and wives often have problems that close friends of the same sex don't have. First, they may not have much to talk about, and second, when they do talk, misunderstandings often develop that lead to major fights. Our research concludes that these problems are particularly resistant to solution. Not only do men and women like to talk about different topics, spoken language serves different functions for the sexes.

Our findings are based on responses to a nationally distributed questionnaire, in-depth interviews and observations of same-sex conversations. We found much variation within each gender and no verbal absolutes to differentiate the sexes. But whether we look at topics of conversation or at the role language plays for each gender, we see enough difference to explain why men and women are, to use Lillian Rubin's book title, "intimate strangers."

One hundred sixty-six women and 110 men, ranging in age from 17 to 80, returned a questionnaire asking how often they discussed each of 22 topics with friends of the same sex. For some topics there is little difference — work, movies and television are, in that order, frequent topics of conversation for both sexes. On the other hand, female friends report more talk than do men about relationship problems, family, health and reproductive concerns, weight, food and clothing. Men's talk is more likely than women's to be about music, current events and sports. Women's topics tend to be closer to the self and more emotional than men's (in another questionnaire item, 60 percent of the women but only 27 percent of the men said that their same-sex conversations were often on emotional topics). A common topic, and one generally reserved for one's own sex, is the other sex and sexuality. Interestingly, women talk about other women much more than men talk about other men (excluding sports heroes and public figures). This includes "cattiness," a feature of conversation that many women wished to see eliminated. "Keep the gossip but get rid of the cattiness" is how one put it.

Of course, there are men who are eager to talk about family matters and women who love to talk about sports, but for a typical couple, there will be areas of personal importance that the other partner is simply not interested in and, in fact, may deride. "Trivial" is a term used often by both sexes to describe topics of obvious significance to the other.

But the difference in topics is not so damaging to intimate male-female relationships as are the differences in the style and function of conversation. For men, talks with friends are enjoyed primarily for their freedom, playfulness and camaraderie. When we asked men what they liked best about their all-male talk, the most frequent answer had to do with its ease. "You don't have to watch what you say" is how one young man put it. Some men commented on enjoying the fast pace of all-male conversation, and several specifically mentioned humor. A number of men said that they liked the practical aspects of these talks. As one wrote, "We teach each other practical ways to solve everyday problems: New cars, tax handling, etc."

A different picture emerged when we asked women what they liked best about talking with other women. While many mentioned ease and camaraderie, the feature mentioned most often was empathy or understanding, which involves careful listening as well as talking. "To know that you're not alone." "The feeling of sharing and being understood without a sexual connotation." "Sensitivity to emotions that men feel are unimportant." In questionnaire responses and interviews, women spoke of their same-sex conversations not as something they merely liked, but truly needed.

Women's greater need for same-sex conversation was shown by responses to other questions. When we asked how important such conversations were, 63 percent of the women, but only 43 percent of the men, called them important or necessary. Women are also far likelier than men to call up a friend just to talk. Nearly half the women in our sample said they made such calls at least once a week, whereas less than one man in five said he did. In fact, 40 percent of the men said they never called another man just to talk (versus 14 percent of the women). Men use the phone a great deal for business, and in the context of a business call they may have friendly conversation. But a call just to "check in" is a rare event.

Consider then the marriage of a man who had most of his conversations with other men, to a woman who has had most of hers with other women, probably the typical situation. He is used to fastpaced conversations that typically stay on the surface with respect to emotions, that often enable him to get practical tips or offer them to others and that are usually pragmatic or fun. She is used to conversations that, while practical and fun too, are also a major source of emotional support, self-understanding and the understanding of others. Becoming intimate with a man, the woman may finally start expressing her concerns to him as she might a close friend. But she may find, to her dismay, that his responses are all wrong. Instead of making her feel better, he makes her feel worse. The problem is that he tends to be direct and practical, whereas what she wants more than anything else is an empathetic listener. Used to years of such responses from close friends, a woman is likely to be surprised and angered by her husband's immediate "Here's what ya do. . . ." Adding to her anger may be her belief, as expressed by many women in our survey, that men don't credit her with good sense and intelligence, and that perhaps that is why he is advising her. The fact is, he does the same with male friends.

Men can be good listeners, of course, and women can give direct advice. But just as women read books and take courses on how to be assertive, men take courses on how to become better listeners. Indeed, whether it was Shakespeare — "Give every man thine ear but few thy voice" — or Dale Carnegie — "Be a good listener"— men have impressed on each other the value of good listening. The advice, however, must often fall on deaf ears. Women continue to be seen as better listeners.

Many books and articles have been written on how language discriminates against women, and there is no doubt that it does. Attempts have been made to change this — in the last couple of years, for example, we have heard men say "he or she" instead of the generic "he" in all-male conversation — but as long as boys play with boys, and girls with girls the sexes will use language in different ways and for different purposes. Whether it is for the feeling of freedom that comes from not having to watch what you say, or the feeling of relief and joy that comes from another human being truly understanding you, we will continue to seek out those of our own sex to talk to. There is no reason each must adopt the other's style. What is necessary is to recognize and respect it.

Discussion

1. What do men and women talk about in conversations with members of their own sex?
2. According to Sherman and Haas, what are the differences in the style and function of conversation between men and women?
3. What do Sherman and Haas suggest that men and women should do about the differences? Do you agree?

4. Consider recent conversations you have had with members of your own and the opposite sex. Are the differences suggested by Sherman and Haas borne out in your own experience?

PUTTING KIDS FIRST   Gail Gregg

It was a blizzard that finally forced the issue into the open. As snow began to fall at noon one wintry New York day, Kenneth S. Schuman, then an associate at the Wall Street investment banking firm of Lehman Brothers Kuhn Loeb, was asked by a senior partner to stand by. A major deal was in the wind, and Schuman soon would be asked to put together a rush report on the project. At 4:45 P.M., his orders finally came through.

Ordinarily, Schuman would have sighed, remained at the office and labored over the complex report until early the next morning. But this evening was different. Schuman's wife, Wendy, a magazine editor, had left for an overnight assignment in Maryland; the teenage babysitter staying with their daughter Cory, then 7 years old, was waiting to be relieved; and outside, the biggest storm of the season was under way. Schuman simply had to get home, important deal or no important deal.

The 39-year-old New Yorker quickly filled his briefcase with the documents he needed and boarded the subway for the half-hour ride to his Upper West Side home. Between intervals of bathing, feeding and entertaining his daughter, Schuman was able to read through some of the complicated financial papers. And once Cory was in bed, he sat up the rest of the night completing his analysis. "I did the best I could, but the pressure was unbelievable to juggle all that," he remembers.

For months, Schuman and his wife had been debating the demands of his job, which he had taken after a two-and-a-half-year tenure as New York City's economic development commissioner. Should Schuman ever become a partner at the firm (now Shearson Lehman Brothers, a subsidiary of American Express) his family would be rich "almost beyond belief." But there were plenty of sacrifices to be made in the interim; his work hours were so extensive and unpredictable, in fact, that Wendy Schuman had vetoed having a second child. "I always felt off balance; you never knew whether you'd be able to make it," Schuman now says of his investment banking days. "You always had to say you'd try to be there, with the family, but you couldn't promise. And when you were home you'd never know when the phone would ring and you'd be called back in."

On the night of the snowstorm, Schuman concluded that the rewards of his high-finance job weren't worth the price. Several days later, he summoned his courage and went to his superiors with his dilemma: "I told them I was happy with my title and salary but unhappy with the unpredictability of the hours," Schuman says. "The response was they gave me a better title and more money. They really didn't seem to understand what I was saying." He tried for several more months to work out some way to remain at the company, but finally he knocked on the door of a senior partner, Peter J. Solomon, to inform him of his decision. He would leave Lehman to start his own company, a real estate investment venture, with two friends who also wanted jobs that permitted them to spend more time with their families.

"I wish I had him back," Solomon now says of Schuman, whom he describes as "very talented." But he confirms that there is little room in the investment banking field for men or women with strong family commitments. "I think the pressures on everybody are destructive and probably get in the way of any balanced life," says Solomon. "Regrettably, if you're going to be a world class player, along with the money and the glamour and the pizazz goes a lack of personal time."

The real conflict for Schuman — and for many other fathers like him today — is that he *did* want to be a "world class player" in business; but he also wanted a "world class" home life. Though few men have yet to forfeit, as Schuman did, high-powered careers and six-digit incomes for family considerations, millions of fathers now are experiencing the same stresses as they try to fulfill longtime career goals and satisfy new family demands. "The male feels not just conflicts, but intense pressures," maintains John Kronstadt, a Los Angeles lawyer and father of two young children. "Society hasn't lowered its level of job performance, but it has raised its expectations of our roles in our children's lives."

A generation ago, men like Schuman and Kronstadt would have had wives to care exclusively for children and home. But today's upwardly mobile father is likely to have a spouse on the fast track, too; the couple must share childrearing and housekeeping responsibilities. And many young fathers of the 1980's seek a more active presence in their children's lives than their hard-working fathers may have had in theirs. Whether they want to have it all, or feel they must do it all, men increasingly are finding themselves victims of a sort of "Superdad" syndrome, similar to the "Supermom" conflicts that plague so many female workers. Dr. Ken Druck, a San Diego clinical psychologist who conducts seminars on the special problems of men, sums up the situation: "Dad can't get away with the old syndrome of coming home and flopping down in a big easy chair as Mom tells the kids, 'Don't bother your father, he's exhausted.' I come home at the same time as my wife. She's just as exhausted as I am."

. . . Government statistics . . . paint a startling picture of just how radically the family has changed since the Ozzie-and-Harriet days of the 1950's and 60's. Fewer than 20 percent of American families with children now fall into the workaday dad, stay-at-home mom variety — a percentage that is expected to drop even further over the next decade. The traditional American family, often cited nostalgically as the moral center of our society, hardly exists except in the imagination. A skyrocketing divorce rate, the rising cost of living and the exodus of millions of women from the home to offices and factories all have combined over the last decade to install a new family in its place — the family in which both husband and wife work or which is headed by a single parent.

Until very recently, these vast changes have been viewed by employers — and by many male workers — primarily as "women's issues." But companies around the country now are beginning to grapple with the fact that both men and women are affected by the new family structures, and that their concerns regularly spill over into the workplace in ways they didn't when breadwinning and homemaking functions were separate. Employee turnover, tardiness and productivity are among the consequences of these family changes.

When a 5-year-old got the measles 30 years ago, for instance, caring for the sick child was part of mom's job. Today, one of the parents has to stay home from work, and it is by no means certain that the parent most free to stay home will be mom. School holidays require special child-care arrangements, very young children need some sort of full-time care, and the fatigue and stress of coping with both a job and heavy household responsibilities take their toll on parents. "It's reaching most families," says Dr. T. Berry Brazelton, a Boston pediatrician and a nationally recognized authority on childrearing. "We've got to recognize that families are being stressed now and they need some backup. I don't think families can survive without it."

Certain to be a key topic at the Labor Department's symposium is how to manage the new generation of fathers who just now are beginning to make family-related demands on their employers. These demands have been slow in coming, in part because many men have feared that their careers would be derailed if they permitted family concerns to trail them into the office. But employers now report that men increasingly are speaking out about their new home responsibilities — and the resultant stress. "These things are just as much on the mind of the male employee," says Arthur F. Strohmer, executive director of human resources, staffing and development for Merck & Company, the pharmaceutical concern. He adds, though, that "You've got an awful lot of traditional thinking to buck" before many managers will take the concerns of new fathers seriously. "Most corporations still operate within a white male value structure," agrees the employment manager of a major high-technology company, who asked not to be named. "There's an expectation that you will give up your family for your job."

Many managers are likely to be men who raised their families in traditional ways and who still view childrearing as a mother's responsibility. Not only do they find it hard to understand the role their male employees now are required to play in the home, but they also can be downright hostile to "new-style" fathers who want to maintain an active involvement with their children. For instance, Catalyst, a New York-based research organization, recently polled personnel directors about their firms' parental benefit policies. It found that, of the 119 major corporations that offered paternity leave, 41 percent nevertheless responded that "no time" was the appropriate amount of time for a man to take off at the birth of a child. "What we're talking about is changing people, not policies," says another personnel executive who wished that his name not be used. "You're trying to tell a 50-to-60-year-old manager who worked his way up the assembly line that Mike's going to come in late every Monday morning."

The seemingly unyielding corporate culture is only one of many reasons that many men have found it difficult to alter their work practices to accommodate new responsibilities at home. Because of the limited earning power of women, many new fathers find that they must shoulder the burden of breadwinning for the family whether they want to or not. And others find that habit and socialization continue to exercise a surprising tug on their work behavior. "There's a lot of romance around fatherhood now." says Dr. Sam Osherson, a psychologist and writer whose book on the subject, "Finding Our Fathers," was published last month. "But a lot of these guys don't feel the romance — they feel frustrated and annoyed."

In contrast to previous generations, though, these lapsed family intentions carry a particularly high cost for men today: acute guilt, stress and, frequently, marital strains. "I hear about it all the time from men who have to work very long hours, and the work situation is expected to come first," says Dr. John Munder Ross, a New York psychoanalyst and authority on the paternal effect on personality development. "These kinds of complaints were so much more submerged in the past. Now they're much more on the surface."

When Ken Schuman gave up a career at Lehman Brothers — a career that could have put him in the top echelon of finance and earned his family a luxurious life style — he found that many of his friends had difficulty making sense of his decision. "You're giving up the American dream," he explains. "And what you're getting is so intangible and hard to explain, not as widely valued in society. It's so gooey compared to what your bonus was."

The modest Greenwich Village office of Affordable Living Corporation is indeed a far cry from the wood-paneled dens of Lehman Brothers. Schuman no longer wears pinstripes to work; a sports jacket will do instead. And gone are expense account lunches at the city's best restaurants or the first-class air flights. But after several years of hard work and financial sacrifice in getting the new venture off the ground, he reports, "It's now become clear that we're going to be successful." The company also has succeeded in reaching its other major goal: its three partners have retained enough control over their schedules that they are able to lead active family lives even as they bring home impressive earnings. "The fast track is alluring," Schuman says, "but when I'm with my kids, taking care of them or playing with them, and I see how much a part of their lives I am, I'm glad I made the decision I did."

Discussion

1. What are some of the causes that forced the traditional family of the 1950s and 1960s to change?
2. What are some characteristics of the typical family of the 1980s, as stated in the article by Gregg? Can you add others?
3. What dilemmas do parents in a family of the 1980s face?
4. Suggest some possible solutions to these problems that parents, their employers, and the government can try out.

FORMAL WRITING

You may wish to explore further the piece you wrote earlier in class. In that case, make sure to use those classmates' comments which you think will be useful in rewriting the piece. Be sure to use as well any interesting ideas you encountered in the readings presented in this chapter.

If, on the other hand, you prefer to write an entirely new piece, here are some suggestions:

The roles of husband and wife in marriage.

Why people get married or divorced.

The rewards and difficulties in marriage.

Remember, you can always turn to the entries in your writer's log for more ideas and information.

Revisions

Now it is time for you to decide how many times you will need to revise your paper before you feel satisfied.

By now you are familiar with several techniques of writing and revising; experiment with as many of them as you can. In fact, some of the prewriting techniques such as brainstorming, memory chain, focusing, and listing can be useful for those parts of your paper in which you feel something is missing, more information is needed, or a fuller explanation is in order.

GROUP READING AND REVISION	Before you write your final draft, present your piece to a group of classmates. Here are some questions they may ask you:

1. Does your essay include a thesis statement that limits your subject to a workable size and presents a viewpoint that needs to be supported?
2. Does each paragraph focus on one particular aspect of this thesis, and do the details in the paragraph support the main idea of the paragraph?
3. Is it possible to look back to your thesis from any point in the paper and know how the material being presented relates to this thesis?
4. Do the ideas presented in this piece represent your beliefs?
5. Will your audience understand as fully as you do the significance of the issue you have elected to write about?
6. Are your sentences complete, your verbs and pronouns correct?

CHAPTER 9

Introductions and Conclusions for the Whole Essay
The World Outside

It takes only a formal introduction and conclusion to transform the compositions you created in the last chapter into full-fledged college essays. You may be somewhat surprised that we are discussing the introduction to your paper *after*, rather than before, its body; however, there are several reasons for doing so. In the first place, an introduction should explain the main point of a whole essay — and few writers know what that main point is until they have written several drafts, and revised their thesis again and again as they work through their ideas. By not embedding their thesis in a formal introduction, they are more relaxed about changing it. Second, an introduction should indicate the specific areas to be discussed in the essay, areas that can be isolated only after a writer has had the chance to try out several approaches. And third, by creating the introduction at the same time as the conclusion, a writer can help keep an essay unified.

The topics about which you are asked to write in Chapter 9 concern issues involving the world outside the private sphere of family, school, and friends — issues that you will consider in terms of how they affect not just your personal life but also the community at large. You are now beginning to recognize that a citywide blackout is not simply a personal experience of fear or fun; it raises questions about the efficiency of our power supply and raises fears about the demons not of darkness but of vandalism and burglary. Fiery flames from an explosion at a chemical factory are no longer something you watch with fascination; such an explosion triggers your concern about lethal gases or chemical spills that may harm entire communities. When you hear of an event such as a concert to raise money for the poor and needy, you feel good even though the event does not affect you directly. And when you read about the miracles of the silicon chip or the promises of space exploration, you are filled with wonder. Thus, as you grow older you realize how events around the globe impinge upon your world of family, friends, and work. The opinions you form or the priorities you establish will vary between you and the next person, but one fact is inescapable: you can no longer meet the world outside by turning indifferent eyes or deaf ears upon it.

Although the world contains too many issues to be covered in one or a few compositions, you will want to isolate those that are of primary concern to you. To help this process, we ask you to create a collage that will highlight the issues you would want to write about, and we show you how to use questions to generate information about your chosen subject.

ACTIVITY   **Making a Collage.** A *collage* is, according to the dictionary, "a composition of fragments of printed matter and other materials pasted on a surface." The word *composition* means a whole — a complete work in which the arrangement and connection between parts are deliberate. The word *fragments*, by contrast, means "pieces" and implies that something is broken or separated. Yet for a collage to work, it must communicate; the fragments within it may not be connected explicitly, but nonetheless they are arranged intuitively or subconsciously.

A truly successful collage can have a substantial impact on viewers because it draws them to make meaning for themselves according to their own conscious inclinations.

Look at the collage on page 166.

1. Can you discover a theme in it?
2. What specific pieces create the theme?
3. Is there one particular piece or a specific group of pieces that stands out most? Why?
4. Why is there only one picture in the collage?

Many writers use the collage as a prewriting technique. A collage is particularly useful when a barrage of apparently unrelated information, responses, and ideas threatens to overwhelm you, for in the very process of making a collage, you create some kind of separation of fragments into groups. A closer look at the collage

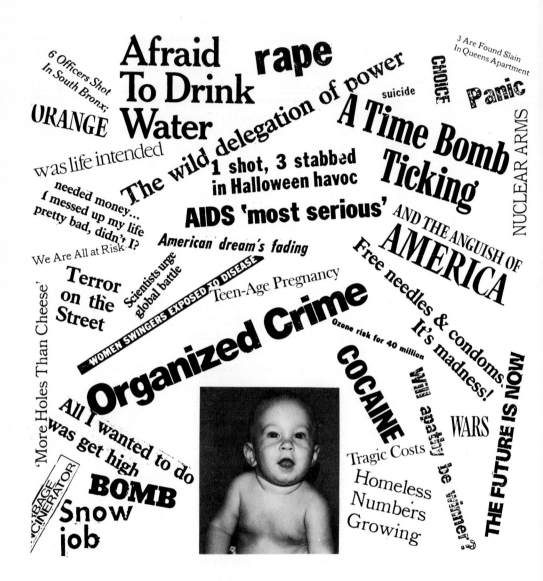

6 Officers Shot In South Bronx;

Afraid To Drink

rape

The wild delegation of power

3 Are Found Slain In Queens Apartment

suicide

CHOICE

Panic

ORANGE

Water

A Time Bomb

NUCLEAR ARMS

was life intended

1 shot, 3 stabbed in Halloween havoc

Ticking

needed money...

I messed up my life

pretty bad, didn't I?

AIDS 'most serious'

AND THE ANGUISH OF

We Are All at Risk

American dream's fading

AMERICA

Terror on the Street

Scientists urge global battle

WOMEN SWINGERS EXPOSED TO DISEASE

Teen-Age Pregnancy

Free needles & condoms,

It's madness!

'More Holes Than Cheese'

Organized Crime

Ozone risk for 40 million

COCAINE

Will apathy be winner?

THE FUTURE IS NOW

All I wanted to do

was get high

BOMB

Snow job

GARBAGE INCINERATOR

Tragic Costs

Homeless Numbers Growing

WARS

above will reveal that although the fragments of printed matter are overwhelming, they seem to have been separated into general areas of problems that the writer sees in the world around her.

Create your own collage of printed matter, pictures, and your own comments about the significant problems or promises that the world presents for you.

WRITER'S LOG	Here are issues to explore as you move along in this chapter. Use your collage to generate more topics.

Topics
1. What I am most afraid of.
2. What I am curious about.
3. If I could change the world, I would . . .
4. Terrorism in the world.
5. How sports can be used to promote peace.
6. Video cassettes in music — their influence on the public.
7. Teen pregnancy.
8. The drug epidemic.
9. Since the world is the way it is, I will/will not have children.

IN-CLASS WRITING	**The Meaning Behind the Collage.** If the maker of the collage on page 166 were to write about the significant problems in the world, she would probably devote a paragraph each to fear of nuclear war, pollution, crime, drugs, teenage pregnancy, spread of AIDS, and concern about the hungry and homeless. Perhaps in the lower half of the collage she is wondering if having children is worth the risk. This is not to say that everyone views the world this way. (Here's an aside: The writer showed her collage to two women friends who walked in as she was finishing it. One of the friends has two children and wants another; the other friend has one child from her first marriage, and she and her second husband are considering adopting a second child. These women's outlook is clearly different. For them, the world has always been full of dangers, yet life goes on and there is always hope.)

Look at the collage you made. Try to discover what the whole implies and what parts connect to make specific points to support that implied statement.

Now write up what you think are the problems and promises of the world we live in.

RHETORIC LEARNING	**Writing the Introduction.** In Chapter 8 you learned to create a thesis. Now you need to learn how to put your introduction together so as to stimulate your readers' interest. The easiest way is to be as clear and concise as possible. Introductions don't have to be very long. In fact, for most student essays four or five sentences are all that is needed. In those sentences you want to let your readers know what your specific topic is, what your thesis is, and why

they should be interested in it. Only when you have a firm idea of the body of your paper are you ready to write a formal introduction.

A formal introduction has three functions to perform:

1. It tells your readers what the topic is.
2. It tells your readers what specific point you want to prove and what the main divisions will be.
3. It helps your readers focus their attention.

For instance, if you were the writer of the collage on page 166, you might want to begin your essay by presenting in some general way an overview of the world; you could then focus on how this situation affects you, and finally you might enumerate the specific reasons for this effect. Such an introduction might look like this:

> Every day we pick up a newspaper or listen to the news on radio or TV and our ears are assaulted with news about people kidnapped and held hostage in one country, or people fatally poisoned or seriously injured from chemical explosions. We hear of people taken ill from contaminated water supplies in one city, from contaminated food in another; of a murder committed on one block of a city, of a suicide on another. Why would anyone want to bring a child into a world over which hovers the threat of a nuclear holocaust; into a country where the young are in turmoil, the old and poor in distress; into a city where pollution or crime can snuff out a life in a moment? But there is always hope; our children are that hope.

Another method many writers use successfully is to begin by mentioning a slightly broader topic than they will be discussing. If you are planning, for instance, to discuss your favorite rock singer, you might begin by mentioning a number of rock singers who are currently popular. You don't have to get any broader than that. You certainly would not want to begin by discussing all music, or even all rock music. You might mention three or four singers, pointing out their special characteristics. The final sentence, your thesis, would then point out the particular qualities of the person you are going to write about. Your introductory paragraph, diagrammed on the opposite page, might look like this:

> Although there are several phenomenal experiments under way in the field of science, the most impressive are occurring in biotechnology. In agriculture, scientists are successfully developing plants that produce their own pesticides and fertilizers, thus removing the danger of poisoning our air. In med-

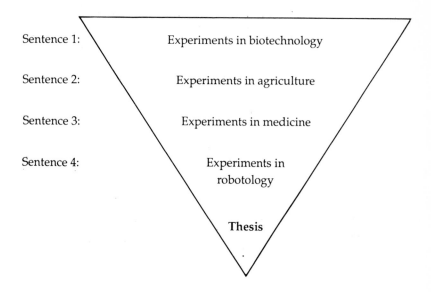

icine, a new drug holds the promise of fighting diseases ranging from the common cold to cancer. But the most breathtaking
experiments are being conducted in robotics, as scientists attempt to develop biochips to replace silicon chips in computers. It is not unlikely that the next generation will enjoy a
life of relative leisure because self-replicating robots will have
removed much of the drudgery, monotony, and frustration of
human labor.

A more elaborate example of an introduction from a professional writer follows. In this case, the writer, Karen Burton Mains,
uses a very brief anecdote to start her essay "Ellen Norton, M.D."
This approach is quite a common one. If you want to give it a try,
notice that it is just seven sentences long, although the article itself
is the equivalent of ten typewritten pages. As you can see, the
introduction is a very small part of the total essay. If you want to
begin in this way, you should be brief as possible.

On the horizon of the great semi-arid plain of northern
Kenya, a camel appears carrying a young girl. She has been
badly gored by an ill-tempered rhino, and under the merciless
African sun, the child is dehydrating rapidly, a fever is raging
and the wound is filled with infection.

But, seemingly airborne, word has gone out across the vast
bush: *Daktari* is camping in the wilderness; the dying girl is
being brought across the dry, trackless plain to healing hands.

The "Daktari" (the Swahili word for doctor) is 49-year-old Ellen Norton, M.D., a medical missionary who practices in the Northern Frontier District, that part of Kenya which nestles against the famine-ridden underbelly of neighboring Ethiopia.

These days people tend to think of missionaries as those courageous but extinct adventurers of a bygone era. But the fact is that such quiet heroes and heroines still do exist. Ellen Norton is one of this rare breed — hardy souls working selflessly in a far-off land and doing this exhausting work for a pittance of what they could earn practicing their profession at home.

Some other ways to write introductions include the following:

1. Using a striking illustration or example. For instance, a description of cold, huddled figures sleeping in the public toilets of bus or train terminals in a city you live in or have passed through might start you on an essay about the plight of the homeless. Here is the introduction to an essay that begins with two short examples before it gets to its thesis:

> A Texas elementary-school teacher gave a reading lesson under her hand-printed sign: "Patient is a virtue."
>
> A Salt Lake City English teacher renowned for his excellence quit the classroom to earn twice as much in another job — driving a truck.
>
> These cases illustrate two sides of a growing crisis in America's public schools: On the one hand, too many classrooms are burdened with teachers improperly prepared for their work. On the other, thousands of competent instructors are being lured from their jobs by more rewarding work elsewhere.

2. Beginning with a point of view different from your own.

> Everyone lives on the assumption that a great deal of knowledge is not worth bothering about; though we all know that what looks trivial in one man's hands may turn out to be earth-shaking in another's, we simply cannot know very much, compared with what might be known, and we must therefore choose. What is shocking is not the act of choice which we all commit openly but the claim that some choices are wrong. Especially shocking is the claim implied by my title: There is some knowledge that a man *must* have.

3. Beginning with a quotation.

"Fathers are a biological necessity but a social accident," Margaret Mead once observed. Contemporary women might take issue with this traditional image of the father as the helpless parent with little talent for or interest in child-rearing. They are likely to argue that the father is just as capable of caring for babies as the mother, and ought to at least share the burdens.

Writing the Conclusion

Perhaps not all writers, but certainly many, whether they are beginners like yourself or veterans, frequently find it nearly as difficult to end a paper as to begin it.

You will be concerned with making your point clearly and logically and with convincing your reader that you are serious and know what you're talking about. Just as there are definite procedures to follow for writing an effective body and introduction, so are there procedures to follow for writing a conclusion. There are also some very specific things to avoid. Let's begin with the don'ts:

1. Don't just stop. How are readers to know you're really finished and there isn't more to come somewhere on a page they don't have?
2. Don't conclude with a detail, that is, with one of the concrete facts you are using to support your position. Details are important to the body of your paper, but you don't want to end your essay with one.
3. Don't bring up a new point in your concluding paragraph.
4. Don't end with an apology. Doing so is the easiest way to convince readers that you don't know what you're talking about.

Now you know what you shouldn't do. How, then, *should* you end your paper? What is the appropriate conclusion that will neatly tie all your main points together and deliver to your readers that satisfying sense of completion? Most writers find, as you probably will, too, that the summary conclusion is the most common ending for expository essays.

The summary conclusion goes back over the main ideas stated in the body and restates the thesis statement. If you choose the summary conclusion, you should keep in mind the length of your essay. One or two sentences in which you restate your thesis may be entirely sufficient when your paper is two pages or shorter. Although your conclusion may be only a couple of sentences, do not forget to indent so that your reader is given a proper signal that you are moving into a new paragraph. Cue words such as *finally, in short, in sum, thus,* and *therefore* indicate to your reader that you are concluding your paper. Concluding paragraphs are necessarily short since they do not develop an idea, as do the paragraphs in the body of your paper.

When your essay is longer, consisting of three or four pages, a summary consisting of three sentences or more may be sufficient. You may also use such lead-off words as *to sum up, lastly, on the whole, as I have said,* and *in conclusion* to open the first sentence of your longer summary paragraph. What is most important, in any summary conclusion, though, is to keep your reader's attention on the thesis statement.

You have other options for concluding your essay, too. Rather than summarize or look back, you can propel your reader forward to new considerations, new implications, possible solutions, and even a call for immediate action.

Read carefully the following examples of kinds of conclusions that you might find appropriate.

1. Summarizing in one or two sentences. For example, a conclusion for the collage on page 166 might be:

   In conclusion, unless we can create a world in which there is a reasonable chance to survive and lead lives relatively free of fear and violence, there is no point in having children.

2. Considering the implications:

   In sum, the result of all this is clear. How can we say we have a free and equal society when half the population cannot enjoy the same privileges as the other half? Sure, I would love to hitchhike across the country during the summer. I want to save money. I have health, energy, and a sense of adventure. But the society I live in tells me in so many words that I would be insane to attempt such a trip, because I'm a woman. We need to look deeper into the meaning of freedom from fear as one of the freedoms our Constitution guarantees.

   The writer's thesis statements was *I would like to hitchhike across the country, maybe alone, but the freedom to do so is not granted to women.*

3. Finding a solution:

   Consequently, as we've seen, there is really only one solution to the problem of finding the perfect summer vacation.

Don't take any. Get a job. Not only will you earn money instead of spending it, which in turn may well make you financially independent for most of the year, but you will probably meet just as many interesting people and have an occasional adventure, to boot. What could possibly make summer vacation more rewarding?

The writer's thesis statement was *Finding the perfect summer vacation may pose a few problems, but keep looking; you'll find it.*

4. Calling for action:

Thus, we have seen that everything the politicians and sociologists have prescribed has proven to be generally ineffective. As I see it, the only way to reduce crime in our cities is for all of us as citizens to take active steps to rid ourselves of those who beat, mug, rob, rape, and kill. I am not suggesting vigilante groups or arming ourselves to the teeth, but in order to defend ourselves and to protect those we love, I say we must organize to plan and act. We must use every available municipal agency to advise and assist us. The time is now; we must act at once.

READINGS The readings that follow present some challenging and thought-provoking possibilities. As you read them, try to discover what each writer's position on the subject is. More important, because some of the information will be new and perhaps surprising to you, write down questions to which you want to find answers in class discussion or through other sources such as the library.

OUR TOXIC-WASTE TIME BOMB

The great toxic-waste mess began oozing into the nation's consciousness about six years ago. "An environmental emergency," declared the Surgeon General in 1980. "A ticking time bomb," warned the Environmental Protection Agency (EPA). The reaction was typically all-American: Congress created a grand-sounding "Superfund," a $1.6-billion, five-year crash program designed in large part to clean up thousands of contaminated sites.

During its early years, the Superfund dribbled away most of its money on a mismanaged effort that, according to critics, did not adequately focus on the enormousness of the task ahead. Last September 30 its funding expired, and the Senate and House haven't at this writing compromised their differences over how many billions of dollars are to be authorized for the next five years.

Meanwhile, fears about toxic wastes continue to grow. Each

day, more and more communities discover they are living near dumps or atop ground that has been contaminated by chemicals whose once-strange names and initials — dioxin, vinyl chloride, PBB, PCB — have become household words. "We have a far bigger problem than we thought when Superfund was enacted," cautions Lee Thomas, the third director of the scandal-tarnished EPA during the Reagan Administration. "There are far more sites that are far more difficult to deal with than anybody ever anticipated." Says Barry Commoner, the environmental gadfly, "We are poisoning ourselves and our posterity."

The Office of Technology Assessment (OTA), a research arm of Congress, contends there may be at least 10,000 hazardous-waste sites in the United States that pose a serious threat to public health. These dumps, where steel drums have been left to rust and leak, letting poisons seep into the earth for decades, are scattered in virtually every county of every state. The cleanup cost, OTA estimates, could easily reach $100 billion for the federal government and $200 billion for local government and industry. Yet between 1980 and 1985, EPA put or proposed putting only 850 sites on its national priorities list. Of these, it managed to clean up just 14 sites — and not very thoroughly at that, critics protest. However, EPA counters that it has cleaned up some 350 emergency sites.

Why has so little been accomplished? "If we're looking for people to blame, the woods are full of them," says William Ruckelshaus, who helped launch EPA as its first director during the Nixon Administration, and was recalled by Reagan in 1983 to try to improve the agency. "The government had never dealt with anything like this before. The fact that there were mismanagement, false starts and mistakes was inevitable." But even he admits that the EPA's toxic-waste performance "didn't have to be as bad as it was."

OTA claims that when EPA tackles a waste site, it seeks only a stopgap solution to the chemical seepage. One dump's wastes are often shifted to other locales better equipped to handle them, "which themselves may become Superfund sites," a 1985 OTA report says. "Risks are [thus] transferred from one community to another and to future generations."

Some critics contend that delaying the expensive cleanup effort will mean greater expense in the future. "Delay not only prolongs the time that people are exposed to toxic hazards," says Michael Podhorzer, director of the National Campaign Against Toxic Hazards, "but every day it means that more toxic chemicals are released into the soil, air and water. The longer we wait, the greater the damage and the higher the final cleanup cost."

But Thomas maintains that EPA has "a good bit of momentum now." It is currently trying to stop the spread of pollution at about 200 sites and is preparing to tackle the cleanup of about 250 others.

By next year, he predicts, "we'll be managing nearly a thousand sites."

The new emphasis at EPA is to stop the seepage of pollutants and protect drinking water first, get rid of the toxic stew later. When wells in Sag Harbor, on New York's Long Island, were found contaminated, for instance, EPA moved swiftly to have two dozen homes hooked up to a city water system to remove the immediate threat.

Acting on a law passed by Congress in 1976, EPA has issued tough regulations designed to trace the flow of toxic chemicals from their manufacture to their eventual disposition, creating a paper trail that should discourage illegal dumping and pinpoint responsibility when contamination occurs. The agency has also vastly tightened its licensing requirements for operators of those landfills permitted to accept hazardous wastes. Such landfills can continue to operate only if they have double liners to prevent seepage. Wells must be bored in the surrounding area to detect any sign of spreading contamination.

Although clearly a necessity, the new rules may take two-thirds of the nation's 1500 licensed disposal sites out of operation, further aggravating the problem plaguing chemical-waste planners: nowhere to go. The public's realization that there is no easy way to bury the toxic-waste problem has fed the ever-present NIMBY (not in my back yard) syndrome. "Something's got to give," says Christopher Daggett, EPA regional administrator for New York, New Jersey, Puerto Rico and the Virgin Islands. "Either we aren't going to have cleanups, or someone's going to bite the bullet and start accepting wastes."

While shuffling wastes from one leaking site to another that may soon turn porous — a bleak game of chemical leapfrog — might seem absurd, there is at present no technology to eliminate landfills as short-term disposal necessities. U.S. industries are generating an awesome 264 million tons of hazardous wastes every year, and science has yet to find a foolproof way of getting rid of all perils. But it has come up with a number of alternatives to simple dumping.

Toxins such as PCBs and dioxin are broken down completely only when burned at temperatures exceeding 2400 degrees Fahrenheit. Some conventional incinerators can generate such heat, but without careful control to maintain it they may occasionally spew toxic gases into the air. Some people fear the fumes could prove as perilous as the chemicals from which they come. But new incinerators may overcome these obstacles.

At Times Beach, Mo., J.M. Huber Corp. has used a mobile electric reactor that heats up to 4000 degrees F. to destroy the dioxin in 100 pounds of soil. Also tested in Missouri is the EPA's mobile incinerator. It got rid of 99.99 percent of the dioxin in 1750 gallons of liquid waste and 40 tons of soil in six weeks, and now can handle one ton per hour. Another movable unit is Westinghouse Electric Corporation's plasma-arc furnace, which reaches temperatures of 9000 degrees F.

Recycling shows promise too. For example, semiconductor manufacturers found that their spent fluid can be used to refine old crankcase oil, helping to eliminate two disposal problems for the price of one.

Perhaps the most innovative technology involves the use of bacteria. A small Texas company called Detox Industries has developed microbes that eat PCBs, creosote and pentachlorophenol. Microbiologist Ananda Chakrabarty of the University of Illinois in Chicago has used a patented "molecular breeding" process to achieve the evolution of a bacterium that can convert the chief ingredient of the herbicide Agent Orange into harmless carbon dioxide, water and hydrochloric acid.

Microbiologist James Whitlock of the Homestake Mining Company found a solution to the problems caused when his company dumped water laced with cyanide (used to leach gold out of ore) into South Dakota's Whitewood Creek. Whitlock took bacteria from wastewater samples, grew them in the lab, then exposed them to increasing levels of cyanide. He installed the survivors in a new $10-million water-treatment plant. Because the "superbugs" possess a sticky body surface, they pick up zinc, iron and other metals in the water. They also eat the cyanide that once threatened to kill the waterway's marine life. Barely a year ago, the creek was too toxic for trout, but now they seem to be thriving.

The increasing cost of getting rid of dangerous chemicals provides a powerful incentive for manufacturers to find ways to capture and recycle them. Minnesota Mining and Manufacturing Co., for example, cut its volume of hazardous wastes in half, mostly by switching from chemical-based glues to water-based glues in making adhesive tape and other coated-surface products. It also burns nearly all of the remaining wastes in a huge incinerator at Cottage Grove, Minn.

While government supervision of toxic-waste sites is vital, only a vast effort by industries that profit from chemicals can get the waste mess under control. That would undoubtedly mean added costs passed on to the consumer, but in the long run it should save money, and the effort must be made.

Manufactured chemicals are a wondrous aid to mankind, alleviating disease, spurring food production and serving as the catalyst for countless useful products. But once discarded, some chemical concoctions, or their by-products, turn killer. The United States has no choice but to curb their lethal ways.

Discussion

1. Why is the article entitled "Our Toxic-Waste Time Bomb"? What do you think will happen if the bomb explodes?
2. What are some of the ways in which the Environmental Protection Agency is attempting to tackle pollution? Do you think these methods are effective? Why or why not?
3. What does the article say are some of the alternatives to dumping? Which alternative do you think is the most promising?
4. If you had to choose between completely giving up manufactured chemicals that are "wondrous aids" or living with the toxins they emit in our soil, air, and water, what would you choose? Why?

ROBOCLONE: A SELF-REPLICATING ROBOT   Robert Freitas, Jr.

The next 20 years may witness the birth of a man-made life form that could lead us into space — and eliminate most human labor here on Earth. Much of the preparatory work toward this dream has already been done.

Picture one possible result of these efforts:

From a rocket that left Earth several years before, an enormous egg drops to Saturn's ice moon Enceladus and cracks open, releasing the robot inside. Stilting spiderlike on the uneven surface, the automaton immediately sets about reproducing itself, using only the materials at hand and feeble light energy from the distant sun.

Soon the robot and its descendants begin their real task: mining Enceladus's ice and building small light-sail tugs to carry the chunks toward the inner solar system. For a time, earthly astronomers see nothing unusual, but eventually a new ring begins to appear around Saturn, surrounding the old ones at about twice the distance. A cloud of replicating-robot vessels spirals outward from Enceladus and then spills in a long stream toward Mars.

Their shipments of ice fall like sparkling meteors onto the Martian surface, melting on impact and thawing the frozen ground. First rivers, then whole seas form. The air grows thick and warm, and soon it rains on Mars for the first time in perhaps a billion years. Within a decade of this transformation human colonists arrive on their new world.

According to Robert A. Frosch, former NASA administrator, such missions are not only possible but necessary. In a talk before the Commonwealth Club of San Francisco, he told his startled audience that to support ourselves in space, we will need self-reproducing robots. They would, he declared, "provide easy access to the resources of the solar system for a relatively manageable investment."

The key to the scheme is a machine that can use solar energy and local materials to build a replica of itself with little or no human guidance. Since generation after generation of offspring would be built, the total number of machines would grow exponentially, the way biological populations expand. So would the machines' output of manufactured products.

NASA is taking this concept very seriously. In 1980 it held a ten-week summer study session at the University of Santa Clara, in California. My group, called the Replicating Systems Concepts Team, studied the idea of setting up a self-reproducing factory on the moon that would eat raw lunar soil and manufacture anything we need from what it ingested.

Our basic plan would put a 100-ton seed full of machinery on the moon. The first robots would emerge to fuse the lunar topsoil into a circular factory site of cast basalt 100 yards across. Then they would install the factory itself and erect a canopy of solar cells to power the system.

The factory has three major sections: One extracts purified elements from the soil; another forms them into machine parts, tools, and electronic components; and the third assembles the parts into useful products. In a year a 100-ton seed could extract enough materials to duplicate itself. If allowed to grow undisturbed for 18 years, the factory output would total more than 4 billion tons per year — roughly the current industrial output of the entire world.

A growing, self-replicating factory could be programmed to mass-produce robot miners and spacecraft — almost anything we need. "It could build a few thousand meter-long robot rovers equipped with cameras, core samplers, and other survey instruments," suggests Georg von Tiesenhausen, assistant director of the Advanced Systems Office at the Marshall Space Flight Center, in Huntsville, Alabama, and a member of the replicating-systems team. "They could cover the moon like ants, mapping it in just a few years. By conventional methods, it might take a century or more to do the same thing."

How soon could such a system be in operation? Von Tiesenhausen says that within 20 years after the project is begun, the United States could produce the first robot able to duplicate itself from raw materials. Former NASA administrator Frosch is even more optimistic. "We are very close to understanding how to build such machines," he says. "I believe that the technology is already available and that the necessary development could be accomplished in a decade or so."

Long before NASA became interested in self-replicating machine systems, the basic theory had already been worked out in some detail; much of it has been around for more than 30 years.

It began in 1948 with the late John von Neumann, a brilliant Hungarian mathematician famed for his early work on electronic computing. In a series of lectures delivered at Princeton, he discussed how automata might reproduce themselves.

According to Von Neumann a self-replicating machine must have at least four distinct components: the builder, the copier, the controller, and the blueprints. Reproduction starts when the controller commands the builder to construct exact replicas of all mechanical systems according to instructions in the blueprints, a sophisticated computer code. The robot would pick the right machine parts from its stockroom and assemble them in order. Then the controller would command the copier to duplicate the blueprints, insert the copy into the replica, and turn the new robot on. *Voilà* — two machines!

Other scientists have also given serious thought to self-replicating automata. Physicist Freeman Dyson, of Princeton's Institute for Advanced Studies, suggests that a small robot adapted to earthly deserts might duplicate itself from the silicon and aluminum in the rocks around it. Powered by sunlight, it would manufacture electricity and high-tension lines. Its progeny could eventually generate ten times the present electrical output of the United States.

Though the robot's potential for destroying the natural environment would be enormous, Dyson believes it would eventually be licensed for use in the deserts of the western United States, probably after bitter debate in Congress. The robot would probably have to carry within itself a memory of the original landscape so that it could restore the site's appearance whenever a location was abandoned.

"After its success here," he speculates, "the company that built it might market an industrial-development kit for the Third World. For a small down payment, a nation could buy an egg machine that would mature within a few years into a complete system of basic industries, along with the associated transportation and communication networks." A spinoff, he suggests, might be the urban-renewal kit, equipped with self-replicating robots programmed to build brand-new neighborhoods from the debris of the old ones.

Computer scientists have received such schemes enthusiastically. Ewald Heer, a robotics specialist at NASA's Jet Propulsion Laboratory, in Pasadena, California, calls self-replicating robots one of the most fascinating ideas for the future of space. "This offers a way to create a self-supporting economy by robot labor," he observes. "Immigrants from Earth could set out, knowing that the means of their survival had already been provided."

Michael Arbib, of the department of computer and information sciences at the University of Massachusetts at Amherst, suggests that they might also be used for interstellar communication. "A self-reproducing machine might carry out its own synthesis from the interstellar gas," he offers. These machines, Arbib says, could reproduce in space, creating an expanding sphere of explorers moving outward toward the far reaches of the universe.

With this scheme in mind, Frank J. Tipler, of Tulane University, in New Orleans has even argued that intelligent aliens cannot exist: If they did, they would have had to build such machines to explore and use the galaxy, and we would see glaring evidence of these machines all around us.

Some machines have already managed to reproduce in primitive ways. Self-replicating computer programs have been written in nearly a dozen different languages, and small machines that can copy themselves from simpler parts have proved remarkably easy to build.

One basic model was developed years ago by British geneticist L. S. Penrose at University College, London. It is an ingenious set of interlocking blocks with clever arrangements of springs, levers, hooks, and ratchets. A two-, three-, or even higher-block assembly can replicate when placed in a box with other loose blocks and shaken gently. One end of the completed assembly hooks on to the loose blocks in the right sequence, building up a duplicate chain and then releasing it when the final block has been connected.

Homer Jacobson, a physicist at Brooklyn College, in New York, built another such device, using an HO train set. In his invention, there are two kinds of programmed, self-propelled boxcars, called heads and tails, that circulate randomly around a loop of track with several sidings. If a pair of boxcars, a head and tail, is assembled on a siding, it can reproduce itself.

Here is how it is done: The head car in the pair waits for a loose head car to come by and shunts it onto the next open siding. Then the next loose tail car to come by is shunted onto that same siding to make a new head-tail pair. Once this happens the first boxcar couple turns itself off and the second pair becomes the active, reproductive one. It can reproduce using the next open siding, and this chain reaction of pair reproduction continues until all sidings are filled or all components are used.

Such experiments sound much too simple to justify calling them reproduction — nothing like the mysterious processes that form a new human life. You might even object that Von Neumann's whole concept is just a general-purpose assembly robot whose output happens to be copies of itself. But after all, observes W. Ross Ashby, a biophysicist at the Burden Neurological Institute, "living things that reproduce do not start out as a gaseous mixture of raw elements." Even human beings require a specialized environment supplied with air, water, and nutrients in order to procreate. Von Neumann's robots happen to be just a little less independent.

In fact some scientists already feel that computers are more than mere machines. John G. Kemeny, president of Dartmouth College and one of the inventors of the computer language BASIC, believes that computers should be considered a new species of life. "Once there are robots that reproduce," he declares, "it would be easy to program them so that each offspring differs slightly from its parent. It would be a good idea to let each robot figure out some improvement in its offspring so that an evolutionary process can take place."

But compact, self-reproducing robots still lie beyond the technological horizon. According to Marvin Minsky, head of artificial-intelligence research at MIT, an automaton today would have to be the size of a factory to reproduce itself from raw materials rather than from prefabricated parts.

Fujitsu Fanuc, Ltd., a manufacturer of numerically controlled machine tools, took a giant step toward that goal with a $40 million robot factory. Robots there are built by other robots, with only 100 humans to supervise and help. The plant produced 100 robots in its first year. Once such a plant can make its own components it can be programmed to make more of itself — to reproduce.

Since we cannot foresee all the problems these robots will have to face on a distant planet, we must supply them with goals and with the problem-solving ability to carry out their assignments in our absence. It seems at least possible that machines this complex will begin to evolve some of the social behavior common with animal populations. This brings us very close to sharing our planet with a form of near-life whose evolution we cannot predict.

At the simplest level, what would happen if one machine began to neglect its production chores in order to reproduce? Its offspring, possessing the same trait, might soon dominate the machine population. Would some form of "kin-preferring" behavior arise? Might the robots even develop a form of "reciprocal altruism" in which the machines behave in seemingly unselfish fashion toward others that are not "kin" to create a more stable "society"?

"If our machines attain this behavioral sophistication," notes Richard Laing, of the department of computer and communication sciences at the University of Michigan, in Ann Arbor, "it may be time to ask whether they have become so like us that we have no further right to command them for our own purposes and so should quietly emancipate them."

And one wonders: Could such self-reproducing robots someday become our enemies? The usual answer is that we can just pull their plugs to regain control over them. But is that really so? We are already so dependent on computers that to shut them down would cause general economic chaos. Of the Santa Claus machines, theologist Ralph Wendell Burhoe, of the Meadville/Lombard Theology School, in Chicago, asks, "Will we become the contented cows or household pets of the new computer kingdom of life?"

And what if the machines learned to defend themselves? The Replicating Systems Concepts Team at the Santa Clara study session concluded that to escape human control, any machine must have at least four basic abilities: It must create new ideas to explain conflicting data, inspect itself completely, write its own programs, and change its own structure at will. A machine that lacked even one of these abilities would almost surely be unable to anticipate or prevent its own disconnection. It seems unlikely that machines will soon acquire these powers, and even if they do, it will be only because human beings make a conscious decision to supply them.

Nonetheless, a few people view the future gravely. James Paul Wesley, associate professor of physics at the University of Missouri, points out that the advent of machines has been amazingly abrupt compared to the billions of years it took carbon-based life to evolve on Earth. Yet the same laws of reproduction apply to both biological evolution and machines.

"Machines," Wesley cautions, "have also evolved toward an increased biomass [quantity], increased ecological efficiency, maximal reproduction rate, proliferation of species, motility, and a longer life span. Machines, being a form of life, are in competition with carbon-based life." The result, he fears, is that silicon life "will make carbon-based life extinct."

Yet there is another possibility. What we are approaching, says NASA computer scientist Rodger A. Cliff, is "cybersymbiosis": eventually humans could come to live inside a larger cybernetic organism. As man and machine evolve, our interactions will cease to be voluntary and become necessary. Cliff views this development with eagerness. Our descendants could live inside large, self-replicating, mobile space habitats, which would act as extraterrestrial refuges and guarantee that humanity is never completely wiped out by some sort of earthly catastrophe.

"Flesh and blood are ill adapted to space," Cliff comments, "but silicon and metal are ideal. Just as our own DNA resides within a protective membrane, and mitochondria are locked within cells, so might humanity live as cybersymbiotic organelles of the space-colony organism. I see these traveling throughout the cosmos, searching for nutrients — asteroids, gas clouds, and so on—growing, evolving, and reproducing. And we will be inside their offspring."

Discussion

1. What is a self-replicating robot? Do you think it is a realistic possibility? Why?
2. In what ways do you think self-replicating robots will affect our society, our culture, our life-style, and our values?
3. Do you think self-replicating robots will pose a threat to humankind?
4. What are the possible benefits to humankind if self-replicating robots are used to explore space?

LANGUAGE LEARNING

Using the Active and Passive Voices. When you were writing your first draft, you may have noticed that sometimes the important part of your point was a person or thing that performed the action, while at other times it was the action and not the performer that was important. Writing forcefully and effectively is possible only when you can make words and sentences achieve your purpose in any written assignment. Knowing the difference between active and passive sentences and knowing when to use each in different contexts will enable you to achieve forceful and effective writing.

An active sentence is one in which the subject is the performer of the action, for example:

$$\underline{\text{S}} \quad \underline{\text{V}}$$
The sheriff drove the old prospector out of town.

The sheriff is the subject of the sentence; *drove* is the past tense form of the verb drive; and *the old prospector* is the receiver of the action.

A passive sentence is one in which the subject is the receiver of the action, for example:

$$\underline{\text{S}} \quad \underline{\text{V}}$$
The old prospector was driven out of town by the sheriff.

Notice the difference between the two renderings: In the passive sentence, the complement or receiver of the action of the first sentence becomes the subject. Notice the verb form: The past tense of the verb to be is used together with the past participle of the verb *drive*. *The sheriff*, which was the subject of the previous sentence, now follows the verb, and is preceded by the word *by*. You may also write the passive form like this: *The old prospector was driven out of town.* As you see, *by the sheriff* has been omitted; the main point is not lost, because in a passive sentence the focus of meaning has shifted to what has happened rather than who did it.

Active sentences have a more immediate effect because they present direct action:

Mary Lou slapped Debbie.

Hal caught the high-fly ball.

A cold spell struck the nation yesterday.

But when we change active sentences to passive sentences, we lose the sense of direct, immediate action:

Debbie was slapped (by Mary Lou).

The high-fly ball was caught (by Hal).

The nation was struck by a cold spell yesterday.

Only the third sentence does not lose force and immediacy when it is shifted to the passive form. But notice too that it is the only sentence that requires the *by* phrase to complete the meaning. Now look at the following sentences and see how each gains by being written in the passive:

In the course of a few days, summer was gone.

We were informed by letter that we would not be rehired.

Pélé was photographed alone on the field, his hands covering his face, crying.

Newspaper writers make frequent and effective use of passive sentences when they focus in on what happened or to whom something happened, especially when the person involved either is a well-known figure or is not identified:

One person was killed and two were injured yesterday when a milk van collided with a Volkswagen near Exit 11 on the Merrick Parkway.

Bobby Deerfield, Grand Prix winner, was taken into custody this morning on charges of assault and mayhem.

An unidentified man was apprehended and prevented from attempting to douse the Eternal Flame at the entrance to the Daniel Boone National Park today.

When referring to a person you can't identify or who isn't important to the point you're making, it is usually better to write passive sentences rather than active sentences that contain the frequently used subject *they*. Look at the following examples:

They told me I should take my form to the bursar's office.

They should not make people wait in line for hours.

They told me I would have to make an appointment with the director.

Each of these sentences could benefit by being in the passive:

I was told to take my form to the bursar's office.

People should not be made to wait in those long lines.

I was told to wait for the director.

FORMAL WRITING

Finding a Topic. You have already done some thinking and writing about the world outside, both for the In-Class Writing assignment and in your writer's log. In addition, the readings in this chapter have focused on critical issues our society faces today. The world outside is not all fear, violence, and danger, however, as you perhaps have already realized. Heroic, generous, humane actions do abound in our world, and some public ones we are all aware of — the Live Aid Concert to aid Ethiopia, Hands Across America in support of the hungry and homeless, CARE, and the Muscular Dystrophy Association telethons, to name but a few. You may have been witness to individual, private actions of human caring and generosity that aroused admiration and hope in you.

What we ask you now is to consider this world we all share and to write about what it means to you. There are several topics you may choose from, but if none of them appeals to you, you are free to come up with one of your own; however, do consult with your instructor to ensure that such a topic is neither too broad nor too narrow for the purpose of this assignment.

Humans — an endangered species.

Space exploration — how it will change the world.

The effects of computers, video music, sports, or medical advances on our way of life.

There is an old saying that asking questions is the beginning of understanding. Since the topic you write about will require a substantial body of information about the world around you, you may find it useful to begin by formulating questions about it. You can generate questions about your subject with the help of the journalist's questions: *who, what, when, where, why,* and *how.*

For example, here are some questions for the second suggested topic, Space Exploration — How It Will Change the World:

1. Who are some of the people who have gone on space expeditions?
2. When was the first/last expedition in space?
3. Where did it go?
4. What did it achieve?
5. Why is space exploration important/unimportant?
6. How will the world be affected by what is learned about outer space?
7. What will the world be like twenty years from now?
8. What more do I need to find out about this topic?

Clearly, answers to these questions will generate a short and choppy first draft. But the essay will be on its way, because you will now be in a position to use any or several of the strategies for prewriting, writing, and revising that have been presented to you in this book.

GROUP READING	**Preparation for the Final Draft.** Here are some additional questions to use in giving and getting feedback from your group:

1. Does the essay have an introduction that contains a clear thesis?
2. Does each paragraph of the body focus on one aspect of the thesis?
3. Does the essay conclude with a paragraph that summarizes the thesis, presents implications, or provides a solution or a call for action?
4. Does the essay use appropriate transitional words or phrases to provide a sense of wholeness?
5. Does the essay use the active or passive voice discriminatingly to get its ideas across?

USEFUL STRATEGIES

Certain strategies for writing papers and taking exams are useful for college work and thus deserve to be presented separately. In college you will frequently be asked to follow a particular form when you prepare papers and take exams.

In Part Four we show you how to work with some of these forms of writing. They do not conflict with any of the other approaches to writing that you have learned thus far. The writing assignments you have done up to now, however, were based on the assumption that the form of a paper will grow out of the material itself and the purpose of the writing, and that you would have several days or even weeks to prepare a paper. Now you will be asked to write papers in prescribed forms and, in one case, in a very limited time.

For many of your college courses, the form of your paper is dictated by the questions your instructor asks you to consider. One common form of college writing is the process paper, in which you describe how some event occurred or how some procedure is carried out. Techniques for writing the process paper are presented in Chapter 10.

Another common form of college writing is the paper of comparison and/or contrast. In this kind of paper you present and evaluate the similarities and differences between two or more items. Chapter 11 provides you with guidelines for constructing this type of paper.

Finally, many colleges now require students to pass a writing examination at some point in their composition sequence. Such tests are usually timed, in-class exams, and there are special techniques you can learn to make the experience somewhat less difficult. Chapter 12 offers guidelines for just such occasions.

CHAPTER 10

Writing About a Process

The narratives you have been writing have been organized chron-ologically; that is, you began at the beginning of the story, told each part as it occurred, and ended with the final moment. The same pattern of organization underlies the first of the expository compositions that you will be writing in this section of the book, the process paper. Remember the first time you tried pedaling down the road on your new bike, your father holding the seat from behind, shouting encouragements and instructions and panting as he ran alongside? Or the time you followed your sister's recipe in order to make the perfect French omelet and ended up with a dry, leathery mishmash that vaguely resembled scrambled eggs from nowhere? Or the time your friend told you how to get to the new disco joint and instead you found yourself at the zoo? But then there was the time you followed the directions in the manual and glowed with pride as you heard a voice say, "10-4, good buddy," over the CB radio you put together yourself.

Learning how to follow directions is often challenging. It's even more challenging to learn how to give them, particularly in writing, since the reader is usually not in a position to ask for clar-ification when confused. So if you have to write a paper to explain, for example, how the human digestive system works or how to make a three-dimensional kite or even how to play chess, you have to explain the steps very clearly and simply. This kind of writing is called *process writing.*

You might wonder what writing a process paper has to do with writing well in college. After all, explaining how to make a kite or play chess is not going to get you an A in your history course, or any other course for that matter. But if you stop and think for a moment, you will realize that assignments for many of the courses you take in college will require you to write process papers. For a term paper for an anthropology course, for example, you might be asked to explain how to read fossils. In a sociology course, you might have to write a paper explaining how to manage a day-care center. You might be assigned a biology paper requiring an explanation of the workings of the human nervous system.

Although narratives and process papers have similar organizational patterns, there is an important difference between them. A narrative describes an event that is interesting and memorable because it was unique — nothing exactly like it had ever happened before — and in your telling, you stressed the specialness of the occasion. In describing a process, by contrast, you will be discussing a series of events that should recur in the same way over and over again. You need to stress those elements that are common to all examples of the process. You will, as always, want to be as precise and as clear as possible.

WRITER'S LOG   Since the work of this chapter centers on explaining how things get done, you might want to use your writer's log to consider problems that you have encountered with other people's efforts to give directions, in addition to exploring the kinds of explanations you yourself might want to present. Some topics might be:

Putting together a toy at Christmas.

The directions that came with the _____.

Important points in explaining how to play _____.

Why someone should know more about _____.

Learning to use the computer.

ACTIVITY   **Writing and Following Directions.** The following experience will help you see the importance of clarity, accuracy, and order in describing a process. You will write instructions for drawing figures; then you will exchange instructions and try to follow someone else's.

First, divide into groups of four or five students each. Make sure that all groups are small enough so that your conversation will not be overheard by the other members of the class. Your instructor will give you picture of a simple figure, and together you will write step-by-step instructions on how to draw such a picture. One person in each group should be assigned to write down the instructions. Be careful not to let the other groups in the class see your figure or hear your instructions.

When you have finished, your teacher will collect the instructions. One person, not a member of the group that wrote the instructions, will read them aloud while another person, also not a member of the group that wrote them, will try to draw the figure on the board.

Discussion

1. Were you surprised to discover how complicated this exercise turned out to be? Why was it so hard to write directions clearly and to follow them closely?
2. When you were able to follow the instructions of your classmates, what were the factors that made their explanations clear? Try to isolate the specific words and phrases that helped you understand the process.
3. When you were not able to follow the instructions, what words and phrases were confusing?

IN-CLASS WRITING   **Rewriting Instructions.** Each student should now take the instructions written by his or her group and rewrite them so that they are perfectly clear. You can check the accuracy of your paper by asking someone to follow your directions. If the person is successful, then you have done your job well.

READING   The short essay that follows is a series of directions telling you how to do something, specifically, how to exasperate your English teacher. The time span covered is one class period, and the directions are given in a sequence starting with the beginning of the class period and continuing, step-by-step, to the end of the period. As you read the essay, underline the words that indicate to you the sequential order of each direction.

HOW TO EXASPERATE YOUR ENGLISH TEACHER   Nila Gandhi

Did you ever want to drive your English teacher up the wall? Most of us have at one time or another but were afraid to try for fear of the consequences. However, here is an almost foolproof method of doing so without the dire possibilities of being suspended from school or flunking the course.

First, stroll into the class about ten minutes late. If you walk in earlier the class may not have settled down, and if you're much later, chances are you'll be asked to leave. Next, offer a polite "Good Morning," and continue at the same slow pace across to the far end of the room, seemingly unaware of the loaded, waiting silence. Then sit for a couple of minutes, shifting around restlessly in your seat as the teacher makes an effort to get going. Once he's really into introducing the lesson, get up and walk to a vacant seat as close to him as possible. By now, he's probably ready to ask in a tense, controlled voice why you are disturbing the class. You will explain, again in a polite voice, that you moved because you wished to hear him better. After he makes another attempt to continue with his explanation and you notice the look of absorption creeping back into his eyes, start chatting with your neighbor. However, make sure that the topic of your conversation has to do with the English class. This time you are sure to hear a slight edge in the voice that demands coldly why you insist on distracting everyone. You apologize contritely and let the teacher continue until the explanation is over and the assignment is given. This relatively lengthy interval will lull his annoyance until, as he looks around at the now silent, busily writing, students, he notices you serenely gazing out the window, apparently lost to the world around you.

Now his voice almost cracks with the effort to maintain his composure. You must pretend to start in surprise as you deliberately stumble over an apology and rummage in your bag for pen and paper. Then, raise a trembling hand and whisper out a request for pen and paper, which, you can't understand why, you have forgotten to bring. With cold anger glimmering in his eyes, the teacher will hand you paper and pencil. Let the pencil drop as you reach for it. If you're skillful enough, you will let it fall so as to break its point and the teacher's composure. Five minutes will be taken up in trying to borrow a sharpener or another pencil from one of the distracted students.

By now, there should be approximately 3 to 5 minutes before the bell rings to announce the end of the class period. Sit quietly as if thinking but keep a close watch on the time for the last pitch. Finally, at exactly 30 seconds before time is up, ask in a loud, earnest voice, "Excuse me, Sir, what is the assignment?"

In writing the essay "How to Exasperate Your English Teacher," Nila did not intend to tell students how to be disruptive; on the contrary, she was trying in a humorous way to do the opposite, to indicate what sorts of classroom behaviors are particularly annoying. This form of writing, in which writers say the opposite of what they intend, is called *irony.*

The ironic tone in the above essay conveys the main reason for writing that particular essay. If you reread the directions you wrote for drawing the figures, you may notice that they do not make very interesting reading. Unless you are just giving directions as in a recipe or the way to get to City Hall, you usually have a reason for writing a process paper. The reason could be, as in the above example, to indicate the necessity for proper classroom decorum. You may want to tell why you enjoy a particular activity or explain why you find the activity easier than most people believe.

IN-CLASS WRITING

Writing About an Activity You Enjoy. Think of an activity you enjoy doing or one that you do particularly well. Spend a few minutes thinking about the particular times you have done that task, focusing as much as possible on a particular occasion. What was the situation in which it occurred? What was your mood at the time? Try to visualize the scene, the time of day, the room in which it took place. Although you may not use these details when you actually write about the activity, they will help you capture the spirit of the occasion.

Try to recall, as well, the particular "tricks of the trade" that make the task easier. And if you have a special way of dealing with the situation when things go wrong, be sure to add them as well.

This is a preliminary writing; you should not expect to have all the details in place. When you have finished, read your paper to some of your classmates. They can help you to see where you need to clarify your presentation or add details.

READING

In the following selection, the process of making an apple pie over a campfire is explained.

WHEN YOU CAMP OUT, DO IT RIGHT   Ernest Hemingway

Outside of insects and bum sleeping the rock that wrecks most camping trips is cooking. The average tyro's idea of cooking is to fry everything and fry it good and plenty. Now, a frying pan is a most necessary thing to any trip, but you also need the old stew kettle and the folding reflector baker. . . .

In the baker, mere man comes into his own, for he can make a pie that to his bush appetite will have it all over the product that mother used to make, like a tent. Men have always believed that there was something mysterious and difficult about making a pie. Here is a great secret. There is nothing to it. We've been kidded for years. Any man of average office intelligence can make at least as good a pie as his wife.

All there is to a pie is a cup and a half of flour, one-half tea-spoonful of salt, one-half cup of lard and cold water. That will make pie crust that will bring tears of joy into your camping partner's eyes.

Mix the salt with the flour, work the lard into the flour, make it up into a good workmanlike dough with cold water. Spread some flour on the back of a box or something flat, and pat the dough around a while. Then roll it out with whatever kind of round bottle you prefer. Put a little more lard on the surface of the sheet of dough and then slosh a little flour on and roll it up and then roll it again with the bottle.

Cut a piece of the rolled out dough big enough to line a pie tin. I like the kind with holes in the bottom. Then put in your dried apples that have soaked all night and been sweetened, or your apricots, or your blueberries, and than take another sheet of the dough and drape it gracefully over the top, soldering it down at the edges with your fingers. Cut a couple of slits in the top dough sheet and prick it a few times with a fork in an artistic manner.

Put it in the baker with a good slow fire for forty-five minutes and then take it out and if your pals are Frenchmen they will kiss you. The penalty for knowing how to cook is that the others will make you do all the cooking.

It is all right to talk about roughing it in the woods. But the real woodsman is the man who can be really comfortable in the bush.

Discussion

1. What was Hemingway's purpose in writing this article?
2. Hemingway used only one transition word throughout this essay. What substitutes might you make for that word?

READING   The following composition is neither a formal essay in the pure sense of the term nor is it included here as a model for you to imitate. We think that you will enjoy reading it and that you may even recognize your own use of these evasions.

BEATING WRITER'S BLOCK: HOW TO CONFRONT THE
TYPEWRITER FEARLESSLY

9:03 A.M.

As every schoolboy knows, writer's block is an affliction every
bit as debilitating as . . . *(Well, as what? Maybe a cup of coffee will
help.)*

Writer's block is a condition that . . .

(Retrieve paper airplanes, empty wastebasket, reread Playboy
*centerfold. Remember the writer who set fire to his apartment to
avoid meeting a deadline?)*

9:25 A.M.

*(Try to beat the clock by leading off with other people's
quotes.)* "Blocks are simply forms of egotism," said Lawrence Durrell . . .

10:32 A.M.

(Maybe this will do it.) What can be done to break writer's
block? There are many traditional answers: change of scenery,
change of work habits, drop everything and see a James Bond
movie. Durrell recommends insulting oneself while shaving and
concentrating on unpaid bills. T. S. Eliot broke his block by writing
poems in French. *(Dabbling in lesser languages removes pressure
to perform in mother tongue.)* Tom Wolfe, totally blocked on his
first famous article, a story about customized cars for *Esquire*,
wrote a really socko memorandum to his editor on the subject. The
editor ran the memo as the article. Wolfe now writes all his articles
as memos. *(On the other hand he is at least three years late with
his current book . . .)*

11:09 A.M.

Los Angeles Psychoanalyst Martin Grotjahn thinks he knows
the cause of the malady. Says he: "People who have strong needs to
love or fight are more prone to writer's block." Most psychiatrists
believe that, just as there is no single explanation for murder or
theft, there is no one cause for writer's block. But Grotjahn, who
discusses the problem in his book, *Beyond Laughter*, believes hos-
tility is the fundamental reason. Writing is an aggressive demand
for attention. It can be blocked when a writer projects his anger
onto reviewers and readers. "It's the fear of being attacked," says
Manhattan Psychoanalyst Walter Stewart, "the fear that you will be
treated as contemptuously as you would like to treat everyone
else."

In fact, Herman Melville was so wounded by critics that he
wrote no fiction at all for thirty years. Says Psychoanalyst Yale Kra-
mer, who is studying Melville's life: "He behaved like a child stub-
bornly remaining silent in a passive attempt at revenge." But even
good reviews can bring on writer's block: they tend to paralyze by
awakening great expectations. As Author Cyril Connolly, a part-

time blockee, expressed it: "Whom the gods wish to destroy they first call promising."

12:15 P.M.

(Word count so far: 385) Short break for inner movie about receiving Nobel Prize for literature. Psychiatrists call this the "grandiose fantasy." This imaginary acclaim is a neurotic compromise between the real self — scared, limited — and the ideal self — a literary conqueror. Says Manhattan Analyst Donald Kaplan: "The fantasy of playing Carnegie Hall may be so gratifying that you can't manage to practice your scales."

This is not to be confused with what Kaplan calls "the Nobel Prize complex" — a compulsive perfectionism that drives the writer to type the opening line of a book 403 times. Every word has to be as good as Shakespeare or Shaw, or there is no use playing the game at all. A subvariation, of course, is that it also has to be perfectly typed. Psychoanalyst Edmund Bergler, a brilliant but erratic writer on the 1950s, has a scatological interpretation of the first-line problem: the writer smearing the empty page with words is the baby smearing mommy's living room wall with diaper residue. Bergler, much admired for his own literary wall smearing, churned out a dozen popular books on psychiatry, all of them arguing that masochism explained *most* of human affairs. He could have used a block or two himself.

1:30 P.M.

(Time to lapse into coherence.) The opposite of the "first-line" problem is the "last-lap paralysis." One screenwriter wrote two-thirds of a script and made the mistake of showing it to friends, who said it was the greatest property ever to hit Hollywood, thus immobilizing the writer.

Fear of success in here. One symptom is short sentences. Fear makes you lose your rhythm and forget how English sentences run. *(Bathroom break, check mail.)* But psychiatrists know that the plucky writer can pull up his socks and finish everything he begins.

Discussion

1. What steps does the writer take to avoid writing?
2. Are there different steps for different sections of the article?
3. How has the writer related the steps of his composing process to the content of the article?

FORMAL WRITING   **Using Process to Make a Point.** For your final writing assignment, you may further develop the process paper you started in the In-Class Writing assignment. Be sure to read your draft to your reading/writing group as described below.

If you prefer, you can write a process paper on one of the following aspects of friendship. If you are planning to write about friendship, you might approach it in either of these two ways:

1. How to meet someone, how to make friends with that person, and how to sustain the friendship
2. How to recognize a bad friend, how to break the friendship, and how to keep it broken

GROUP READING AND REVISION

New Questions. You may want to add the following questions for your group's consideration of a process paper:

1. Are there any terms they do not understand?
2. Is the sequence of events clear and in order?
3. Do the transition words help the readers to understand the order? Are there places where additional transition words might help?
4. Can your readers tell why you wrote about this particular process?

CHAPTER 11

Writing the Comparison/ Contrast Paper

Often in writing, you will be asked to deal with several ideas, people, places, things, or situations. You might, for example, have to write about two approaches to physical fitness, the main characters in two short stories, the three candidates for mayor, a traditional and an innovative design for an elementary school classroom, or a particular approach to alcoholism and its relationship to programs for alcoholics in your town. In these essays, you will probably want to discuss the similarities and differences between the different things you are writing about, and to conclude which is better or more useful or to propose a viable combination of the best aspects of each. Expository essays that show how ideas, people, places, things, or situations compare, or are similar, and how they contrast, or are different, are called *comparison-contrast* essays. Such an essay, like the others you have been learning about, has an introduction containing a thesis, a body of several paragraphs that develop your ideas, and a conclusion that summarizes your main points. In comparison-contrast essays, though, there are different ways to organize the body. This chapter presents those approaches.

You have been comparing and contrasting things all your life. When you were five and chose to play with the dump truck instead of the blocks, or when you were fourteen and chose to go to Burger King instead of McDonald's, you were reaching your decisions almost unconsciously by comparing and contrasting. It is natural to recognize similarities and differences and then, on these bases, to determine what suits you best at that moment. You also use the process frequently to convince someone of something. Remember when your parents didn't want to leave you home over the weekend because of what happened the last time they left you alone? You explained to them that you had changed and that they could now rely on you. You compared and contrasted the way you are today with the way you were then in order to convince them of your trustworthiness.

Comparing and contrasting are useful in decision making, explaining, understanding, and convincing. You rely on the process often in your daily life, and you will have considerable use for it during your academic career. In this chapter, you will have an opportunity to note how familiar you are with the process as you learn to write well-organized comparison-contrast essays.

ACTIVITY   **Comparing and Contrasting: An Everyday Experience.**
Think of some small decision you have to make. Perhaps you are considering one of several options regarding tonight's dinner, or maybe you have a choice to make about how to spend your evening or how to handle your time over the weekend. Select the decision you are going to deal with and write down the two or three options you have.

1. Under each option, list all of the reasons *for* selecting the particular choice.
2. Next, under each option, list all of the reasons for *not* selecting this possibility.
3. Finally, read over your lists and make a tentative decision.

One way to test out a decision is to try it out on someone else. Join with a partner and spend the next few minutes trying to convince each other that the decision each of you reached is the best one to have made.

After you have both had a turn, go back over all the work you just did and notice where and how you used comparing and where and how you used contrasting, both to make your decision and to convince your partner of the rightness of your decision. Notice how familiar you are with these two thought processes.

WRITER'S LOG   Possibilities for comparison-contrast entries in your writer's log might include:

Two different schools

Two different jobs

Two different rock singers

Two different TV shows

Two different college majors

Writings that point out similarities are called *comparisons;* writings that make the reader aware of differences are called *contrasts.* When you write a paper that compares, contrasts, or does both, there are two patterns you can use to organize your information. The readings that follow are similar in content but different in organization. When you read them, compare and contrast them.

THE COURTSHIP OF ARTHUR AND AL   James Thurber

Once upon a time there was a young beaver named Al and an older beaver named Arthur. They were both in love with a pretty little female. She looked with disfavor upon the young beaver's suit because he was a harum-scarum and a ne'er-do-well. He had never done a single gnaw of work in his life, for he preferred to eat and sleep and to swim lazily in the streams and to play Now-I'll-Chase-You with the girls. The older beaver had never done anything but work from the time he got his first teeth. He had never played anything with anybody.

When the young beaver asked the female to marry him, she said she wouldn't think of it unless he amounted to something. She reminded him that Arthur had built thirty-two dams and was working on three others, whereas he, Al, had never even made a breadboard or a pin tray in his life. Al was very sorry, but he said he would never go to work just because a woman wanted him to. Thereupon she offered to be a sister to him, but he pointed out that he already had seventeen sisters. So he went back to eating and sleeping and swimming in the streams and playing Spider-in-the-Parlor with the girls. The female married Arthur one day at the lunch hour — he could never get away from work for more than one hour at a time. They had seven children and Arthur worked so hard supporting them he wore his teeth down to the gum line. His health broke in two before long and he died without ever having had a vacation in his life. The young beaver continued to eat and sleep and swim in the streams and play Unbutton-Your-Shoe with the girls. He never Got Anywhere, but he had a long life and a Wonderful Time.

MORAL: It is better to have loafed and lost than never to have loafed at all.

ARTHUR AND AL, RETOLD

Once upon a time there were two beavers named Al and Arthur. They were both in love with a pretty little female.

Al was a young beaver. The pretty little female looked with disfavor upon his suit because he was a harum-scarum and ne'er-do-well. He had never done a single gnaw of work in his life, for he preferred to eat and sleep and to swim lazily in the streams and to play Now-I'll-Chase-You with the girls. When Al asked the pretty little female to marry him, she said she wouldn't think of it unless he amounted to something. He had not even made a bread-board or a pin tray in his life. Al was very sorry, but he said he would never go to work just because a woman wanted him to. Thereupon, she offered to be a sister to him, but he pointed out that he already had seventeen sisters. So he went back to eating and sleeping and swimming in the streams and playing Spider-in-the-Parlor with the girls.

Arthur was the older Beaver. He had never done anything but work from the time he got his first teeth. He had never played anything with anybody. The pretty little female looked upon Arthur with favor because he had built thirty-two dams and was working on three others. So she married him one fine day at the lunch hour — he could never get away from work for more than one hour at a time. They had seven children and Arthur worked so hard supporting them, he wore his teeth down to the gum line. Arthur's health broke in two before long and he died without ever having had a vacation in his life. Al continued to eat and sleep and swim in the streams and play Unbutton-Your-Shoe with the girls. He never Got Anywhere, but he had a long life and a Wonderful Time.

MORAL: It is better to have loafed and lost than never to have loafed at all.

Discussion

1. In what ways are the two selections similar? different?
2. What is the patten of organization used in the first selection? What is it in the second?

RHETORIC LEARNING

Organizing the Comparison-Contrast Paper. There are two main ways to organize a comparison-contrast paper: point-by-point organization and block organization.

Point-by-Point Organization. In the story as told by Thurber, the characteristics of Arthur and Al are compared and contrasted point by point. As each aspect of the event is told, both Arthur and Al are discussed. You first learn that both beavers love the same "pretty little female." You then read about their very different lifestyles, about Arthur, the hard worker, and Al, the playful ne'er-do-well. Next you find out what happens to their marriage proposals, and finally you are told that later on in life Arthur, tooth-less and joyless, dies, while Al, who "never got anywhere," has a "long life and a wonderful time."

A picture of this point-by-point comparison-contrast looks like this:

Introduction	There are two beavers named Al and Arthur.
Body	
Circumstances:	Al loves the pretty little female.
	Arthur loves the pretty little female.
Life-style:	Al is a playful ne'er-do-well.
	Arthur is a hard worker.
Proposal:	Al's marriage proposal is rejected.
	Arthur marries the pretty little female.
Later life:	Arthur works hard, loses his health, dies young.
	Al continues to play, lives long, and has a wonderful time.
Conclusion	It is better to have loafed and lost than never to have loafed at all.

Block Organization. In the second version of the piece, the information is organized in blocks. The body consists of two paragraphs, the first of which tells everything about Al, and the second of which tells all about Arthur.

A picture of this method of organizing the comparison-contrast looks like this:

Introduction	Arthur and Al love a pretty little female.
Body	
Al:	1. Ne'er-do-well, playful life style.
	2. His marriage proposal is rejected.
Arthur:	1. Hard worker.
	2. Marries the pretty little female.
Conclusion	Arthur dies.
	Al lives.
	It is better to have loafed and lost than never to have loafed at all.

When you write essays that include or consist entirely of comparison and/or contrast, you will have to decide which pattern of organization — the point-by-point pattern or the block pattern —

is best. The nature of the information you are comparing or contrasting and the purpose of your essay (your thesis) will affect your decision.

IN-CLASS WRITING

Writing Your Own Fable. Following are several well-known proverbs. Select one and write a fable in which you use comparison and contrast to support it. You may use the proverb as stated, or, like Thurber, you can change it around. Once you select the information you will include to support the proverb, look it over and select the organization pattern that seems most appropriate.

Proverbs
1. Early to bed and early to rise makes a man healthy, wealthy, and wise.
2. Too many cooks spoil the broth.
3. A stitch in time saves nine.
4. A bird in hand is worth two in the bush.
5. Better late than never.
6. The early bird catches the worm.
7. Honesty is the best policy.
8. 'Tis better to have loved and lost than never to have loved at all.

Change the proverb if you wish.

ACTIVITY

Comparing Photos. On pages 204 and 205 are two pictures, taken at different times, of the section of New York City now known as Times Square. In both instances, the scene is clearly a large urban center. However, the nature of the scene has changed substantially in the thirty years that have elapsed between the two photographs.

Look at each photograph carefully and then make a list of everything you see in each one, as shown below.

Picture A   **Picture B**

_____   _____

_____   _____

_____   _____

_____   _____

A

204

B

When you have finished, compare your lists with your fellow students'. Add any details they have listed that you may have omitted.

In completing your lists, you have taken the first step toward writing a comparison-contrast paper. Using the block method of organization, you would have a paragraph describing the main features of the area as it appeared in the 1900s and a second paragraph noting the similarities and differences in the 1930s. However, you also need a statement that provides a focus for your comparison. What do you feel is the nature of the change that has occurred? Your answer to that question will provide the controlling idea for your comparison, just as the proverbs suggested as morals for the In-Class Writing assignment provided the main idea for your fables. Reread your lists, select the eight or ten details that best prove your thesis, and then make two lists, like those below.

Thesis: _____

Picture A   **Picture B**

_____   _____

_____   _____

_____   _____

Now you will reorganize your material to prepare a paper using point-by-point organization. Look over your original lists for each of the pictures and see what categories of details you can isolate. You will probably have one on the differences in the buildings you see, another on the kinds of transportation shown, and a third on the activities. Using the same thesis, regroup your material into three paragraphs, each of which discusses a different category.

Thesis: _____

Category 1: _____

Picture A _____

_____

Picture B _____

_____

Category 2: _____

    Picture A _____

    _____

    Picture B _____

    _____

Category 3: _____

    Picture A _____

    _____

    Picture B _____

    _____

FORMAL WRITING

Choosing a Place to Live. The two pictures you see on pages 208 and 209 show living environments that are quite polar opposites. Picture A presents an environment of solitude, space, and isolation, whereas Picture B, in stark contrast, characterizes an almost boxed-in, close-quartered existence.

Study these two pictures; then think about where you would like to live if you had the choice. Let your own felt needs guide your decision. List the special features of the place you have chosen, or write a few sentences describing your choice.

Then look at the two pictures again, and compare and contrast your choice with the worlds they illustrate. List all the similarities and differences you can find between your choice and the environment in Picture A. Do the same for Picture B.

My Choice versus Picture A

Similarities   *Differences*

_____   _____

_____   _____

_____   _____

My Choice versus Picture B

Similarities   *Differences*

_____   _____

_____   _____

_____   _____

A

B

Which of the two pictured environments is closer to the world you prefer?

Now write a paper in which you use your comparisons and contrasts to tell why your choice is better than the world in the picture that is *closer* to it. What similarities will you include? What differences will you want to emphasize? The similarities will help you get started, and the differences will each supply a reason for the body of your paper.

GROUP READING AND REVISION

You and your reading/writing group members should check one another's papers for the following additional considerations:

1. Which method of organization is used? Is it used throughout the paper?
2. Does the comparison and/or contrast support a point? Is that point the same as in your thesis?

CHAPTER 12

Writing the In-Class Essay

Thus far, we have emphasized writing assignments on which you could spend as much time as you wish. With increasing frequency, however, colleges are requiring students to write essays in class within a specified time period, usually less than an hour, as a way of measuring writing ability. And, of course, for most content courses in-class writing assignments are usually part of the examination process. In both cases, the writing assignments may be as brief as a single paragraph or as extensive as a four- or five-paragraph essay. But whatever the length, you are still expected to produce a well-organized composition, to use vivid, precise words, and to explain your meaning clearly and concisely — that is, to apply all the knowledge you have gained from this composition course.

Having to write an essay in a limited amount of time creates a special set of pressures that require special strategies to deal with them. Many students, for instance, suffer from test anxiety: they find the situation so threatening that they are unable to write as well as they could in other circumstances. Even students who are not fazed by exams often find themselves unable to marshal their resources as quickly as they need to. In this chapter you will learn a number of approaches for helping you through such assignments; you will learn ways to ease your fears and techniques to help you produce your best work.

ACTIVITY **Reading the Question.** It may seem unnecessary to say that the first step in taking an examination is to read the question carefully. But unfortunately, many students receive failing grades because they do not pay sufficient attention to this small but vital matter. These students assume they know what is being asked of them after one hasty reading; they do not realize they have gone off on a tangent until it is too late.

Look at the paragraph below, and answer the discussion questions that follow. Notice how many chances there are to miss the point.

> The crime rate in the United States has been increasing steadily in the past few years and shows no sign of declining despite increased expenditures for police and other crime-fighting forces because these agencies have not focused on the real reason for the increase. The chief cause of the increase is the tremendous attention paid to crime and criminals in the newspapers, on TV, and in books and magazines. To combat crime, all media coverage should be controlled by a national censor who will have the power to limit the amount and the nature of public information on this subject.

Discussion

1. What topic might you think was going to be discussed when you finished reading the first sentence?
2. What topic did you think was going to be discussed when you finished reading the second sentence?
3. What topic did you think was going to be discussed when you finished reading the third sentence?

As you can see from your answers to the discussion questions, students who focus only on the first sentence might believe they are expected to write an essay about the increase in crime, while students who focus only on the second sentence might think they are being asked to write about violence and the media. Although both sets of students could write excellent essays, both would be in danger of failing because they did not notice that the question actually asks them to write about censorship.

How do you avoid this danger? Obviously, reading the whole question carefully — at least twice — is the necessary first step. If the question is presented in a two- or three-sentence paragraph, you need to decide which sentences provide background information and which ones you are expected to respond to. You need to ask yourself, "What is the issue here?"

PRACTICE	**Determining the Issue.** Working alone or in a small group, determine what each of the following questions asks you to do.

1. Teenagers frequently ignore the advice of parents and teachers, preferring instead to follow the suggestions of their peers. Their behavior might deal with actions as uncomplicated as choice of hairstyle, or it might involve matters as complex as sex and drugs. What do you believe might result from this situation?

2. The change from high school to college is far greater than most freshmen expect it to be. To a student who has been out of school for several years, the nature of college work may seem totally foreign. What steps would you advise an entering student to take to make the first year of college successful?

3. The freedom to change jobs attracts some people, while the security derived from staying in the same workplace appeals to others. Some people focus on the chance for advancement that change offers, while others are aware only of the risk of failure. Compare these two attitudes to show the advantages and disadvantages of the two approaches.

As you can see, your instructions may be given in the form of a question or, in the case wherein you are asked for your opinion, in the form of a sentence that includes words like *should* or *must*. A key question to ask yourself is, "What is the issue here?"

ACTIVITY	**Planning.** As important as it is to read the question carefully, it is equally important to plan out your essay before you write a single word in your test book. Unlike the essays you work on at home, in which you can write and revise and even start over, the compositions you write in class must be as close to perfect as possible the first time you put your words on paper. You need to know what your main points will be and what supporting materials you will rely on.

Often students regard such planning as a waste of valuable time. They argue that by using the time to write rather than plan, they can produce longer essays. But these students forget that an essay's length is not the only, or even the chief, consideration; it is the quality of the essay, its organization and its substance, that determines its success or failure. Sometimes it is better to "make haste slowly."

There is, of course, only a limited amount of time. If fifty minutes or an hour is allotted for the exam, you should plan to spend about ten minutes organizing your thoughts. Even if you have only twenty or thirty minutes, you should expect to spend about five minutes thinking about what you want to say and how you want to present it.

To make the best use of your time, you should have some strategies that will enable you to tap your best thinking as rapidly as possible. There are a number of approaches you can use, some of which work better for certain types of questions than for others. Particularly useful are (a) making lists, (b) constructing a chart, and (c) creating categories.

PRACTICE   **Listing Pros and Cons for an Argument Essay.** When you are asked to write an essay in which you agree or disagree with a proposition, you need quickly to come up with the best possible reasons why you are either in favor of or opposed to the ideas being presented. In such cases, making lists of reasons can be extremely helpful; following are two ways to approach the task.

Look at the question about crime and censorship on page 212. The question asks you to agree or disagree with the idea of having a national censor to limit the amount of information about crime and violence made available through the media.

1. Suppose you feel very strongly one way or the other about the issue. In this case, you should make a list of all the reasons you can think of to support your position. Do not try to decide whether a reason is a good one or not; at this point, doing so would be a waste of time. Once you have listed several — at least four or five — reasons, select the two or three that seem the most useful. Although you may be tempted to quit after you have listed two reasons, since two are probably all that you need, resist the temptation. Otherwise, you run the risk of omitting a better reason than your first choices simply because it did not come to mind as quickly as the others.

2. If you are not sure about how you feel on the issue, you should make two lists of reasons, one that lists why you might agree with the proposition and another that lists why you might disagree. Again, do not waste time censoring your lists by trying to decide whether the reasons are good ones or not; just list anything you can think of. Once you have several items on each side, reread your lists and choose with which position — pro or con — you feel most comfortable. Although you might

worry that the resulting essay does not reflect your ideas completely, you should realize that test readers are basically concerned with determining whether a student can present and develop an idea, not with how "sincere" the particular views are.

One problem that you need to address when you use the list-making approach is the potential for confusing an example with a reason. A reason tells why; an example shows the reason in action. Scrutinize your lists to ensure that they contain reasons, not examples.

Working alone or with a small group of students, make lists of reasons agreeing and disagreeing with the proposal on page 212 about censoring media coverage of violent crime. Spend ten minutes creating the lists, and then write a sentence that expresses your opinion and gives two reasons to support it. Finally, compare your sentence, reasons, and lists with those of other members of your class.

PRACTICE   **Constructing a Chart for a Process Essay.** Making a chart is a particularly useful technique for planning a process paper. Here you construct a chart to show the various steps in a process and how those steps fit together. Look at the question on page 213 that asks you to recommend steps to take in achieving success in the first year of college. A chart for this topic might consist of a single chain or might involve two or three parallel chains. The work you did on process writing in Chapter 10 would be useful here. For example, the steps in a chain might start off with the idea that a person should join clubs that interest him or her. From that, the person could meet people with similar interests. The chart might look like the one on the next page.

Working alone or with a small group of your fellow students, create one or more charts for the question about success in college. Look at your chart, and isolate those steps which are major ones; then write a sentence that lists the major steps. Finally, compare your sentence with those of other students or groups in your class.

PRACTICE   **Creating Categories for Comparison-Contrast or Cause-Effect Essays.** Sometimes it is useful to make a list of categories you might use in answering a question. The work you did in Chapters 9 and 10 on these organizational strategies of this book would be helpful here. Essentially what is called for is some idea of how

Chart for In-Class Process Essay

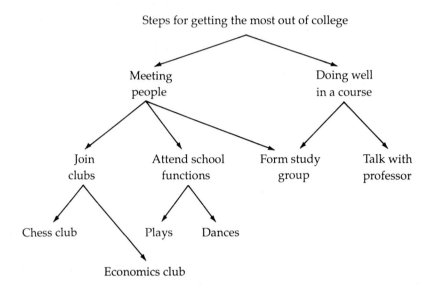

Steps for getting the most out of college

Meeting people — Doing well in a course

Join clubs — Attend school functions — Form study group — Talk with professor

Chess club — Plays — Dances

Economics club

you could group your information when you go about writing your answer.

Look at the questions on page 213 about (a) teenagers following their peers and (b) changing jobs. For both of these questions, you need to have some sense of the categories, or groups, you can use to organize your paper. For the question on jobs, you might consider such categories as the nature of the work, social factors, and family responsibilities.

Working alone or in small groups, spend ten minutes creating categories for either of the questions mentioned above. Then write a sentence that lists those categories, and compare your sentence with those of other class members.

ACTIVITY   **Planning the Paragraphs.** Because in-class writing allows so little time for thinking and revising, it is useful to have a sense of not only what your main idea is going to be and how you will support it but also what each of your main body paragraphs will include. To a large extent, the work you have done in formulating thesis statements has given you a good start in this direction. Each of the reasons, steps, or categories you have identified will give you the substance for a body paragraph; your only remaining task is to decide what else to include in those paragraphs.

One of the most important ingredients to supply, if you can, is a specific example — that is, a brief retelling of an incident in which the problem could be seen. You should also add sentences that will answer the question, "What do I mean by that?"

Look back over each of the plans you have made for the four kinds of essays we have presented thus far — the argument essay, the process essay, the comparison-contrast essay, and the cause-effect essay. Pick any two or three you want to work on. For each one, choose one of the main points that you have mentioned in your thesis sentence, and then make a list of the possible ideas you could include in the paragraph that discusses that point.

Writing a Conclusion

The conclusion of an in-class essay is the least important part of the paper. One sentence that restates your thesis is all that is necessary; one or two more sentences that suggest new areas of action would be a possible addition. But in truth, there is little you can add to your paper at this point that will turn a poor essay into a good one. And if your essay *is* a good one, it is extremely doubtful that any reader would condemn it for lacking a full conclusion.

Overcoming Text Anxiety

For students who suffer from test anxiety, none of the foregoing information on writing an essay exam is of much use. Test anxiety is one of the most painful experiences that students can face. Instead of being able to tap their usual ability to think up ideas, students with test anxiety find that they "freeze" — their minds go blank and remain that way until almost the end of the time period. As they stare at the empty paper, they become more and more anxious. Only when the test is almost over do some of them find that they can begin to write; however, by then it is usually too late to produce a satisfactory composition. Certainly it is too late to show how skillful they really are.

It would be comforting to believe that there is some magic cure for this problem, but none has come to our attention as yet. Until one does, students with test anxiety will have to rely on strategies like the following, which we have found to help many of our students. First of all, you need to force yourself to relax. Take several deep breaths, filling your lungs with as much air as they can hold and then releasing it slowly. Stretch out your legs and arms — standing, if possible — and slowly stretch your neck by moving your head from one side to the other.

In addition to releasing the tension in your body, you need to release the tension that is tying up your mind. One way to do so is to empty your mind by staring at some distant object, repeating a nonsense syllable, and gently erasing any thoughts that come into your head. Try to do this for four or five minutes before a test is due to begin.

Another technique students use to release their minds comes through freewriting. For ten minutes or so, write down anything that comes into your head. You will find that frequently these thoughts involve problems from other areas of your life or expressions of anger about the situation. Since no one but you will see the freewriting, you can feel safe in writing it all out, and in this way you will be able to clear your mind for at least the time needed to finish a test.

These strategies have helped many students, and a combination of them will undoubtedly help those of you who suffer from the problem of test anxiety. But perhaps the most valuable lesson was that taught by President Franklin D. Roosevelt, who said, "You have nothing to fear but fear itself."

IN-CLASS WRITING

The Handwriting Problem. Once you have planned your essay, formulated your thesis statement, and sketched out your body paragraphs, your essay is well on its way. You are ready to start writing.

The physical act of writing, however, raises a few minor matters that sometimes interfere with student performance. Some students worry excessively about the neatness of their papers and the readability of their handwriting. Although they are correct in being aware of the fact that readers can be annoyed or confused by illegible handwriting or hard-to-follow lines, such students also need to realize that with an in-class essay, neatness is only a relative matter. Readers are not concerned with finding no mistakes, nor do they care about exemplary penmanship. All that they ask is to be able to follow the ideas without needing a map.

In their excessive zeal, some students first write a draft of their paper and then try to copy it over. This is without a doubt the single worst thing they can do — there is simply not enough time to produce both a good draft and a clean copy. DO NOT EVER TRY TO COPY OVER YOUR ESSAY. You can, however, take a number of steps to make your paper more readable.

1. Use wide margins and write on every other line. The extra space on the edges and between lines makes even difficult

handwriting easier to follow. It also provides space for you to add additional information. With in-class writing, more often than not, you will think of ideas that belong in paragraphs you finished earlier in the period. By skipping lines, you will be able to add the new information on the blank line above the place where it belongs, as in the following example:

There should be some way to
                    such as Miami Vice
control TV shows, that have a lot

By leaving wide margins, you will also be able to add information there, if necessary. Having the extra space is also useful when you are proofreading your work and discover that you have omitted a word or phrase.

2. Do not waste time using white-out. Many students, when they need to cross out a word, a line, or a paragraph, worry about the resultant appearance of their paper. Some take the time they might otherwise use for thinking or writing to carefully white-out the portion of their paper they want to revise. Such students are not aware of the fact that a reader expects that thoughtful students will want to change their papers several times during the course of writing. Readers do not regard the crossed-out passages as mistakes; rather, they consider them a sign of a careful thinker. Whiting-out is not only unnecessary but also a waste of valuable time. All that is needed is to draw a single line through the offending word or words and then go on to writing, using the next empty space on the line.

   At the other extreme are students who are so annoyed at their mistakes that they scratch them out with X's, circles, and all kinds of ugly and messy lines. These markings are indeed irritating to a reader and are equally unnecessary, except perhaps for those writers who use the method to vent their rage. If you must make harsh doodles, do so on a separate piece of scrap paper, and then simply draw a single line through the words you wish to omit in your actual composition.

3. Use a pencil to write in words that you are unsure how to spell. Sometimes students create visually unattractive papers when they are using a word they do not know how to spell. They write the word, then write over it to change one or two letters, and then write over it again, changing the same or other letters, and so on. In the end, the reader must guess what word was intended.

It is not difficult to avoid such blots, especially if you know you have trouble with spelling. All you have to do is make sure you have both a pencil and a pen when you come into the classroom to take the test. Every time you come to a word whose spelling you are unsure of, write the word *in pencil* as best you can at the moment, and then go on. In this way you will not have interrupted your creative process but you will have a copy that a reader can follow. When the time comes to proofread your paper, you can go over each of these words. If using a dictionary is permitted, you can look up all these words at the same time (again a time-saving procedure); if not, you will still have time to think about the spelling when you are not caught up in worrying about what the next sentence will say.

4. Add large blocks of writing at the end of your essay. Occasionally you will discover that you need to add a full paragraph's worth of information somewhere in the middle of an essay. How can you do that without making a mess? Easy. Just put a star (*) at the point where you want the paragraph to go, and then put another star several lines below the end of your essay, beginning your new paragraph there. This method of starring is a standard practice with which all members of a college faculty are familiar. Instead of being confused, they will silently compliment you on knowing this academic convention.

LANGUAGE LEARNING

Editing and Proofreading Your Answer. The most difficult but crucial part of writing an in-class paper is the final editing and proofreading. Most in-class writing assignments for a fifty-minute time period suggest that you spend ten minutes on this part. Unfortunately, few students realize the importance of the task. They are so concerned with finishing their papers that they use the time to continue writing.

Make sure you don't fall into this trap. When you still have ten minutes left, stop writing. If there is time after you have checked your paper, you can write another few sentences to finish it off. Remember, your paper will be judged by the quality of what you have already produced, and the reader's decision will have already been tentatively formulated by the time the first paragraphs have been read. Your readers will base their judgment of your ability as a writer on what they see on the pages you have already written. The mistakes that are there, that you did not correct, will influence their decisions. What you did not write cannot help or hurt you.

The procedure for editing and proofreading an in-class paper is different from that for editing and proofreading a paper you have had time to create. Read over the following steps.

1. Because you have been involved so completely in the creative process of writing your paper, you need to make a deliberate effort to change your thinking pattern. Relax, stretch your arms and legs, and stare at the ceiling or lean your head on the desk for a minute or two. Do anything you can think of to separate yourself from your paper.

2. Reread your paper slowly, to yourself. Although you will not want to read it aloud and disturb your neighbors, do read it slowly enough so that you can actually hear the words. If you point to each word as you read it, you may be able to see it more clearly and notice if you actually wrote the word as you intended.

3. Ask yourself: "Is my position clear? Do my reasons support that position? Do my examples support my reasons?" If you feel you have omitted a significant detail, you can add it now. Many students are careful to leave wide margins or to skip every other line, just to have room for these additions.

4. It is almost impossible in an in-class writing situation to read your paper for mistakes in the usual way of simply reading it over. You are too close to it, and there is not enough time to make the necessary separation. The following suggestions can help you find the most common student errors.

   a. Look at the first word of every sentence. If it is a connecting word such as *because, although,* or *since,* stop and read the sentence carefully. Does it express two complete thoughts? If there are not two subject-verb units, something is wrong. In most cases of this sort, the unit that begins with *because* belongs to the previous sentence. Read that sentence together with the one you have isolated to see if they fit together. Or add the missing material.

   b. Look at each sentence to see if you have used a form of the verb *to be (am, is, are, was, were, be, been, being)* or the verb *to have (have, has, had).* Then see if there is another verb with it. That second verb needs an ending, usually *-d* or *-ed.*

   c. Skim through your paper to find every place you put a comma. If the word following the comma is *he, she, it, I, you,* or *they,* stop and read the sentence more carefully. Are there two subject-verb units? Is there a connecting word? If the answer to the first question is yes, and to the second question no, you need a period instead of a comma.

FORMAL WRITING   **The In-Class Essay.** Read the following four paragraphs carefully and select one to write about. You will have fifty minutes to write your answer. Plan to use your time as follows: ten minutes to plan your essay, thirty minutes to write it, and ten minutes to edit and proofread it.

A. In the past twenty years the quality of education has declined at an extraordinary rate. Today, students are graduating from high school lacking the requisite skills of reading, writing, and arithmetic. To counter this trend, students should be retained at each grade for as many years as it takes for them to master these necessary skills.

Write an essay in which you agree or disagree with the above statement.

B. The policy of the American government has been to preserve as much land as possible in national parks for the recreation of all citizens. Now that our national resources such as oil, coal, and minerals are being used up, we can no longer afford the luxury of maintaining these wilderness areas.

Write an essay in which you discuss what you think would be the results if we were to develop our national parks for their natural resources.

C. Women have demanded and frequently received equal rights to all kinds of jobs, from construction workers to lawyers. But while women have received equal opportunities, they have not been expected to assume equal responsibilities. This situation is most apparent in the armed forces, where women now serve in significant numbers but are not expected to fight on the front lines.

Write an essay in which you compare the advantages and disadvantages of adding women to the fighting forces.

D. One of the most difficult moments in life is the time when a relationship with another person is about to end. Although it is not possible to prevent all pain, it can be limited.

Write an essay in which you describe the steps that an individual could take to end a relationship with the least amount of suffering. Be sure to tell why you included each of the steps you did.

Afterword

Whether you thought it would ever happen or not, it has. You have finally reached the end of this book. You might like to take a moment or two here to consider the distance you have traveled as a writer and to think over where things began to fall into place along the way. Somewhere along the path this book has forged for you, did an awareness emerge that made you feel you were becoming a competent writer?

You may even want to take out some of the assignments you did and arrange them in the order in which they occurred in this book. As you do this, look at your teacher's comments to see if they reflect something that was beginning to happen in you. Maybe they are telling you that writing well is neither a mystery nor an accident. You can actually make it happen whenever you wish. Your growing ability as a writer may have come about without your having realized it. We think you should know if it has happened.

Finally, as you look at yourself as a writer, remember that writing is an experience, and since it is, you ought to feel as good about it as possible. This good feeling is best defined as confidence. From page 1, the goal of our book has been to help you develop that confidence in yourself. As you move into more advanced writing courses, you will experience further growth and greater confidence. Accept our best wishes. We are confident of your success.

The Authors

Appendix
A Grammar, Punctuation, and Spelling Refresher

Throughout this text we have assumed that you have a basic understanding of language, and we have tried to provide you with techniques that will help you build on that knowledge in order to create more varied and interesting ways to express your ideas. This section of the book is intended to provide a brief review of a few areas with which students have particular difficulty. Here you will find a more complete definition of the sentence, a fuller explanation of the verb system, a more thorough review of the main punctuation marks, and consideration of common problems of spelling.

All writers, even the most skilled, refer to handbooks from time to time, and although this section is not a complete handbook, you can develop the habit of consulting it.

I. THE SENTENCE

The Sentence Core

The sentence is the basic unit of thought in the English language. A sentence must contain at least one kernel made up of two elements — a verb and a subject — and provide a unit of information.

A *verb*

    tells what the action of the sentence is.

    links the ideas together.

    tells the time at which the action occurred.

    may tell if the action is done by one or more persons or things.

    may be one word, or may include several auxiliary (helping) verbs (or may require a completer).

A *subject*

> tells the person, place, thing, or idea that performs the action of the verb.
>
> answers the question, Who or what did the action?
>
> usually comes before the verb.

The following are all examples of sentence kernels:

> Maria laughed.
> Paul is smiling.
> James feels comfortable.
> Voting is a privilege.
> They threw the ball.

Problems, Exceptions, and Situations to Watch Out For

1. In some sentences the word *there* precedes the verb instead of the subject.

   There *was* a *lot* of water damage on Ms. Taylor's kitchen floor. There *were* several other *homeowners* in the hardware store buying books on repairing.

   In these sentences, *there* is not the subject; it marks the position of the subject that follows the verb.

2. Sentences that give commands often do not have a subject.

   Keep out!
   Come one, come all, to the greatest show on earth.

   In these sentences, the subject, *you,* is understood.

3. The main verb in a sentence kernel often consists of two or more words — the action word plus one or more helping verbs:

   John *should have been writing* in his journal.

All of the italicized words in the last example are considered part of the main verb. The additional words are called helping verbs, or auxiliaries.

One of the main functions of the auxiliaries is to tell whether the action is taking place in the present, took place in the past, or will take place in the future. Look at this sentence:

> Paula is working.

Here we know that the action is taking place in the present because of the *is*. If that word had been omitted, and the sentence was only

Paula working.

we would not know whether the writer meant past, present, or future.

If you are not sure whether the verb in your sentence needs an auxiliary, see if it tells when the action is taking place. If it does not, you need an auxiliary.

For a fuller explanation of verb forms, refer to page 233.

Adding Modifiers and Avoiding Fragments

Modifying Words

Modifiers add life to sentences. Although a subject and a verb are the basic core of the sentence, they do not by themselves make for very exciting reading. Few people would be content with a steady fare of two- and three-word sentences. The precision and complexity of mature thinking require precise and complex sentences.

One of the simplest ways to expand your sentences is by adding modifying words and phrases, which can transform dull, vague sentences into ones that are both vivid and specific. For example,

The man laughed.

can become:

The *broad, dark* man *with the thick walrus mustache* laughed *scornfully.*

As you can see from the above example, descriptive words can be placed in front of a noun. Words that indicate, for instance, size, shape, color, or texture help the reader to sense the person or object. Usually two or three such words are enough; only in exceptional cases would you want to use more.

A *slimy green* snake slithered by.

Descriptive words can also be used to tell how an action was performed. These words, often ending in *-ly* give your reader a better grasp of your meaning.

The small green Honda swerved *dangerously.*

Modifying Phrases: Prepositional Phrases

Phrases can be used to add additional details and are especially helpful when you have already used a few modifying words in front of a noun subject.

The lean, gray dog *with the long, thick tail* sniffed warily.

Phrases can also add details that make your meaning more specific. By using phrases that begin with *in, at, under, behind, through, of,* etc., you can add a great deal of valuable information. Much of this information supplies answers to such questions as *where?* (at the store, under the table); *when?* (in a few minutes, by tomorrow afternoon); and *where to?* (to the movies).

Modifying Phrases: Words with *-ing* Endings

A verb ending in *-ing* cannot be the main verb in the sentence without a helping verb, or auxiliary. However, verbs in this form are useful for adding ideas to your sentences. Look at the following two sentences:

Mary walked out of the classroom.
She left her gloves on the chair.

These two sentences, while grammatically correct, create an unpleasant, abrupt sensation as you read them. A smoother result is achieved if they are combined in the following way:

Mary walked out of the classroom, leaving her gloves on the chair.

Problems to Watch Out For

You know that a unit such as *singing and dancing under the stars* is not a complete sentence. There are, however, a number of instances when you add such phrases to your writing. They are added sometimes even when you have already added a period to the sentence to which it should be joined. The result looks like this:

The guests enjoyed the party. Singing and dancing under the stars.

It is important to check every sentence that begins with an *-ing* word to make sure that there is a subject-verb kernel to make it a complete sentence. Now correct the example above.

Modifying Phrases: Using Words with *-ed* Endings

Since the *-ed* ending is the usual one for regular verbs in the past tense, we automatically create a sentence when we put a noun in front of a verb with this ending.

John walked.
Mary talked.

But this ending is also used for some words that can bring new ideas to our basic sentence.

John, *tired from his long journey,* fell asleep at the kitchen table.

This same sentence could be written:

John fell asleep at the kitchen table, *tired from his long journey.*

However, sometimes the writer will end the sentence after *table* and add a period because he or she has finished the sentence. Then the writer adds the extra idea but starts it as a new sentence. Then we have:

John fell asleep at the kitchen table. Tired from his long journey.

The reader must now guess where the phrase *Tired from his long journey* belongs. Writers should always try to make their meaning as clear as possible.

Other Modifying Phrases: Afterthoughts

Often when you are in the midst of writing a sentence, you get a few extra ideas and want to add them. Unless you intend to write a new sentence with a subject and a verb, these added bits of information belong to the sentence you are working on.

When Karen hit a home run, everyone cheered wildly, *especially her boyfriend, Joe.*
There are many sports you might want to try at the beach, *such as snorkeling, scuba diving, and surfing.*

In these sentences it would be a mistake to place a period before *especially* or *such as,* for the units that follow have no subject and no verb, and therefore are not sentences. Words that frequently introduce this kind of fragment are:

such as	including
especially	for example
also	except
for instance	

Most fragments of this kind can be corrected by being attached to the preceding sentences.

Joining Words

Using *And* and *But*

Two short sentences with a close connection to each other may be combined to provide a smoother flow to your writing:

From: George joined the Caligari softball team. He proved to be the leading hitter.

To: George joined the Caligari softball team, and he proved to be the leading hitter.

One problem to watch out for is noting the difference in meaning between *and* and *but*. *And* indicates an additional idea that continues the main drift of the sentence; *but* indicates an additional idea that sets up an exception to the main drift of the sentence. Notice the difference between this example and the one we have just seen.

George joined the Caligari softball team, but he never got a single hit.

Adverbial Clauses

As you learned in Chapter 6, words like *because, after, while,* and *although* are used to join two ideas together. If only one of the ideas is given in the sentence, the meaning is unclear and the reader is confused. When the joining word comes between the two ideas, you can spot it fairly easily and correct it.

Wrong: Bill kept his eyes on the floor. Because he did not want the teacher to call on him.

Correct: Bill kept his eyes on the floor because he did not want the teacher to call on him.

The *because* should join the two ideas, and so you can correct the sentence simply by removing the period and the capital *B*.

The problem, unfortunately, is not always that simple, for the joining word is often put at the beginning of the sentence, and then it may be difficult to remember which sentence it belongs to. You should not stop beginning sentences with these words; in fact, it is an important way to add variety to your sentences. But it does put an added burden on you, and you must check each sentence carefully.

Who, Which and *That* **Clauses**

Another group of joining words that can be used to build sentences is *who, whom, whose, which,* and *that.* These words operate differently from those we have discussed above for they perform a double function. First, they act as pronouns, taking the place of the nouns to which they refer. The forms of *who* are used for people; *which* is used for places and things; and *that* may be used for all. And, as pronouns, these words can be subjects and objects, just as other pronouns can. Second, they act as joining words. Suppose you write the following two sentences, which you want to combine into one:

> Charles is the lead singer for the Ginger Peachy rock group.
> Charles sang the tenor solo in the church choir.

If you substitute *who* for *Charles* in the second sentence and insert the whole unit between *Charles* and *is* in the first sentence, your new sentence would be:

> Charles, who sang the tenor solo in the church choir, is the lead singer for the Ginger Peachy rock group.

As you can see, *who* is both the joining word that connects the two ideas and the subject of the verb *sang.* Like all joining words, *who, which,* and *that* are signals to your readers that there will be two ideas in the sentence. Whenever you use one of these words in a sentence, you must check to see that you have included two subject-verb cores, each expressing an idea.

Avoiding Run-Ons

Every sentence needs one subject-verb core, but one is enough. If you omit the period between two complete sentences, or if you put in a comma where a stronger separation is needed, you will create confusion in your reader's mind.

Often when you write, you think of a connection between two ideas, but by the time you transfer your thoughts to paper, you leave out the word that connects those ideas. For instance, you might write:

> Gladys gave a loud cheer, she had passed Chemistry 101.

What you probably were thinking was that Gladys gave the cheer because she had passed Chemistry 101. You may have left the connecting word out on the theory that your readers would automatically know what the connection was, but in this example and in many others like it, your readers could have thought of several other possibilities. They might, for instance, have substituted *when, since, after,* or *for.* You need to make your exact meaning clear. Sometimes you may want to put a comma between *cheer* and *she,* but as explained in Chapter 6, a comma cannot be used to separate two complete thoughts.

The run-ons that result from this kind of omission, which is sometimes called a comma splice, can be corrected by putting a period at the end of the first thought and starting the next word with a capital letter. But the result in most cases would be two choppy sentences. It is far better to use a connecting word, which not only fixes the error but conveys your meaning as well.

Note: In many run-ons or comma splices caused by the substitution of a comma for a connecting word, you will find a *he, she, it, they, we, you, this, that,* or *I* in the middle of the sentence. Any sentence in which one of these words appears in the middle should be checked carefully. Read it out loud if necessary. Count the subject-verb cores, and if there is more than one, make sure there is a linking word, or rewrite it as two sentences.

Confusion over Joining Words

Certain words appear to be connecting words, but although they are important ways of connecting ideas, they are not words that can join sentences. The following words fall into this category:

now	then
therefore	however
moreover	consequently

If, by mistake, you have used these words to join sentences, you can correct your error either by inserting a period before the word and then starting a new sentence with a capital letter or by placing a semicolon before the word. (*Note:* You may need a comma following each of these words.)

John read the textbook three times, studied his lecture notes for twenty hours, and made up an outline of three answers to possible essay-exam questions; consequently, he received an A+ on his sociology exam.

If the joining word can be moved to another position in its own clause, you need either a period or a semicolon between the units.

II. VERBS

In the discussion of sentence structure, we introduced the subject of verbs by providing a brief view of their function. But many writers have trouble selecting the particular form of verb they need in a specific situation. In this section, we will review some of the main problem areas in the selection of verbs.

Recognizing the Main Verb in the Sentence

The Function of Verbs

The verb is the word (or words) in a sentence that tells the action. When the sense of action is strong, there is usually no problem:

The acrobat *leapt from the platform.*
The diver *paced* down the board, *leapt* high in the air, *arched* his back and *spread* his arms, in a perfect swan dive, then *plunged* into the pool.

Often the verb merely presents a state of being, in which case it is less easy to recognize:

The swimmers *were* happy that they had won the meet.

If you can form a sentence kernel by adding a subject to a word, then that word is being used as a verb:

Maria smiled (*smiled* is a verb).

The unit "Jim *coffee*" does not make sense; therefore you can see that *coffee* is not a verb.

The Form of Verbs

Because verbs perform many functions in a sentence besides telling action — whether the action takes place in the present, past, or future; whether one or many are performing the action — their forms make a number of changes. The following chart presents the most common forms of the active voice.

In discussing verbs, people usually distinguish three forms: the infinitive, or base, form; the past tense; and the past participle — *talk, talked, talked.*

Situation	Form	Examples
1. To tell what happens now	*Present Tense*	I, You, We, They *talk.*
2. To make a statement that is generally true	Base, or infinitive, form + *-s, -es* when *He, She, It* are subjects	He, She, It *talks.* The sun *rises* in the east. Now the children *talk.* They *talk* too much.
3. To tell what happened at a specific time in the past	*Past Tense* Base form + *-d* or *-ed* for regular verbs or proper form of irregular verb	(All subjects) *talked, saw.* Yesterday they *talked* to me. Yesterday they *saw* me.
4. To tell what will happen in the future	*Future Tense* *will* + base form	(All subjects) *will talk.* I *will talk* tomorrow about the problem.
5. To tell what happened in the past and continues in the present or to show what happened in the past at an unstated time	*Present Perfect* *have* (or *has* for *he, she, it* as subjects) + base form + *-d* or *-ed* or proper form of irregular verb	I, You, We, They *have seen, have talked.* He, She, It *has seen, has talked.* The children *have talked* all morning. He *has* always *talked* too loud.
6. To tell an action in the past that was finished before another past action	*Past Perfect* *had* + base form + *-d* or *-ed* or	The children *have seen* the movie. He *has seen* the movie many times.

Situation	Form	Examples
	+ proper form of irregular verb	(All subjects) *had talked, had seen.* Marie *had talked* before her mother asked for silence. They *had seen* each other last week.
7. To tell an action that will be completed before a specific time in the future	*Future Perfect* *will have* + base form of verb + -d or -ed or proper form of irregular verb	(All subjects) *will have seen, will have talked.* By tomorrow morning, Marie *will have talked* for twenty-four hours without stopping.
8. To tell an action that is going on now	*Present Continuous* *am* (subject is *I*) *is* (subject is *He, She, It*) *are* (subject is *You, They*) + base form of verb + -ing ending	I *am talking.* She *is talking.* Marie *is talking* to you. I *am talking* to Marie. They *are talking* to me.
9. To tell an action that was going on in the past	*Past Continuous* *was* (subject is *I, He, She, It*) *were* (subject is *You, We, They*) + base form of verb + -ing ending	He *was talking.* We *were talking.* Yesterday Marie *was talking* all through dinner. Yesterday you *were talking* while I *was trying* to study.
10. To tell an action that will be going on in the future at the same time as another action	*Future Continuous* *will be* (all subjects) + base form of verb + -ing ending	I *will be talking.* Marie *will* still *be talking* when we go to bed.

Present Tense — Special Problems

Simple Present Tense — Using -s

One of the greatest difficulties is knowing when to put -s at the end of a verb.

Whenever you use the present tense, you will need an -s on the main verb when the subject of the sentence is *he, she, it,* or words that can substitute for them.

> Joe's radio blares all day long. (It blares.)
> He likes to keep it very loud.
> Joe thinks the music sounds better that way. (He thinks; it sounds.)

Special Verbs in Present Tense. The verb *to be* (that's the infinitive form of *is, are,* etc.) uses a form ending in -s for both the present and the past form when the subject is *he, she, it,* or words that substitute for them.

> John is hoping to be a disc jockey.
> He was working on the school radio station.

Interfering Words — Present Tense and Verb Choice

Sometimes we have words between the subject and the verb that make it difficult to recognize the exact subject.

> One of the men drives to school.
> All of the women wear jeans.

Although the phrases *of the men* and *of the women* provide some necessary information about the subject of the sentences, they are not the subjects. *One* is the subject of the first sentence; *all* is the subject of the second sentence.

> The grain in the fields looks ripe. (It looks.)
> A group of workers is fighting for a raise. (It is.)
> The teacher, together with his students, stays for the school play. (He stays.)

In order to decide whether or not you need an -s, find the verb in a sentence, and then ask yourself who or what is doing the action. When the answer is one person, one place, or one thing or idea, or if you can substitute, *he, she,* or *it* for the subject, be sure there is an -s on the verb if it is in the present tense.

Words That Cause Confusion

There are two groups that are difficult to work with.

Anyone, **etc.** *Anyone* refers to just one person, as you can see if you look at the word carefully (see the *one*?). There are a number of words like *anyone* that always refer to just one person or one thing. When you use these words as the subject of the sentence in the present tense, you need an *-s* on the verb. Here is a list of the most frequently used of these words:

no one	anybody	everything
someone	nobody	nothing
everyone	somebody	something
each	everybody	
neither		
either		

Everybody wants to be a winner.
Everything costs too much.

In order to decide whether or not you need an *-s,* check to see if the word you are using as the subject of your sentence in the present tense ends in *-one, -body,* or *-thing.* If it does, you know it will need an *-s.* The other words that require the *-s* will have to be memorized.

Words Ending in -s. Some words end in *-s* even though they refer to just one thing. Some of these words are

measles	economics	athletics
mathematics	news	
mumps	physics	

Despite the *-s,* these words are not plural forms; they need a verb with an *-s* in the present tense.

The news is good today, for a change. (It is.)
Mathematics is my best subject. (It is.)

Here **and** *There.* We often use the phrases *here is, here are, there is,* and *there are* (also with *was* and *were*) to begin a sentence. *Here* and *there* are not usually the subjects of these sentences. In such sentences, the subject comes after the verb.

Here is a beautiful skateboard.
There are five reasons why you should quit school.

In order to decide whether or not you need an *-s*, find the verb and ask yourself who or what is (or are). If the answer to that question is one person, place, thing, or idea, you need the *-s* form.

Past Tense — Irregular Verbs

Although most English verbs form the past tense by adding *-ed*, a number of the most common ones do not follow this general rule. Instead they change their forms completely. Once you have memorized them, the only problem will be to make sure that you have used the appropriate forms. In the list of irregular verbs that follows, three forms of each verb are given. The first is used for the present tense, the second is used for the past tense, and the third is used with a form of *have* (*have, had, will have*). Here is an example of the use of *see* (present), *saw* (past), and *seen* (with *have*):

Tom and Bill *see* a movie every Saturday. (present)
Joe *saw* a play last week. (past)
We *have seen* all the movies in town. (form used with *has, have, had*, and *will have*, called the past participle)

Present	Past	Past Participle
am (is)	was	been
arise	arose	arisen
awake	awoke	awakened
bear	bore	borne
beat	beat	beat(en)
become	became	become
begin	began	begun
bend	bent	bent
bet	bet	bet
bid	bade	bidden
bid	bid	bid
bite	bit	bitten
bleed	bled	bled
blow	blew	blown
bring	brought	brought
build	built	built
burst	burst	burst
buy	bought	bought
catch	caught	caught
choose	chose	chosen
come	came	come
cost	cost	cost

Present	Past	Past Participle
creep	crept	crept
cut	cut	cut
deal	dealt	dealt
dig	dug	dug
dive	dived	dived
do	did	done
draw	drew	drawn
drink	drank	drunk
drive	drove	driven
eat	ate	eaten
fall	fell	fallen
feel	felt	felt
fight	fought	fought
find	found	found
fly	flew	flown
forget	forgot	forgot, forgotten
freeze	froze	frozen
get	got	got, gotten
give	gave	given
go	went	gone
grow	grew	grown
hang	hanged	hanged (execute)
hang	hung	hung
have	had	had
hear	heard	heard
hide	hid	hidden
hit	hit	hit
hold	held	held
hurt	hurt	hurt
keep	kept	kept
know	knew	known
lay	laid	laid
lead	led	led
leave	left	left
lend	lent	lent
let	let	let
lie	lay	lain
lie	lied	lied (tell an untruth)
light	lighted, lit	lighted, lit
lose	lost	lost
make	made	made
mean	meant	meant
meet	met	met
pay	paid	paid
put	put	put
quit	quit	quit

Present	Past	Past Participle
read	read	read
rid	rid	rid
ride	rode	ridden
ring	rang	rung
rise	rose	risen
run	ran	run
say	said	said
see	saw	seen
sell	sold	sold
send	sent	sent
set	set	set
shake	shook	shaken
shine	shone	shone
shoot	shot	shot
shrink	shrank	shrunk
shut	shut	shut
sing	sang	sung
sink	sank	sunk
sit	sat	sat
sleep	slept	slept
slide	slid	slid
speak	spoke	spoken
spend	spent	spent
spread	spread	spread
spring	sprang	sprung
stand	stood	stood
steal	stole	stolen
sting	stung	stung
strike	struck	struck
stick	stuck	stuck
swear	swore	sworn
sweep	swept	swept
swim	swam	swum
swing	swung	swung
take	took	taken
teach	taught	taught
tear	tore	torn
tell	told	told
think	thought	thought
throw	threw	thrown
understand	understood	understood
upset	upset	upset
wake	waked, woke	waked, wakened
wear	wore	worn
weave	wove	woven
wed	wed	wed

Present	Past	Past Participle
weep	wept	wept
wet	wet, wetted	wet, wetted
win	won	won
wind	wound	wound
wring	wrung	wrung
write	wrote	written

III. PUNCTUATION AND MECHANICS

The various marks of punctuation in a sentence are simply ways to make your meaning clear to your reader. In general they indicate groups of words that should be seen as a unit. When we read, we use these punctuation marks to govern the length and nature of the separation between units. Like markers on a highway, they tell us when we should slow down, make a brief pause, or come to a full halt.

Knowing when to use periods and commas helps us to make our written work more easily understood by others. But this knowledge is not a substitute for understanding the basic form of the sentence. Unfortunately, many problems in punctuation are the result of improper sentence structure. If your understanding of sentences is hazy, refer to the first section in this Appendix, pages 225–233.

Marking the End of a Sentence

The marks listed below indicate a full stop.

The Question Mark

Use a question mark when the sentence is asking for information:

Where is the nearest gas station?

Can someone fix my flat tire?

A question mark is not necessary when you are giving a report of a question rather than seeking information. For a full explanation, see page 251–252.

The Exclamation Mark

Use an exclamation mark at the end of a sentence that expresses a strong feeling:

> At last!
>
> A friend in need is a friend indeed!
>
> It's the greatest show on earth!

Exclamation marks should be used with caution. Too many of them in your writing limits their effectiveness.

The Period

Use a period to mark the end of a sentence that is neither a question nor an expression of strong emotion. A period is the most frequently used endmark:

> Now is the time for all good men and women to come to the aid of their country.
>
> Life is just a bowl of cherries.

A period is also used after an abbreviation:

> Dr.   M.D.   A.M.
>
> Ms.   Wed.   Fla.
>
> B.A.   Inc.

Marks Within the Sentence

Marks within a sentence are less than full stops. The four marks discussed here are the strongest that can be used within a sentence.

The Colon

The colon is used primarily in formal writing — in documents such as the Declaration of Independence, lawyers' briefs, and scholarly articles. Most of the writing you will be doing in college is considered informal writing, for which the colon is rarely needed. In a few situations, however, a colon would be the best choice.

Use a colon when a long list follows a complete statement:

> The following books were on the best-seller list last year: *Comstock Lode, East of Eden, People's Pharmacy 2, Sylvia Porter's New Money Book for the 80's,* and *What Color Is Your Parachute?*

Use a colon between the hours and minutes in giving in time:

7:32 A.M.

Use a colon after the opening of a formal business letter:

Dear Mr. President:

Use colons between titles and subtitles of books and articles:

Palm Sunday: An Autobiographical Collage, by Kurt Vonnegut

If you look closely at the punctuation used in this and other sections of the Appendix, you will notice that a colon has been used between most statements of a rule and their examples.

The Semicolon

Use a semicolon between two complete sentences whose meaning is so closely connected that a period would feel like too abrupt a break:

John and Mary were married in 1949; they have lived together for thirty-three years.

Semicolons are frequently used with *however, therefore,* and *consequently*:

Suddenly the storm erupted, pouring torrents of rain on the open meadow; that was, therefore, the end of our picnic.

Our meeting had to be cancelled; however, it has been rescheduled for next Tuesday.

Use a semicolon for a list that includes many commas. The semicolon will indicate where the main divisions in the list occur:

The librarian ordered the following books for the library: *The Company of Women,* by Mary Gordon; *Ellis Island,* by Mark Helprin; *The Hour of Our Death,* by Phillipe Aries; and *The Shock of the New,* by Robert Hughes.

Use a semicolon to correct a comma splice. Semicolons are a useful way to correct a situation in which two complete sentences have been joined together, separated only by a comma.

The Dash

Use a dash to show an interruption in the thought of a sentence. The dash can also serve as an informal substitute for a colon or can add material to a sentence in a way that avoids confusion. It can also substitute for a comma, but it gives the separation much more emphasis.

> It's a rare consumer who doesn't know how charge and credit cards — Visa, Mastercard, American Express, or Diner's Club — work.

> But the electronic fund transfer system — the transfer of money from your account to the merchant's account when you make a purchase — is practically unknown.

Because dashes are a dramatic sort of punctuation, they should be used sparingly; however, dashes are better than parentheses ( ) to indicate an added but interfering idea.

The Comma

Of all the marks of punctuation, the comma seems to cause the most confusion to beginning writers. For the most part, commas indicate small separation inside a sentence. But not all separations require a comma, and many beginning writers put commas in places where they are not only unnecessary but wrong. If you thoroughly learn the five situations in which a comma must be used and then use a comma only in those places, you will probably avoid some serious errors.

Dates, Addresses, Openings and Closings of Letters, and Numbers. A comma is necessary between name of the day and month, as well as between the date and the year:

> Wednesday, May 13 , 1988

A comma is necessary between the street address and name of city, as well as between city and state:

> 735 Park Avenue, Plainfield, New Jersey

A comma is needed to separate hundreds from thousands, thousands from millions, millions from billions:

> 4,750,639,217

A comma is necessary after the opening greeting and after the closing of a letter:

> Dear Mr. Smith,

> On Monday, January 27, 1987, I took the civil service examination for pothole inspector at your headquarters at 179 Wrat-

tling Road, Bumpton, New York. Although 4,280 other men and women also took the exam, no one has yet been hired. When will the results be published?

Yours truly,
B. Roken Axelrod

Direct Quotations. A comma is necessary to set a direct quotation off from the rest of the sentence:

"Pet cobras are fun," said Maizie, "especially when they are as cute and cuddly as my Spot."

Joining Words. Use a comma before *and, but, for, so,* and *or* when these words connect two fairly long sentence units. Before you use a comma in this situation, be sure there is a connecting word (*and, but,* etc.). The comma cannot substitute for the connecting word.

Many people think that tame cobras do not make good pets, but they should read Dr. Venom's book *Owning Cobras for Fun and Profit.*

Separating Items in a Series. When you have several items together in a sentence, you need commas to separate them:

Cobras like a warm place to sleep, a juicy rat to eat, and someone to love.

Maizie's cobra has black, white, and brown spectacle-shaped marks on his hood.

Spot raises his soft, limpid, beady eyes whenever Maizie whistles.

Separating Interrupters. When you add words that interrupt the flow of the sentence, separate them from the rest of the sentence with commas:

Spot, who loves to warm himself on the windowsill, slithers to the door when Maizie comes home.

If she is late, however, he sulks in the corner.

Be sure that the words you set off actually interrupt the sentence and are not necessary to identify which person, place, or thing:

The snake that bit Josephina was not Spot.

Since the words *that bit Josephina* are necessary to the meaning, you do not need commas.

After Introductory Material. When you supply information before the main part of the sentence, you need to separate it with a comma:

> When Spot learned that he was accused of biting Josephina, he pouted for three days.

> Looking soulfully at the ceiling, he ignored all of Maizie's efforts to cheer him up.

> Finally, he consented to leave his corner when Maizie offered him a plump field mouse.

If you begin with only a short phrase, you do not need a comma:

> In the morning Spot was his usual cheerful self.

Capital Letters

Names

The use of capital letters varies from country to country and from one age to another. Spanish- and French-speaking countries use capital letters much less frequently than English-speaking lands, but at the same time their use in the United States has declined in the past two hundred years.

The general rule is to use a capital letter for:

1. The name of a particular person, place, or thing.
2. The first word of a sentence.

A capital is used when a word names a particular person, place, or thing. If there is a title with a person's name, it should also be capitalized:

Ms. Monica Aldrich	Nigeria
Senator Daniel Webster	Pikes Peak
Rear Admiral Farragut	Red River
General Stephen Decatur	Wok-Do Restaurant
Nikki Giovanni	the Golden Gate Bridge
Hepzibah Pyncheon	Sears Tower
Mother Jones	Maple Street
France	

Certain words are always capitalized: names of cities, countries, languages, months of the year, days of the week, holidays, sacred names, the word *I* (when writing about oneself):

On Monday, September 6, 1987, while living in Cairo, Egypt, I began an intensive study of the Koran in the original Arabic.

Even when you are using words derived from these names, you need the capital letter:

Every New Yorker should know some Spanish.

If a word is used in a general sense, it is not capitalized.

Words like *country, lawyer, ocean,* and *father* are capitalized only when they are part of a particular name. For example, when the word *river* is part of the name of a particular river, the *r* is capitalized; if the word *river* is used to refer to an unspecified body of water, the *r* is not capitalized. In the preceding examples, the words *mother, peak, river, restaurant, golden, gate, bridge, tower, maple,* and *street* are all capitalized because they appear as parts of particular names; otherwise they are not capitalized.

Other kinds of names that need capitals are names of business organizations, religious and political groups, associations, unions, and clubs. In other words, names of particular groups are capitalized:

General Motors Corporation has signed a special contract with the United Auto Workers Union to cover the Buick assembly plant in Flint, Michigan.

Names of commercial products are also capitalized:

On April Fool's Day, my little sister covered a cake with whipped Crest toothpaste instead of RediWhip. We took one taste and rushed to the bathroom to wash our mouths out with Listerine.

Titles of books, magazines, movies, television shows, newspapers, articles, stories, songs, and record albums also use capitals for the main words. You do not need to capitalize *of, an,* or *the* unless they are the first word.

The Caine Mutiny

Gone with the Wind

Death Comes to the Archbishop

Capitals to Start Sentences

The first letter of the first word of a sentence must be capitalized:

My lawyer assured me I would win my case if I could find one witness who would say he saw me in the bar that night.

The first word of a sentence in a direct quotation is capitalized:

Maggie said, "Arthur is too gentle to be a boxer."

Even when the words quoted do not make a complete sentence, the first letter is still capitalized:

Joe answered, "Why not?"

But if the sentence of the direct quotation is interrupted by naming the speaker, you do not need to use a capital for the continuation of the quote:

"If Arthur would only get mad," answered Joe, "he'd knock out three men with one punch."

Apostrophes

Use an apostrophe with the letter *s* to show possession:

the shopper's guide

the children's toys

Zenobia's passion

Adam's fall

If the word already ends in an -*s* or a -*z*, use only the apostrophe; you do not need to add another -*s*:

the girls' dresses

the boys' shirts

Notice that it is the existence of the -*s* that is significant, not the fact that the words are plural. If we wanted to discuss the books the children own, we would write *the children's books,* even though the word *children* is plural. Use an apostrophe to form the plurals of numbers, letters, and signs:

There are two e's in eel.

On the midterm exam there were five A's and four C's.

It was hard to tell the +'s from the −'s on the math test.

Use an apostrophe in the spot where a letter has been omitted. You can use an apostrophe to change *do not* into *don't; don't* is called a contraction. Here the apostrophe takes the place of the omitted *o.* In some cases, if you forget to put in the apostrophe, you will create confusing sentences.

It's/its. In the word *it's*, the apostrophe takes the place of the omitted letter *i* of *it is*, or the *ha* of *it has*. *It's* = *it is* or *it has*. These are the only meanings *it's* can have.

It's not easy to learn to spell. (It is not easy to learn to spell.)

It's been difficult finding a job. (It has been difficult finding a job.)

Note: The word *its* (without the apostrophe) has a completely different meaning. *Its* is used to show ownership:

The country faced *its* problems with courage.
The art museum brought *its* pictures to the community.

You're/your. The apostrophe in *you're* takes the place of the *a* in the word *are*, and so *you're* = *you are*.

You're going to be late for work if you don't leave now. (You are going to be . . .)

Note: Your (without the apostrophe) shows ownership:

You will forget *your* books if you leave them under the chair.

Who's/whose. The apostrophe takes the place of the *i* in *who is*, so that *who's* = *who is*. That is the only meaning of *who's*.

Who's going to the dance tonight? (Who is going to the dance tonight?)

Note: Whose (without the apostrophe) shows ownership:

Whose book is on the window ledge?

They're/their/there. The apostrophe in *they're* takes the place of the *a* in *are*, so that *they're* = *they are*.

They're going to the dance tonight. (They are going to the dance tonight.)

Note: Only if the subject and verb of your sentence are *they* and *are* do you need the apostrophe. (We will discuss the differences between *their* and *there* more fully later in this section.)

Hyphens

Use a hyphen to separate a long word between syllables when it comes at the end of a line and you do not have room to write it out completely. The hyphen goes above the line, next to the last letter of the syllable. The requirement that the separation come between syllables is an important one to note, since your reader's understanding of your meaning may otherwise be confused. If you are not clear about the precise end of a syllable in any particular word, you should check it in a dictionary. For example, *propane* can be separated at *pro-*; if you separated it at *prop-*, your reader would miss the pronounciation of the total word.

Use a hyphen to join some compound words, such as *father-in-law, seventy-five,* and *pro-abortion.*

Note: Most writing problems with hyphens occur when you are writing a descriptive passage. You need hyphens when you want to change the thought *The baby was six months old* into a modifier in another sentence: *The six-month-old baby.* In some cases you will have to add *-ed* or remove an *-s.*

Quotation Marks and Indirect Quotations

Use quotation marks to mark off the exact words that a person has said. All the words that are spoken — but only those words — are enclosed within the quotation marks:

> Donald Hall says, "Writing well is the art of clear thinking and honest feeling."

The phrase that identifies the speaker, called a dialogue tag, is never enclosed in quotation marks; if you wish to put it within the quote itself you have to close the quotation before the dialogue tag and open it again after the dialogue tag:

> "Writing well," says Donald Hall, "is the art of clear thinking and honest feeling."

Notice that you always need two quotation marks, one to open the quote and the other to close it. All punctuation that belongs to the quote goes inside the quotation marks, and commas are used to set off the dialogue tag.

Use quotation marks for the titles of short works. Titles of poems, one-act plays, essays, and short stories are set off with quotation marks:

> "Stale Air and the Plastic Esthetic" is an essay in *Kicked a Building Lately?* by Ada Louise Huxtable.

Note that the titles of long, book-length works are italicized, as above.

Reporting a Statement

When you wish to state what someone has said but do not want to use the exact words, there are a few — but important — changes that need to be made.

Suppose you want to change the following sentence from an exact quotation to a report of that statement:

Nila said, "I went home to India last year."

You would first have to remove the quotation marks. Then, since you, rather than Nila, are now the deliverer of the message, you would have to change the *I* that Nila used to *she*. And the verb that was in the past needs to be put into the past perfect form. The new sentence would read:

Nila said that she had gone home to India last year.

For an indirect statement:

1. You do not need quotation marks. Since you are not giving the exact words, you do not have to separate the words from the rest of the sentences in the paper.
2. The verb tense will usually have to be moved one degree further into the past.
3. The pronouns that refer to the speaker and listener need to be changed.
4. You may wish to add *that* between the speaker and the words.

The following examples show the changes necessary for different speakers and different time periods:

From: Carol, Jim, and Elaine said, "We are glad you came back to New York."

To: Carol, Jim, and Elaine said *they* were glad *Nila had come* back to New York.

From: Nila replied, "I never knew how much I loved New York until I left."

To: Nila replied that *she had* never *known* how much she loved New York until she left it.

From: Carol said, "I will come to see you tomorrow."

To: Carol said *that she would* come to see *Nila* tomorrow.

Remember that *you* in an essay refers to the reader and *I* refers to the writer of the essay.

Reporting a Question

The same changes that need to be made in changing a statement from a quotation to a report of the statement are also necessary for reporting a question. There are also a few other considerations:

1. The question mark is no longer needed. It should be replaced with a period to mark the end of the sentence:

   From: Carol asked, "When did Nila's plane land?"
   To: Carol asked when Nila's plane had landed.

2. The reverse order of subject and verb that is used in questions is returned to the normal order:

   From: Elaine asked, "How *was* the flight?"
   To: Elaine asked how the *flight was.*

3. The use of a form of *do,* common in asking questions, is changed to the regular past forms with *have*:

   From: Jim asked, "How *did* you sleep?"
   To: Jim asked how she *had* slept on the plane.

4. When the question is not introduced by a questioning word, such as *how, why, what,* or *when,* the word *if* or *whether* is added:

   From: Nila asked, "Will you tell me what has happened?"
   To: Nila asked *if we* would tell her what had happened.

IV. SPELLING

Words Frequently Misspelled

Students from other countries who learn English as a second language often make their strongest complaints about its spelling. Despite the efforts to find some guidelines — and there are a few rules that help — most writers find that the only way to cope with the problem is to memorize the spellings of those words which give them the most trouble.

Two approaches are necessary: (a) You need to make your own personal list of problem words. Keep a special notebook in which you list each misspelled word. Write each word four or five times, looking at it carefully as you write and even spelling it out loud. Force yourself to actually see and hear each letter. (b) Study the words listed on page 256–257, which are the most frequently misspelled words in the language. Try to learn a few words each day. But don't try to learn too many at one time; a steady pace of five words a day is more efficient than twenty-five words all at once. If there are any words that are unfamiliar to you, look them up in the dictionary.

Adding an Ending

Some of the spellings of English words derive from certain rules about pronunciation. If you understand some of the underlying principles of the pronouncing system, then many of the spelling rules will make sense and will be easier to use.

In English, the combination of vowel-consonant-vowel usually requires that the first vowel be given a long sound, like the *a* in *cake*. (Vowels are *a, e, i, o,* and *u*; all other letters are consonants.) If a word ends in a vowel-consonant or a vowel-consonant-consonant, the vowel sound is short, like the *u* in *run* or the *a* in *park*. When you add an ending, you either drop a letter or add a letter to preserve the sequence:

> *write* becomes *writing* (vowel-consonant-vowel preserved) or *written* (vowel-consonant-consonant to change pronunciation)
>
> *admit* becomes *admitting* (vowel-consonant-consonant; letter doubled to preserve pronunciation)

The letter *y* sometimes functions as a vowel. When it does, the *y* is usually changed to *i* when an ending is added:

> *baby* becomes *babies*

When it does not function as a vowel, the *y* is retained when an ending is added:

> *delay* becomes *delays*

Words Frequently Confused

Two/to/too. These tiny words can cause big problems.

Two is the number 2. If you are counting a number of items, this is the spelling you want:

> I had *two* apples and Elaine had two pears.

To indicates direction. If you want to tell where someone or something went, you need *to*:

> Betty went *to* church every Sunday.

When you want the word that goes before a verb, you want *to*. (*To* plus the verb is called an infinitive.)

> *To* succeed in college, you have *to* work.

Too means more than enough, or very. If you mean "also," you need *too*:

Carol is *too* busy to help us.

Will you read your paper to the class, *too*?

Where/were. These words should be pronounced somewhat differently, but sometimes the two are confused.
Where tells us at what place:

Where did you leave your surfboard?

Were indicates the action or part of the action of the sentence. It is a verb. If you are giving the verb in the sentence, use *were.* Note that when you use *were,* you should be talking about the past:

The men *were* working on the car.

The women *were* happy.

There/their (they're). We have already talked about *they're* when dealing with apostrophes, and so you already know that *they're* can only mean *they are. There* refers to place:

I left the basketball *there,* by the water fountain.

There is also used as part of opening phrases:

There are three main causes of the Civil War.

Their shows ownership:

The boys left *their* jackets on the grass.

Then/than. The pronunciation is slightly different. *Then* rhymes with *hen* and *than* rhymes with *can.*
Then shows a time relationship. If you are talking about a sequence of events, this is the form you want:

First I turned off the alarm clock. *Then* I went back to sleep.

Than is used in comparisons. If you are showing similarities or differences, this is the word you want:

Jim's task was more difficult *than* mine.

Road/rode. These words are pronounced the same.
Road is the name of a long narrow stretch with a smoothed surface used for traveling:

All *roads* lead to Rome.

Rode is the past tense form of the verb *to ride*:

> This morning Elaine *rode* in Jim's new car.

Lead/led. *Lead*, when it refers to the heavy, silver-colored metal, is pronounced in the same way as *led*:

> The *lead* sinker fell off the fishing line.

Led is the past tense and past participle form of the verb *to lead*, used to mean "the action of commanding or showing the way":

> George Washington *led* the Continental Army during the Revolutionary War.

(*Lead*, pronounced differently, is also the present tense form of the verb *to lead*).

Piece/peace. Both of these words are pronounced the same. *Piece* refers to a section of something:

> Jim ate a second *piece* of cake.

Peace refers to the absence of war or fighting:

> After World War II, everyone hoped there would be many years of *peace*.

Knew/new. *Knew* is the past tense form of the verb *to know*, used to mean "to understand or have knowledge about":

> Carol studied so hard she *knew* the work by heart.

New indicates recent origin:

> Nila bought some *new* saris in India.

Know/no. *Know* is the present tense form of the verb to know, used to mean "to understand or have knowledge":

> I *know* how to swim.

No is a negative indicating absence:

> We have *no* bananas today.

Lose/loose. The pronounciation is different.
> *Lose* rhymes with *fuse*. It is a verb whose action refers to not winning:

> If we don't score more goals, we will *lose* the game.

Loose rhymes with *goose*. It refers to being free from restraints or unfettered:

> After she got hit in the mouth, Johanna had a *loose* tooth.

Chose/choose. Both are forms of the verb *to choose*, meaning "to select." *Choose* is the base form; *chose* is the past tense form. They are not pronounced alike. *Choose* rhymes with *lose*; *chose* rhymes with *hose*:

> I *choose* my shirts with care.
> Yesterday I *chose* a blue-striped shirt to wear with my tan suit.

Dye/die. Both are pronounced the same. *Dye* refers to the color or the act of coloring. *Die* indicates the loss of life. (The past tense of *dye* is *dyed*; the past tense of *die* is *died*.)

> Marilyn *dyed* her hair purple.
> All the roaches *died* after we sprayed the kitchen.

Words Most Frequently Misspelled

accept	during	marriage
accommodate	embarrass	medicine
acquire	enough	necessary
across	exaggerate	occasion
advertisement	except	occurred
all right	excitable	opinion
among	exercise	particular
analysis	existence	personal
analyze	experience	personnel
apparent	familiar	playwright
argument	fascinate	precede
bargain	forty	preferred
beautiful	fourth	prejudice
beginning	fulfill	privilege
believe	guarantee	professor
benefited	height	pursue
conscious	hoping	quiet
curriculum	huge	receive
definitely	interest	recommend
description	jealous	referring
develop	license	rhythm
discipline	lonely	sacrifice
dropped	losing	seize

separate   technique   useful
similar   thought   vacuum
source   together   weird
succeed   transferred   writing
suspense   unnecessary   yield

Pages 104–106. "On the Way to Being Real" from *Person to Person: The Problems of Being Human* by Carl Rogers and Barry Stevens. Reprinted by permission of Real People Press, Box F, Moab, Utah 84532.

Pages 111–112. Excerpt from *A Walker in the City* by Alfred Kazin, copyright 1951, 1979 by Alfred Kazin, reprinted by permission of Harcourt Brace Jovanovich, Inc.

Pages 112–114. Excerpt from *The Woman Warrior: A Childhood Among Ghosts* by Maxine Hong Kingston. Copyright © 1975, 1976 by Maxine Hong Kingston. Reprinted by permission of Alfred A. Knopf, Inc.

Pages 129–130. "How to Make People Smaller Than They Are," by Norman Cousins, reprinted from *Saturday Review,* December 12, 1978, by permission of the author.

Pages 131–135. "Career Planning" by Selbourne G. Brown, *The Black Collegian,* September/October 1985. Copyright © 1985 by Selbourne G. Brown. Reprinted by permission of the author.

Pages 135–138. Excerpted from "Managing Your Time" in *Getting Things Done: The ABC's of Time Management* by Edwin Bliss.   Copyright © 1976 by Edwin C. Bliss. Reprinted with the permission of Charles Scribner's Sons, an imprint of Macmillan Publishing Company..

Pages 155–157. Sherman and Haas, "Man to Man, Woman to Woman," *Psychology Today,* June 1984. Reprinted with permission from Psychology Today Magazine. Copyright © 1984 (PT Partners, L.P.)

Pages 158–162. Gail Gregg, "Putting Kids First," *The New York Times* Magazine, April 13, 1986. Copyright © 1986 by The New York Times Company. Reprinted by permission.

Pages 173–176. "Our Toxic Waste Time Bomb," as condensed from "A Problem That Cannot Be Buried," *Time,* October 14, 1985. Copyright 1985 Time Inc. All rights reserved. Reprinted with permission of *Time* and *Reader's Digest* from the March 1986 *Reader's Digest.*

Pages 177–182. Robert Freitas, Jr., "Roboclone," *Omni,* July 1983. Copyright 1983 by Omni Magazine and reprinted with the permission of Omni Publications International Ltd.

Pages 193–194. From Ernest Hemingway, "When You Camp Out, Do It Right," *Toronto Star Weekly,* June 26, 1920, p. 17. Reprinted by permission of Alfred Rice for the Estate of Ernest Hemingway. © Ernest Hemingway.

Pages 195–196. "Beating Writer's Block," *Time,* October 31, 1977. Copyright 1977 Time Inc. All rights reserved. Reprinted by permission from *Time.*

Pages 200–201. "The Courtship of Arthur and Al" by James Thurber. Copr. 1940 James Thurber. Copr. 1968 Helen Thurber. From *Fables for Our Time,* published by Harper & Row. Reprinted by permission.

ART CREDITS
Page 27: Courtesy James Vaughn.
Page 33: Frank Siteman/Stock, Boston.
Page 166: A. J. Cyr Photographics.
Pages 204 and 205: The Bettman Archive.
Page 208: © Yvonne Freund/Photo Researchers, Inc.
Page 209: J. R. Holland/Stock, Boston.

Index